SOUNDING COMPOSITION

**PITTSBURGH SERIES IN COMPOSITION,
LITERACY, AND CULTURE**

David Bartholomae and Jean Ferguson Carr, *Editors*

SOUNDING COMPOSITION

*Multimodal Pedagogies for
Embodied Listening*

STEPH CERASO

University of Pittsburgh Press

Published by the University of Pittsburgh Press, Pittsburgh, Pa., 15260
Copyright © 2018, University of Pittsburgh Press
Manufactured in the United States of America
Printed on acid-free paper
10 9 8 7 6 5 4 3 2 1

Cataloging-in-Publication data is available from the Library of Congress

ISBN 13: 978-0-8229-6533-6

Cover art: photo by B. Rosen licensed under CC BY-ND 2.0
Cover design: Adam B. Bohannon

To my family: This book—this career—would not have been
possible without you.

And to Dan, the most patient and generous listener I know.

CONTENTS

Acknowledgments   ix

INTRODUCTION: TOWARD EXPANSIVE LISTENING AND SONIC
COMPOSING PRACTICES   1

1. SOUNDING OUT RHETORIC AND COMPOSITION AND SOUND
STUDIES: RESONANCES, PERTURBATIONS, PROVOCATIONS   14

2. SOUNDING BODIES, COMPOSING EXPERIENCE:
(RE)EDUCATING THE SENSES   28

REVERBERATION: MY LISTENING BODY   51

3. SOUNDING SPACE, DESIGNING EXPERIENCE: THE ECOLOGICAL
PRACTICE OF SONIC COMPOSITION   68

REVERBERATION: MAPPING SOUND   91

4. SOUNDING CARS, SELLING EXPERIENCE: SOUND DESIGN IN
CONSUMER PRODUCTS   105

REVERBERATION: SONIC OBJECTS   124

CONCLUSION: MULTIMODAL LISTENING PEDAGOGY AND
THE FUTURE OF SONIC EDUCATION   143

Notes   155
Works Cited   169
Index   187

ACKNOWLEDGMENTS

IF THERE WERE A SOUNDTRACK for writing this book, it would be crowded with the sounds of many intelligent, warm voices. I'll do my best to amplify those voices here.

First and foremost, I want to thank all of the students who helped me develop and refine multimodal listening pedagogy over the years. A loud shout-out goes to the students in my 2014 "Sound, Composition, and Culture" seminar at the University of Maryland-Baltimore County, particularly David Coursey, Meghan Cusack, Sam Manas, and Imani Spence. This book could not exist without you all.

I want to thank a number of friends and colleagues who read and provided invaluable feedback on this manuscript. Casey Boyle, Byron Hawk, Eric Detweiler, Jon Stone, Carolyn Kyler, Pamela VanHaitsma, Patricia Suzanne Sullivan, and Ruth Osorio—you helped make this a better book. A few of these people deserve special recognition. Carolyn, who has been commenting on my work since I was an undergraduate, has been a patient and wonderful reader. I would be nowhere without her mentorship. Casey offered sage advice on multiple occasions and has been a fantastic interlocutor throughout the writing of this book. I also want to acknowledge Patricia, who volunteered to read the *entire* manuscript in the final stages of this project, and Ruth, who helped me create an accessible design for the book's website.

I am grateful to have been a part of Pitt's doctoral program in "Composition, Literacy, Pedagogy, and Rhetoric," which allowed me to pursue intellectual questions that do not fit neatly into disciplinary categories. I want to thank my amazing committee, Don Bialostosky, Steve Carr, Annette Vee, and Jess Enoch, for sharing their knowledge, kindness, and energy with me. I owe a hearty thanks to Don, who stepped in as chair when I needed him most. It has been a real pleasure working with such an attuned thinker and listener.

Many thanks to Dame Evelyn Glennie, who took time out of her busy world tour to let me interview her—a thrilling experience for me as a scholar and a fan—and to the acoustic designers who were nice enough to answer my questions (even if they did not understand why someone from an English department would be interested in sound design and architecture).

I am indebted to the anonymous reviewers who offered commentary that proved to be a tremendous help in revising this manuscript. Acquisitions editor Joshua Shanholtzer has been a reliable sounding board throughout the revision process, and my sincere thanks goes to editors David Bartholomae and Jean Ferguson Carr for their feedback and for publishing my work in this distinguished series. An earlier version of Chapter 2 appeared as "(Re)Educating the Senses: Multimodal Listening, Bodily Learning, and the Composition of Sonic Experiences" in *College English* 77.2 (November 2014), pages 102–23. I received permission from the National Council of Teachers of English (copyright 2014) to include a revised version of the article in my book. Thanks to former *College English* editor Kelly Ritter and the two reviewers, Stephanie Kerschbaum and Kyle Stedman, who provided excellent commentary on the article. Alongside Kati Fargo Ahern, I also wrote about the idea for the Design a Sonic Object Project I discuss in Chapter 4's Reverberation in a short article titled "Composing with Sound," which appeared in *Composition Studies* 43.2 (2015), pages 13–18.

I am appreciative of the feedback I received on various parts of the book from faculty and graduate students at a number of institutions where I gave invited talks, including the Maryland Institute for Technology in the Humanities at the University of Maryland-College Park, Duke University, and Georgia State University. The writing of this book spanned multiple states and jobs, and I am thankful for the support of my students and colleagues at the University of Pittsburgh, Georgetown University, the University of Maryland-Baltimore

County, and the University of Virginia. Additionally, being interviewed by Eric Detweiler for his *Rhetoricity* podcast helped me clarify some of the main arguments of this book. Thanks to Eric for inviting me to voice my ideas. And the scholars who participated in "Rhetoric and Sensation," a seminar at the Rhetoric Society of America's 2015 Summer Institute led by Debbie Hawhee and Vanessa Beasley, set my brain on fire. There are too many of you to name, but thanks for your brilliance.

A thriving interdisciplinary community of sonically-minded scholars have contributed to my thinking in this book. I appreciate Jennifer Stoever, Jonathan Sterne, Mary Caton Lingold, Darren Mueller, and Whitney Trettien taking the time to talk with me about my project and giving me opportunities to share my work with the larger sound studies community. I am especially indebted to Jennifer. As editor-in-chief of *Sounding Out*, she supported and published my work when I was a graduate student, and I am forever grateful for her encouragement. Jennifer and the *Sounding Out* team have been highlighting the work of women, minorities, and early-career scholars for years, introducing many new voices to the field of sound studies. This work does not always get the recognition it deserves. On behalf of sound nerds everywhere, I want to say "thank you" to Jennifer and the *Sounding Out* crew, Liana Silva and Aaron Trammell. You are valued more than you know.

The sound community in rhetoric and composition has also grown substantially in recent years, and I am thankful for conversations with so many smart and lovely people, including Steven Hammer, Mary Hocks, Courtney Danforth, Harley Ferris, Nathaniel Rivers, Michelle Comstock, Jonathan Alexander, Crystal VanKooten, Michael Faris, Timothy Oleksiak, "Guest DJ" Scott Wible, Devon Randall Kehler, Cassie Brownell, and Jon Wargo. I also want to thank the many friends, teachers, and colleagues who have supported me throughout the writing of this book: Jody Shipka, Jim Seitz, Nancy Welch (who started it all), Dahliani Reynolds Temte, Jean Bessette, Danielle Koupf, Stacey Waite, Erin Anderson, Trisha Campbell, "mixtape goddess" Maura McAndrew, Kerry Banazek, Matt Pavesich, Lisa Phillips, Jim Brown, Alison Booth, Mary Kuhn, Jocelyn Sheppard, Lindsay DiCuirci, Kim Hufhand, Corey Dall, Arlan Hess, Leah Hampton, Travis Vogan, and Anne Garland Mahler. And thanks to Lulu Miller, queen of the sound nerds, who helped to reignite my passion for this project in the final stages of revision.

Pamela VanHaitsma deserves a paragraph of her own. Pamela is my peer mentor extraordinaire. She has been providing feedback on this and other projects since graduate school. Her positivity and wisdom have helped me navigate the ups and downs of academia, and I am beyond grateful for her insight and friendship.

Last but not least, I want to thank my family, especially my parents, Tim and Deb Ceraso, and my grandmothers, Lynda Koleck and the late Janet Ceraso, for their love and support. Thanks to my brother, Matt Ceraso, and my unofficial sibling, Courtney Hufhand, who shared my excitement about sound from the start. Our cassette tape recordings and pretend *Rolling Stone* interviews (I was the reporter, they were the rock stars) prepared me for this book in unexpected ways. Thanks also to Molly Ceraso, for reminding me to break out in dance every now and again, and to Geoff and Harriet Brown for their cheerleading. Finally, I want to thank Dan Brown for his devotion and encouragement and for forcing me to take breaks when I desperately needed them. Dan reminds me daily that there is much more to life than work, and I am lucky to get to spend my life with him.

SOUNDING COMPOSITION

INTRODUCTION
TOWARD EXPANSIVE LISTENING
AND SONIC COMPOSING PRACTICES

On the way to class I pass an active construction site. I can feel the sounds of the loud machinery in my chest cavity, and I am suddenly anxious. I start to walk faster toward the building where my classroom is located. When I arrive at the digital lab there are twenty-five students already in their seats—all of them staring at screens. It is quiet enough to hear the electric hum of the computers. Though I am glad to have escaped the uncomfortable construction sounds, the awkward near silence does not relieve the tension in the body. I watch the clock on the screen of my phone and wait impatiently to begin class.

~

Starbucks is bustling. The blend of hissing, clanking appliances, lively conversations, and store music creates a welcoming environment. Muffled sound is leaking from the earbuds of a woman standing in front of me, giving me an unwanted sample of her "private" sonic experience. I order my coffee and find a table in the corner. The songs on the corporate playlist sound similar—upbeat yet indistinct enough to fade into the background like unobtrusive sonic wallpaper. I barely notice the soundscape as I evaluate student projects on my laptop.

~

On the drive home from campus I listen to a podcast. There is something comforting about the acoustics of the car. The sounds from the world outside are diminished, making it seem like I am in my own listening booth. By interacting with the material features of the car, I can regulate the speaker's volume and position as well as the interior temperature. I can adjust the position of the seat to make my body feel more relaxed. Listening to this podcast in my car is a sensorially pleasing experience, and it puts me in a good mood. I pull into my driveway and continue to sit there. I do not want to tear myself away from the narrative world of the podcast or from the sonic world I am inhabiting—my customized listening cocoon.

THESE SONIC SCENES FROM MY everyday life capture an important quality of sonic interactions. Though listening is often thought of as a practice that involves paying attention to audible information, sonic experiences engage much more than our ears and brains; they also affect our physical and emotional states. Indeed, all sonic encounters have subtle, sometimes powerful, effects on our bodily experiences in different situations and settings. Consider the various ways that sound influences our feelings and behaviors as we move through the world. We inhabit countless strategically designed sonic environments every day, whether or not we are aware of it: shopping malls, grocery stores, churches, hotels, restaurants, offices, parks. These acoustically designed spaces are intended to persuade us to feel or act in certain ways. For instance, the sound in a store might be employed to try to elevate our mood so we linger there longer and buy more; a hotel lobby might be intentionally loud to encourage people to talk and be social. The objects in our lives also provide sonic feedback that sometimes stirs our emotions. You can probably hear when your washing machine is on the fritz, or perhaps the sight and sound of an ice cream truck triggers a feeling of nostalgia for your childhood. Sonic encounters can be intense bodily events—like when you stand close to gigantic speakers at a concert and feel the vibrating, thumping bass in your stomach and throat. And, many technologies enable us to design personalized sonic experiences: noise-cancelling headphones, apps that reproduce the sounds of a coffee shop to help writers concentrate in their too quiet home offices, music platforms that offer customized playlists for every occasion, white noise machines that promise a better night's sleep. There is even technology that gives listeners the power to adjust and manipulate the sonic world around them in real time using two wireless earbuds and a smartphone app (*Here One*).

As these examples illustrate, engaging with sound entails much more than hearing audible information. Sonic experience is complex, varied, multisensory, and contextual.

Given the rapid development and wide accessibility of new sonic technologies and experiences, this is an opportune moment to reconsider the role of sound in rhetoric and composition—to think expansively about what it means to listen to and create with sound in the twenty-first century. There has been a huge boost in scholarship on sound by authors from across the humanities and social sciences. Yet little work has been done on how to teach students to design or participate critically in sonic interactions. The sonic boom that we are now experiencing in academia and everyday life amplifies the need for developing more extensive pedagogical approaches to sound and listening. I see this moment as an opportunity for rhetoric and composition scholars to build upon and invigorate our long disciplinary history with sound.[1]

Sounding Composition introduces a robust sonic education for rhetoric and composition—and multimodal composition in particular—by reimagining the teaching of listening to account for a broad range of sonic experiences and composing practices. To that end, in the following chapters, I develop a pedagogical framework that is based on listening and composing techniques from an eclectic mix of contemporary sound practitioners. These professionals practice what I call *multimodal listening,* or attending to the ecological relationship among sound, bodies, environments, and materials. As I will argue, multimodal listening is a practice that can help all of us take advantage of the affordances[2] of sound and become thoughtful, sensitive listener-composers in any setting. This book offers a capacious, explicitly embodied approach to sonic education that strives to provide teachers and students with a more holistic understanding of the sonic world.

WHY SONIC EDUCATION MATTERS NOW

In order to consider how we might transform pedagogical approaches to sound in rhetoric and composition, we must first reflect on how digital technologies have changed our relationship to sound and listening. More often than not, using digital technologies involves disengaging with one's immediate environment.[3] Sound seems to be one of the most effective and desirable modes of disengagement. This is most likely because, unlike visual media, sonic media allow us to multitask with ease. You cannot, for example, watch a movie on your phone while walking down the street without the risk of crashing into people or objects, but listening to sonic media allows you to free up your eyes and the rest of your body. It is possible to run, type, clean, and do any number of activities while listening to music, audio books, or podcasts.

While consuming digital sound is convenient, the widespread adoption of digital audio technologies has also influenced the ways that many people are conditioned to listen. For instance, plugging in to digital devices like MP3 players and smartphones encourages people to pay attention to some sounds and ignore others; these technologies train (hearing) listeners to pay attention to the sounds being funnelled through their ears. People use digital audio technologies to create sonic boundaries around themselves, and any sound that happens to permeate their personalized sonic bubbles is a distraction. Using technologies to create private listening experiences is certainly not a novel practice. The gramophone, car radio, Walkman, and many other consumer products were employed to do this long before digital devices became available. What *is* new and significant about digital technologies is their pervasiveness in home, work, and public environments. It is easy and often preferable to be plugged in as much as possible. While there are many advantages to being able to access a gigantic library of sonic content at the tap of a finger, plugged-in listeners also miss out on the larger world of sound in which they are situated. In other words, digital audio technologies play a role in training people to develop selective listening habits by encouraging them to tune out the sonic environment around them. As I will argue throughout this book, too much tuning out, or selective listening, can lead to an impoverished understanding of how sound works and affects people in different environments and contexts.

In some ways, then, digital audio technologies have played a role in perpetuating restrictive listening practices. At the same time, they have enhanced listeners' capacities to consume and compose with sound. One of the key affordances of digital audio technologies is that they allow users to design and manipulate sound in ways that were once limited to professionals. By watching video tutorials or simply tinkering with software, scores of people have taught themselves to produce high quality podcasts, songs, audio documentaries, and more. Computers and tablets have become viable substitutes for professional sound studios. Listeners also have more access than ever before to downloadable audio files. Smartphones and MP3 players serve as massive storage devices that make it possible for listeners to carry their entire audio libraries in their pockets, which they can choose to consume, organize, share, and remix. The sheer number of accessible audio files and the fact that listeners are no longer beholden to a physical medium (e.g., record, tape, CD, etc.) has profoundly changed how music and other audio is consumed as well. Because people are now able to purchase individual MP3s of songs, instead of having to buy full albums, the kind of sustained listening associated with playing an album in its entirety is becoming increasingly rare; many contemporary audio libraries are more like digital mixtapes than comprehensive collections. Generally speaking, contemporary audio technologies enable users to engage with and control sound in ways that were not possible for the average listener before the mass popularity of personal computers and mobile devices.

Bearing in mind the various ways that digital technologies have changed our relationship to sound, this cultural moment demands a listening pedagogy that takes into account the distinct sonic habits and experiences that have emerged during the twenty-first century. Clearly, digital technologies provide new avenues for teaching with sound. At the same time, our dependence on digital technologies—especially the earbudded experience of consuming digital audio—has resulted in a selective understanding of how sound works as a mode of composition and an affective, rhetorical force in the world at large. Thus, the challenge for teachers is this: How can we help students cultivate relevant listening practices that allow them to capitalize on the affordances of sound in digital contexts while retraining them to become perceptive listener-composers in any setting?

In response to this challenge, *Sounding Composition* provides a collection of possibilities for teaching students to be smart, sensitive listeners during the production of multimodal compositions and in their experiences with a variety of sonic media, environments, and objects. This book is pedagogical both because it presents practical applications for the multimodal composition classroom and because it proposes listening practices that can help anyone learn to be more reflective about their sensory interactions with the affectively rich sonic world. In a culture where being plugged in to digital devices is a common occurrence, when so much of what we pay attention to is streaming through earbuds or flashing on screens, I am calling for a reeducation of our senses—a bodily retraining that can help listeners learn to become more open to the connections among sensory modes, environments, and materials. In addition to listening in to digital content, it is time that we learn to listen up, out, through, and around.

MORE THAN EAR-ING: MULTIMODAL LISTENING

To provide an expansive framework for sonic education, this book introduces a pedagogy based on the concept of *multimodal listening*. I define multimodal listening as the practice of attending to the sensory, contextual, and material aspects of a sonic event. Multimodal listening moves away from ear-centric approaches to sonic engagement and, instead, treats sonic experience as holistic and immersive. Unlike practices in which the listener's primary goal is to hear and interpret audible sound, multimodal listening accounts for the ecological relationship among sound, bodies, environments, and materials.

Multimodal listening is quite different from listening practices that depend upon the ears exclusively, or what I call *ear-ing*. Ear-ing involves focusing on a particular kind of audible information, such as spoken language. It is how most people interpret what it means to listen: paying attention to audible content.[4] Ear-ing relies on undistracted attention. In contrast, to listen multimodally, one must attend to the distractions. Instead of only homing in on specific content, multimodal listeners are attuned to how sound is connected to and intertwined with different senses, spaces, and objects. Multimodal listening allows for dispersed attention—a general openness to the sonic world and its complexities. Put differently, multimodal listening enables listeners to understand how their bodily experiences in specific contexts shape and are shaped by sound. In this sense, multimodal listening echoes the kind of nonlinear, distributed attention that is associated with digital environments; it is a practice that is aligned with the learning habits that we have already been developing via interacting with computers and mobile devices.

At first blush, *multimodal* may seem like a term that does not adequately represent the dynamic sonic experiences and listening practices I am setting out to examine. One of the limitations of the word *multimodal*, as Thomas Rickert points out, is that it "indicates various, discrete modes that are then combined" (*Ambient* 142). In other words, *multimodal* implies that there are separate modes (visual, aural, etc.) that are isolated and need to be put back together. While the separation of different modes may work on a conceptual level, it is a far cry from actual bodily interactions with the world. When one observes a plane taking off or a tree rustling in the wind, one does not experience the image, then the sound, and so on. Rather, these sensory modes are experienced simultaneously. By isolating individual modes to make meaning of and with them, *multimodal* approaches tend to ignore how sensory modes work together, ecologically.

However, the implied separation of the senses in the term *multimodal* is in part what makes it an apt word to describe the listening pedagogy I introduce in this book. Multimodal listening pedagogy is both an acknowledgment of and a response to the fact that we have learned to attend to different sensory modes in isolation. People separate modes at the level of attention all of the time, and the privileging of particular senses is rooted in cultural learning (Classen and Howes). Sight, for instance, has historically been the dominant sensory mode in most Western cultures while hearing is considered secondary (Erlmann). Further, not everyone has access to all of the senses. Individuals with disabilities often rely on a particular sense out of necessity. For example, many blind people develop an acute sense of hearing to compensate for a lack of visual information (Bates). Because we have learned to treat the senses as discrete modes, multimodal listening pedagogy necessarily proposes practices that involve an ecological engagement with and understanding of sensory interactions. The goal of multimodal listening, which relies heavily on a conscious, heightened awareness of the body, is to reeducate people to attend to how the senses that they have access to work together to shape their unique embodied experiences. Multimodal listening pedagogy requires reflecting on one's personal sensory habits and unlearning those ingrained habits in order to approach bodily interactions with sound in more holistic ways.

Multimodal also serves as a tactical term. Like Matthew Kirschenbaum, I understand *tactical* to be an insistence "on the reality of circumstances in which it [the term tactical] is unabashedly deployed to get things done" (415). The frequent use of the term *multimodal*, as well as the serious consideration it has been given in rhetoric and composition scholarship, has helped to facilitate and justify new pedagogical approaches and innovative courses in many composition and rhetoric programs. In addition, scholarship on multimodality and the journals and conferences that continue to encourage its production have enabled scholars to receive legitimate recognition for their nontraditional work, such as nonprint-based projects. What *multimodal* offers as a tactical term, then, is a way to connect multimodal listening pedagogy to the well-known corpus of scholarship on multimodality that has allowed people to take risks—"to get things done"—in rhetoric and composition (415). Multimodal listening pedagogy provides teacher-scholars with a familiar touchstone that can help them validate the unfamiliar, experimental kinds of sonic composing and listening practices that I recommend in this book.

Lastly, using the term *multimodal* to describe the listening pedagogy I am proposing will add momentum to critical discussions about multimodality in the field. In recent years scholars have been pushing conceptions of multimodality by moving beyond strictly digital environments and accounting for the distinct affordances of different modes and materials.[5] *Sounding Composition* extends this exciting work by offering a nuanced, body-centric pedagogy. Specifically, this book attempts to expand how multimodality is defined in the discipline by arguing that multisensory experience needs to play a central role in how multimodal composition is understood and practiced. In this way, my project resonates with Kristin Arola and Anne Wysocki's collection, *Composing (Media)=Composing (Embodiment)*, which lays the groundwork for "wider sensuous engagements in writing classrooms" (8).[6] I believe that a deeper focus on sound and listening can move the field toward more sensuous and capacious multimodal pedagogies. Indeed, a rigorous examination of any single mode will inevitably expose that mode's *multimodal-ness*; as I will show, sound is always connected to and experienced with multiple senses. To further clarify how this book contributes to ongoing disciplinary conversations, I want to turn briefly to a discussion of how multimodal listening diverges from typical uses of multimodality in rhetoric and composition.

REIMAGINING MULTIMODALITY VIA MULTIMODAL LISTENING

My choice to emphasize the role of bodily experience in multimodality differs from the majority of scholarship on the subject. Leading scholars of multimodality—namely the New London Group, including Gunther Kress and Theo Van Leeuwen—discuss multimodal communication practices through a semiotic framework (Cope and Kalantzis). The end goal of this research is meaning-making. As Kress writes in *Multimodality*, "There are domains beyond the reach of language, where it is insufficient, where semiotic-conceptual work has to be and is done by means of other modes" (15). Although scholarship about multimodality acknowledges modes that are extradiscursive, the ultimate pursuit of meaning-making positions multimodal approaches in the same realm as the discursive—a realm where objects are analyzed and interpreted.[7]

The semiotic framework introduced by the New London Group has had a powerful influence on conceptions of multimodality in rhetoric and composition. In 2005, Cynthia Selfe and Gail Hawisher dedicated a special issue of *Computers and Composition* to Kress's work, and Selfe's adoption of the term *multimodal* in her own teaching and research has popularized the New London Group's approach to multimodality in the field (Lauer). The National Council of Teachers of English's (NCTE) Position Statement on Multimodal Literacies, for instance, defines multimodal literacies as the "integration of multiple modes of communication and expression that can enhance or transform the meaning of the work beyond illustration or decoration" ("NCTE"). In fact, many publications that inform the ways that rhetoric and composition scholars understand and teach multimodality stress the fundamental role of meaning-making: Lutkewitte's *Multimodal Composition: A Critical Sourcebook*; Bowen and Whithaus's *Multimodal Literacies and Emerging Genres*; Arola, Sheppard, and Ball's *Writer/Designer: A Guide to Making Multimodal Projects*; and Selfe's *Multimodal Composition: Resources for Teachers*, among others. The aforementioned scholarship has been essential to the growth of multimodal composition in the discipline, as well as my own research and teaching. Together, this body of work has redefined how composition is practiced and taught, making it possible (and legitimate) to design innovative assignments and projects that go beyond alphabetic text.

What I want to suggest, however, is that there is more to multimodality than the search for meaning. Multimodality should not be treated only as an enhanced hermeneutic or as a category that is subsumed by hermeneutics. Alongside and in addition to semiotic approaches to multimodality, it is necessary to adopt approaches that take up the affective, bodily, *lived* experience of multimodality. The multimodal listening pedagogy I describe in this book extends previous scholarship on multimodality by offering sonic practices that encompass the semiotic and the bodily aspects of multimodal experiences, which I see as inseparable. While many scholars of multimodality—including Kristie Fleckenstein, Christina Haas, and Patricia Dunn—have foregrounded the role of the body in relation to writing and images, I contend that a more acute attention to the body in relation to listening and sonic composing can result in roomier, explicitly sensory multimodal pedagogies.

This book uniquely contributes to scholarship on multimodality in rhetoric and composition by showing that sound is an ideal mode for exploring the multisensory nature of multimodal interaction. Interactions between sound and the body depend on vibration, which can serve as "a basis for thinking about relations between the senses" (Trower 5). Low sound frequencies (below 20 Hz) produce vibrations that are felt (e.g., the tactile experience of feeling the pulsing bass blasting from a passing car). It is also possible to see sound. Sonic vibrations from a band playing at a restaurant might disturb the water in your glass. Even the simple act of seeing the source of a sound you hear and/or feel can play a role in shaping your listening experience. Instead of emulating the typical ways that multimodality has been approached in the field by isolating and examining particular modes in order to make meaning, throughout this book I will demonstrate that sound is an especially effective—and affective—mode for understanding how the senses work together *ecologically* in multimodal experience.

SOUNDING BODIES, ENVIRONMENTS, AND OBJECTS

My choice to use the word *sounding* in the title and chapter titles for this book is strategic. *Sounding* signifies that sound is being made or emitted from someone or something. The fact that *sounding* is a verb, that it implies action, is pertinent to the arguments I make in *Sounding Composition*. The listening pedagogy I propose does not simply ask students to make meaning of sound as if it were a passive object of study. Rather, in multimodal listening pedagogy, engaging with sound involves experiencing and attending to the senses as they are activated by sound; it entails treating sonic events as physical encounters. Multimodal listening pedagogy is also associated with action in that it is aimed at helping students produce sonic compositions. The action of *sounding*, Julian Henriques writes, "encompasses everything, everyone and all the activities that go into the making of sound" (xxix). Similarly, multimodal listening pedagogy encompasses the range of activities associated with sonic production; it connects listening with making and doing things with sound.

The activity of *sounding* is integral to Chapters 2, 3, and 4 of this book, which focus on different kinds of sound practitioners: a deaf percussionist; acoustic designers; and automotive acoustic engineers, respectively. I have chosen these distinctive practitioners because they each demonstrate a particular kind of *sounding* that amplifies a key attribute of multimodal listening. Chapter 2 examines the body-centric listening and composing practices of deaf percussionist Evelyn Glennie, concentrating specifically on how multisensory approaches to listening can inform multimodal composing projects. Chapter 3 explores acoustic designers' practices for engaging with and composing sonic environments to offer an ecological understanding of multimodal composition. And Chapter 4 turns to automotive acoustic engineers—and product designers in general—to consider how the sonic practices used for enhancing human relationships with designed objects can inform our everyday interactions with things. Together, this three-part investigation of sound in relation to the *body*, the *environment*, and *objects* lays out the foundational concepts and practices for multimodal listening pedagogy. To be clear, I am not calling attention to the practices of sound professionals so that they can be replicated exactly in the classroom. I instead offer these extradisciplinary practices as heuristics for reimagining listening pedagogy to help teachers and students cultivate productive habits that can be applied to multimodal projects and sonic experiences in their own lives.

In order to initiate this kind of reimagination, I provide different pathways and possibilities for teaching with sound throughout the book. Each of the three chapters mentioned above is followed by a related interchapter that includes an example assignment, a pedagogical discussion, student work, and resources for teaching. I refer to these interchapters as *Reverberations*. A *reverberation* is an acoustic design term for the persistence of sound in an environment after the original source of the sound has ceased. It is a phenomenon that occurs when reflections from the original sound blend together and linger in a space (Brooks 21). Likewise, the assignments I provide represent the persistence and blending together of ideas from each chapter after it has ended. On a larger scale, I hope that these assignments will reverberate in classrooms as they are adopted and modified by teachers long after they have read this book. The Reverberation interchapters are also enriched by a correlating website (www.stephceraso.com/reverberations) that features media from the example student projects referred to in the text. Traditionally, teaching materials in books are relegated to appendices. However, my decision to position the Reverberation interchapters throughout the book has to do with emphasis. Moving them to the end of the book might signal that they are not as important as the main chapters—that they are an afterthought. Yet, these concrete pedagogical discussions deserve as much attention as the discussions of case studies and scholarship. I take seriously the notion that both classroom practices and research should be approached with the same degree of care and thoughtfulness. Thus, I have tried to enact this concept through the book's structure.

The primary audience for *Sounding Composition* includes teachers, scholars, and students of rhetoric and composition who have an interest in sound and multimodal composition pedagogy. While pedagogy is the central theme, this book has much to offer beyond pedagogical theory and applications. For instance, the case studies and everyday examples woven throughout the core chapters are relevant to the growing number of scholars interested in sonic rhetorics, or the ways that sound—in conjunction with other elements of an environment or interaction—operates as a material, affective force that influences listeners' bodily states, moods, thoughts, and actions. Audiences from other disciplinary subfields might also find different parts of the book useful. Rhetoric and composition scholars concerned with feminist rhetorical work on listening and embodiment, as well as scholars interested in disability studies, may be drawn to the exploration of deafness and multisensory sonic experiences in Chapter 2. Indeed, issues of accessibility in relation to sound and multimodal composition are discussed throughout the book. Scholars of spatial rhetorics might find significant the emphasis in Chapter 3 on the strategic design of sonic environments. And, the focus in Chapter 4 on the use of sound in product design could be informative for rhetoric and composition scholars interested in materiality/material rhetorics or design more generally.

In addition to multiple audiences in rhetoric and composition, this book is meant to be a resource for teachers, scholars, and students from a variety of academic disciplines that deal with sound, listening, multimodality, multimedia, and digital production. Most notably, readers associated with the field of sound studies constitute an important secondary audience for this book. In Chapter 1, I elaborate on how the main arguments of *Sounding Composition* have been influenced by sound studies work and pinpoint a number of scholarly areas that can bring together the fields of rhetoric and composition and sound studies in more explicit ways.

Sound plays an undeniable role in shaping experiences of all kinds. As educators, we cannot afford to ignore sound or brush it off as less attention-worthy than the visual. There is a genuine need for new pedagogical approaches that can help students cultivate critical listening and sonic composing practices in both scholarly contexts and in their daily lives. Thus, I conclude the book with a discussion about how multimodal listening pedagogy can contribute to a twenty-first century sonic education that is relevant to everyone—not just a particular field or discipline.

Sounding Composition loudly calls attention to the importance of listening in what has become a "plug-in and tune-out" society. It offers ways to sharpen and invigorate students' engagement with digital audio technologies while teaching them to be attuned listeners in their everyday interactions with the world. Implementing the multimodal listening pedagogy I propose in this book requires a willingness to treat the body as a real site of intellectual work rather than just a house for the mind. This pedagogy asks teachers and students to listen generously and expansively; to regard sound as a locus of inquiry as opposed to content to be mined for meaning; to embrace experimentation and unfamiliar sonic practices. Ultimately, the ideas I share in this book are intended to create a *BOOM* that will shake and unsettle disciplinary approaches to sound and listening. My hope is that this felt noise will result in a more imaginative, inclusive, and transformative sonic education. Like sound itself, the pedagogical suggestions and practices I offer are malleable and should be revised or altered to meet the needs of different disciplines, teachers, and students. In short, this book should be played with, not simply read. I want to encourage readers to sample, mangle, hack, remix, and reinvent its contents.

ONE

SOUNDING OUT RHETORIC AND COMPOSITION AND SOUND STUDIES

Resonances, Perturbations, Provocations

WHILE THE INTRODUCTION SITUATED MULTIMODAL listening peda-
gogy within disciplinary conversations about multimodality, this chapter out-
lines the ways that the field of sound studies has informed my thinking in this
book. *Sound studies*, according to Jonathan Sterne, is "a name for the interdisciplinary ferment in the human sciences that takes sound as its analytical
point of departure or arrival . . . it redescribes what sound does in the human
world, and what humans do in the sonic world" ("Sonic Imaginations" 2). My
participation in sound studies—attending conferences, contributing to publications like *Sounding Out* and *Provoke! Digital Sound Studies*, teaching a wide spectrum
of sound studies literature—has been crucial in shaping my understanding of
sound as a scholar of digital writing and rhetoric. As someone who has been
listening in to both rhetoric and composition and sound studies for over a
decade, in this chapter I intend to sound out, to explore the nature of, possible connections between them.

This is not the first attempt to put these fields into conversation. A 2013
Rhetoric Society Quarterly article titled "Auscultating Again" (Gunn et al.) started to
map some key similarities and differences between rhetorical studies and sound
studies, emphasizing that "sound has been relatively little studied—arguably,
repressed—for the last several decades as a respectable scholarly topos in many

areas of communication and rhetorical studies" (476). More recently, rhetoric and composition scholars have been engaging with sound studies work in explicit ways by discussing theories of voice, sonic archives, and soundscapes (Anderson 2014; Stone 2015; Rickert 2013; Hocks and Comstock 2017). Yet, at the time of this writing, there has not been a consideration of how the field of rhetoric and composition (broadly conceived) and the field of sound studies (also broadly conceived) might be put into dialogue.

Below I identify a number of scholarly areas that can serve as sites of generative exchange between rhetoric and composition and sound studies. I situate the main arguments of *Sounding Composition* within each area, describing how my conception of multimodal listening pedagogy stems from both fields. I want to be clear that this is not meant to be a comprehensive overview of sound studies or sound-related scholarship in rhetoric and composition. Sound studies is a disparate, interdisciplinary field that takes up a huge variety of topics, methods, and approaches; it is impossible to capture all the complexity of sound studies in a single chapter or book.[1] There is also a large body of sound-related work in rhetoric and composition that warrants much more than a chapter. Instead of attempting an all-inclusive review, then, I focus selectively on the connections and productive tensions between rhetoric and composition and sound studies that have most influenced my thinking and writing about multimodal listening pedagogy. In other words, the subjects I identify—listening, agency, space, digital production, and pedagogy—serve as possible points of intersection between rhetoric and composition and sound studies *and* as terms that animate my examination of sound in relation to bodies, environments, and objects in the chapters that follow. I argue for more expansive notions of sound and listening in rhetoric and composition via a deliberate engagement with sound studies, as well as offer some future possibilities, challenges, and trajectories for scholarship in both fields. Finally, because this brief chapter is meant to initiate a conversation, it can also serve as a pedagogical tool. My hope is that teachers and students will continue to flesh out, revise, and build upon these ideas in their own classroom discussions.

LISTENING

I begin with listening because it is an important term in rhetoric and composition and in sound studies. Unsurprisingly, there is a plethora of sound studies scholarship on listening. Many scholars have attempted to identify different modes or types of listening practices (Truax 1984; Chion 1994; T. Rice 2013). Sound studies scholars have also discussed listening in relation to various technologies (Bull 2000, 2007; Sterne 2003; Hagood 2011), environments (Schafer 1977; Corbin 1998; Smith 1999), cultures and identities (Feld 1982; DeNora 2000; Novak 2008), race and embodiment (Weheliye 2005; Henriques 2011; Stoever 2016), and more. This is only a small sampling of the diversity of approaches to listening in sound studies scholarship. The fact that there is such a large body of research on listening is an indication of the richness of listening as a theoretical concept and practice.

There is also a long history of listening scholarship in rhetoric and composition, as well as in the related field of communication studies.[2] Scholars have discussed listening with regard to written and oral communication (O'Reilly 1927; Nauer 1975), pedagogy (Mersand 1951; Macrorie 1951; Comstock and Hocks 2006; LaVecchia 2017), technology (Rockwell 1939; Tallman 1948; J. Rice 2006), understanding and empathy (Chancellor 1944; Stratton 1948; Booth 2004; Campbell 2017), and archives (Stone 2015; Bessette 2016), among other topics. While listening scholarship in the history of rhetoric and composition has at times been sporadic and dispersed, here I want to draw attention to an area of research that has been gaining momentum for over a decade: feminist rhetorical work on listening. I call attention to this research not only because it is a cohesive and growing corpus of listening research in the discipline, but also because its emphasis on embodied experience is relevant to multimodal listening pedagogy.

Initially, feminist rhetorical research aimed to recover listening, a practice that had been undervalued and neglected in rhetorical scholarship. It was also a response to an urgent need to find ways for feminist scholars to better communicate across racial and cultural difference. Scholars such as Jacqueline Jones Royster (1996), Cheryl Glenn (2004; 2011), and Krista Ratcliffe (2006) have underscored the role of situated, embodied experience in listening interactions. For example, in *Rhetorical Listening*, Ratcliffe explores how listening to language can "expose troubled identifications with gender and whiteness both in our culture and in our lives" and "conceptualize tactics for negotiating such troubled identifications" (8). Ratcliffe's work has also inspired scholars to explore other aspects of identity in relation to listening, such as queerness (Oleksiak and Tiffe 2015). What I find most valuable about feminist rhetorical scholarship is its acknowledgment that listening practices are not merely contingent upon words but are also shaped by context-specific embodied experiences. This feminist rhetorical work highlights the importance of reflecting on one's own identity to better understand the intricate, often subtle, dynamics of a listening situation.

While feminist rhetorical scholarship has helped to restore listening as a vibrant area of inquiry in rhetoric and composition, I want to suggest that this work can contribute to sound studies as well. Cross-conversations about listening between sound studies and feminist rhetorical scholars could result in a more robust body of research on listening and identity. Indeed, the emphasis on embodiment in feminist rhetorical work has the potential to enrich sound studies conversations about listening and gender, race, sexuality, disability, and class—topics that deserve increased attention in sound studies. At the same time, bringing sound studies research into conversation with feminist rhetorical work can offer more capacious notions of listening and sonic engagement in rhetoric and composition. Much feminist rhetorical work on listening is still focused on the interpretation of language (as opposed to nondiscursive sound). It is also frequently used as a metaphor (e.g., "listening" to text). Feminist rhetorical scholarship has considered the role of embodiment in terms of identity categories, but it has not yet developed fully the relationship between listening and sensory experience or the ways that senses other than hearing figure into listening practices.[3] I submit, then, that sound studies' attention to nondiscursive bodily engagements with sound could expand feminist rhetorical approaches to listening, as well as other sound-related work in rhetoric and composition.

I see multimodal listening pedagogy as an initial attempt to bring together ideas about listening from rhetoric and composition and sound studies. To resound and broaden the discourse that feminist rhetorical scholarship has initiated about embodied listening experiences, multimodal listening pedagogy puts a more pronounced emphasis on felt experience—on engaging with nondiscursive sound via multiple sensory modes. I use multimodal listening pedagogy to offer an explicitly embodied, sensory approach to listening. In this respect, my pedagogy has been influenced by the work of sound studies scholars, such as Salomé Voegelin (2010), Steve Goodman (2012), Julian Henriques (2011), Nina Sun Eidsheim (2015), J. Martin Daughtry (2015), and Jennifer Lynn Stoever (2016), who take up the bodily nature of listening in their work in diverse and provocative ways.

While *Sounding Composition* synthesizes ideas about listening from rhetoric and composition and sound studies, my concept of multimodal listening also offers a distinct approach to listening. That is, multimodal listening is a practice that is tied to multimodal production; it is a listening practice that is especially valuable to media makers. One of the key arguments in this book is that we need listening practices that involve more than the ears to become savvy designers of sonic media. As I will demonstrate, treating listening as a multisensory practice allows composers to produce more sensorially engaging sonic projects. Again, there are many listening theories and practices across rhetoric and composition and sound studies, and I am not suggesting that multimodal listening should preclude other modes of listening; different contexts and occasions call for different responses to discursive and nondiscursive encounters with sound. Instead, the body-centric orientation to listening I offer in this book responds to the need for more dynamic sonic practices in relation to multimodal interaction and production—an orientation that I believe can be beneficial to rhetoric and composition and sound studies as well as related fields that deal with media production, such as digital humanities and media studies.

AGENCY

Examining listening in relation to the body raises questions about agency. In fact, the question of whether or not humans are in control of their sonic experiences encapsulates one of the biggest differences between sound and listening research in rhetoric and composition and sound studies. Rhetoric and composition approaches to sound have relied heavily on semiotics, treating sound as an object of analysis or mode of composition rather than a bodily experience. Sound is often discussed as a thing that can be studied, controlled, and manipulated. While sound studies scholars also use semiotic approaches, there has been a strong push in sound studies work to examine the materiality of sound. Scholars such as Frances Dyson (2009), Steve Goodman (2012), Shelley Trower (2012), and J. Martin Daughtry (2015) have explored sonic encounters as multisensory, vibratory events. This work illustrates that sound is not just another object to pay attention to or make meaning of (though we can certainly do those things), but sound also impinges upon bodies causing uncontrollable—sometimes even harmful—responses.

This vibratory conception of sonic experience has the potential to radically perturb notions of sound in rhetoric and composition; to disrupt our dependence on meaning-making and open up new possibilities for theorizing sonic interactions. As Daughtry describes, "Moments like this, in the street or near powerful loudspeakers or amid gunfire or near explosions—moments when sound acquires the appearance of mass and texture, of being big and heavy and rough, of being both an acoustic and haptic event—these moments compel us to acknowledge that sound is not only a text for us to interpret, but a force for us to reckon with" (162). The moments that Daughtry portrays in this passage amplify the fact that sound itself has agency. Sound affects and transforms bodies in a variety of ways with or without our consent. In extreme situations such as warfare, these sonic effects and affects can be immediate, jarring, and physically traumatic. In less intense sonic situations, like walking to work along a heavily trafficked street, sound might cause subtle physical responses that elude our conscious awareness. Daughtry also implies that, due to its agential powers, sound can direct our attention. This idea resonates with Thomas Rickert's discussion of attention in *Ambient Rhetoric*: "Attention attends to the salient, but the bringing forth of salience is itself a complex activity that has ambient dimensions" (xi). In other words, it is not just that we pay attention to sound, but that sound challenges our practices of attention via "the bringing forth of salience." Even when we make an effort to pay attention to a particular kind of sound—speech or music, for instance—our attention can be diverted by other sounds: the backfiring of a car engine, the rumbling of a garbage truck, the howling of an ambulance siren. The agential power of sound is also determined by how a sound is shaped and distorted by the materials and spaces in which it occurs. The sound of someone coughing in a reverberant, mostly empty space like a large church might demand more attention than the sound of someone coughing in a crowd at an outdoor concert. When it comes to sonic encounters, then, agency is distributed among sound, bodies, environments, and materials.

Acknowledging the agential aspects of sonic experience can problematize and enrich areas of rhetoric and composition that approach sound as a kind of text to be interpreted, as well as inform areas that have not yet made sound a primary concern. For example, discussing sound as a vibrational event could be a worthwhile approach for rhetoric and composition scholarship on new materialism, object-oriented ontology, posthumanism, and similar areas of inquiry that attempt to complicate notions of agency and control—to move beyond representation, meaning-making, and critique. Rhetorical theorists have already begun this work through investigations of language, images, objects, and, to a lesser extent, sound. Lynn Worsham (1987), Victor Vitanza (1991; 1997; 2000), and Diane Davis (2000) have attended to the materiality and excess of language, showing how language cannot simply be controlled and instrumentalized. Laurie Gries (2015) has examined the agential power of images—specifically, various iterations of the viral Obama Hope image—as they circulate, transform, and coproduce the world. In their 2016 collection *Rhetoric, Through Everyday Things*, editors Scot Barnett and Casey Boyle feature work that explores "how various material elements—human and nonhuman alike—interact suasively and agentially in rhetorical situations and ecologies" (2). And, Thomas Rickert has argued that the rhetorical effects and affects of "an environment, including sound, even designed sound, cannot be reduced to the intentions of any party" (*Ambient* 145). Taking a cue from Rickert's initial exploration of ambient sound and agency, I want to propose that a more extensive focus on sound has the potential to sustain and expand this exciting area of rhetorical theory, and that sound studies can offer new critical pathways for rhetoric and composition scholars to study the material, agential nature of sound.

Sound studies work that is centered on affective experience instead of or in addition to attention and meaning can enhance and complicate rhetoric and composition scholarship on sound, and it has certainly informed my thinking about multimodal listening. However, the goal of multimodal listening pedagogy is not to move (entirely) beyond attention and meaning. My reasoning here has to do with multimodal listening pedagogy's connection to the design and production of sound. Composing with sound necessarily involves a conscious attention to one's own and others' listening experiences, as well as conscious choices about how to employ sound in various situations and settings. Attention and intention are chief concerns of sonic composition. Moreover, because rhetoric and composition scholarship on sound has not focused primarily on the body or senses, attending to how meaning is constructed in and through bodily experience is a necessary part of the listening pedagogy I develop in this book.[4] That said, I recognize that sound is not just another object that can be brought into the classroom for analysis and interpretation, which is why multimodal listening pedagogy asks teachers to design more explicitly embodied activities that do not assume a position of remove from sound. In addition, while I concentrate on deliberate multimodal listening and composing practices, I do acknowledge disruptive moments of sonic agency throughout the book. As sound studies work has made clear, sound cannot always be controlled; thus, the unpredictability of sound needs to be considered even when attention and meaning-making are essential. The agential power of sound is an idea I only begin to touch on, and I hope that other rhetoric and composition scholars will continue to develop this line of thinking.

SPACE

Scholarship on the relationship between sound and space is another potential point of intersection between rhetoric and composition and sound studies. In sound studies, this category of scholarship is generally associated with soundscapes. The term *soundscape*, coined by R. Murray Schafer and popularized through his World Soundscape Project in the 1960s and early 70s, attuned scholars to the ecological relationship between humans and the sonic environment. Schafer underscored the negative effects of sounds in locations that were becoming more and more industrialized, arguing that such sounds were a kind of pollution that needed to be eradicated. Since Schafer's initial use of the term *soundscape*, many scholars have critiqued and extended his exploration of sonic environments, using different terms and definitions.[5] Soundscape studies continues to be a thriving area of sound studies that is constantly evolving.

Rhetoric and composition scholars have also referenced the concept of soundscape in their research. In their 2006 article about teaching with sound—"Voice in the Cultural Soundscape"—Michelle Comstock and Mary Hocks include an "understanding of our soundscapes as cultural artifacts" in their definition of *sonic literacy* (n.p.). More recently in "The Sounds of Climate Change" (2017), Comstock and Hocks explore the soundscape as a kind of sonic rhetoric that communicates vital information about climate change and extinction. Likewise, Thomas Rickert investigates sound as a suasive force in ambient environments (2013). As I will discuss in Chapter 3, Kati Fargo Ahern and Jordan Frith have also taken into account the affordances of mobile technologies in their examination of *social soundscaping*, a practice that involves listening to, contributing, and editing geolocated sounds in specific spaces (n.p.). Together this work has helped to accentuate the compositional and rhetorical potential of sonic environments.

I want to suggest that, in addition to existing rhetoric and composition scholarship on soundscapes, research on spatial rhetorics could benefit from a more direct engagement with sound studies. Scholars of spatial rhetorics, such as Roxanne Mountford (2003), Nedra Reynolds (2007), Jessica Enoch (2008), David Fleming (2008), and Greg Dickinson, Carole Blair, and Brian Ott (2010), have analyzed an array of fascinating spaces: museums, religious sites, cities, national parks, and memorials, among others. Much of this work explores the multimodal, sensory experience of navigating spaces.

Sound (and silence) is sometimes discussed, though, in general, it tends to receive less attention than the visual and material aspects of space. However, as I see it, the focus on the sensory experience of environments in scholarship on spatial rhetorics presents an opportunity to attend to soundscapes more closely. Sound studies research could prove useful in this regard. At the same time, spatial rhetorics offers sound studies frameworks and methods for better understanding people's affective engagements with spaces, why spaces are given value or purpose, and how and why certain behaviors and practices occur in a space. In short, spatial rhetorics scholarship could inform and add nuance to sound studies research on soundscapes.

In terms of this book's intervention in conversations about sound and space in multimodal composition, I draw from and broaden soundscape studies through considerations of digital environments. That is, I treat digital spaces as soundscapes—as ecologies of sound, bodies, materials, technologies, and aesthetics that are similar to, yet distinct from, the physical spaces we inhabit. In Chapter 3, for example, I examine the relationship between attending to the soundscapes of physical spaces and designing sound for digital spaces. I demonstrate how training listeners to become attuned to a range of different soundscapes can heighten their sensitivity to the functions, effects, affects, constraints, and possibilities of sound in screen-based environments; in turn, this sensitivity can help composers use sound in more compelling ways.

DIGITAL PRODUCTION

Rhetoric and composition's extensive history of producing digital scholarship can offer sound studies informative models for taking advantage of the affordances of sound in digital spaces. Long before *digital humanities* became a buzzword in higher education, rhetoric and composition scholars were experimenting with digital modes of composition. For decades journals such as *Kairos*, *Computers and Composition Online*, and *Enculturation* have provided scholars with opportunities to break away from the rules of traditional, print-based models of academic publishing. *Enculturation*'s 1999 issue "Writing/Music/Culture" is especially significant in terms of paving the way for future investigations of sound in the field. In addition to amplifying discussions about the role of music in digital environments, "Writing/Music/Culture" featured sonic content to showcase sound as an effective medium for scholarship in digital spaces. By the mid-2000s, rhetoric and composition scholarship about sound, including audible scholarship, had become a well-established part of the field. *Computers and Composition* and *Computers and Composition Online* published two distinct but related special issues on "Sound in/as a Compositional Space" (Ball and Hawk 2006) that explored sound as a mode of composition from theoretical and practical perspectives. More recently, special issues in *Currents in Electronic Literacy* (Davis "Writing with Sound" 2011) and *Harlot* (Ceraso and Stone "Sonic Rhetorics" 2013) have encouraged the field to turn up the volume and listen to sonic work.

Conversely, the vast majority of sound studies scholarship is silent. While digital journals like the *Journal of Sonic Studies* and *Sound Effects* have cropped up in recent years, these and other sound studies publications still rely primarily on alphabetic text.[6] To my mind, then, rhetoric and composition scholarship on multimodal production could be helpful to sound studies scholars interested in developing more dynamic, audible scholarship. For instance, rhetoric and composition work on the affordances and limitations of sound (Shipka 2006; McKee 2006; Alexander 2015), multimodal design (Arola, Sheppard, and Ball 2014; Alexander and Rhodes 2014), and accessibility in digital spaces (Yergeau et al. 2013; Zdenek 2015) present practical models and theoretical frameworks—many of which I build upon in the following chapters—that could inform the production of sound studies scholarship. I do not mean to imply that rhetoric and composition scholars have taken full advantage of the possibilities of sound or other modes in digital publishing environments. The technical production aspects of rhetoric and composition scholarship still have a long way to go before catching up with our research. That said, rhetoric and composition has in many respects led the way in experimenting with digital forms of scholarship and can, therefore, be a valuable resource for sound studies scholars interested in producing more soundful digital work.

While rhetoric and composition provides sound studies with models and frameworks for digital scholarship, sound studies offers rhetoric and composition approaches to sound that move beyond computers. As I elaborate on in Chapter 2, thus far multimodal composition scholarship has discussed sound mainly in relation to digital spaces—we analyze, create with, and listen to sound on screens. Thinking about sound in digital environments is important and, as noted above, rhetoric and composition is ahead of the curve in many ways when it comes to digital production. However, I find curious the emphasis on digital sonic interactions since the field seems to agree that multimodality entails more than the digital (Shipka 2011; Palmeri 2012; Alexander and Rhodes 2014). While the calls of scholars to redefine multimodality have resulted in an interest in various forms of visual and material composition that occur off screen, sonic work in multimodal composition remains tethered to computers. Treating sound as something that is associated exclusively with computer interaction leaves out crucial considerations of nonscreen-based multimodal experiences with sound and other modes.

To clarify, I am not insinuating that there is a hard distinction between digital and nondigital interactions. As Jason Farman points out in *Mobile Interface Theory*, mobile devices often blur the lines between digital and nondigital experiences. Considering the ways that digital processes inform so many aspects of our lives—from personal banking to healthcare—the digital is no longer a category that can easily be switched off. Rather, the digital is now an ambient condition that is integrated seamlessly into our everyday activities. The point I am trying to make, however, is that there is a big difference between the computer-intensive digital sound work that is encouraged in multimodal composition courses and experiences with nondigitized sound. For example, because digital audio is compressed, it does not contain a full range of frequencies. Thus, it cannot be felt in the same way as nondigitized sound. While digital sound has its advantages, it offers a diminished sonic experience at the level of the senses. Sound studies research, which deals with sound in relation to a wide range of environments and situations beyond the computer screen, can therefore productively expand notions of sound and multimodality in rhetoric and composition.

Additionally, in multimodal composition sound is often treated as an isolated mode that is disconnected from other modes (e.g., there are distinct labels like "sonic rhetoric," "visual rhetoric," etc.). Sound studies scholars, on the other hand, have begun to acknowledge that sonic experience intersects with other senses. Karin Bijsterveld writes, "Scholars in sound studies have recently taken a step back from their beloved topic, stressing that 'we' should not 'hyposthasize' sound as something that needs our exclusive devotion at the expense of what we can see, smell, taste, and touch. This claim echoes earlier recommendations in sensory studies not to either defend or attack the dominance of one sensory modality in particular societies or situations, but to start out from the 'multisensoriality' of experience" (Pink 2009: 19) (*Sound and Safe* 18). Rather than isolating sound or cutting it off from other sensory modes—as multimodal composition scholarship frequently does—sound studies work has become more open to examining sensory interconnections. In this respect, sound studies' emphasis on the "'multisensoriality' of experience" has informed one of the most significant disciplinary interventions in this book—to challenge the notion that listening and sonic composing are simply ear-centric experiences. Multimodal listening pedagogy redefines what sonic engagement means in rhetoric and composition by advancing bodily, ecological listening and composing practices that can be used in a variety of settings. Such practices, I contend, can help our students create more lively and immersive sonic projects.

PEDAGOGY

Despite the impressive breadth of subjects that sound studies has addressed so far, pedagogy has received little attention. *Sounding Out*—a digital hub for sound studies conversations—has initiated some energizing pedagogical conversations, but there are still few resources that provide examples or methods for teaching with sound. In stark contrast, the vast majority of rhetoric and composition scholarship on sound is pedagogical. Rhetoric and composition scholarship on sound covers topics from sonic literacy to composing rhetorically effective podcasts. Most of this work deals with strategies for teaching students to produce their own sonic projects. Put simply, rhetoric and composition scholarship offers pedagogical expertise that is not currently available in sound studies—or in most disciplines for that matter—which is why I believe it could be of significant use to sound studies teachers.

Notably, the host of pedagogical research on sound in multimodal composition does not include many discussions on how to teach listening. Listening is often mentioned in multimodal composition scholarship on sound but rarely elaborated on or explained as a practice. There is no shortage of listening scholarship in sound studies, as mentioned above, and I would argue that this work could be of value to multimodal composition. In fact, despite its need for more substantial pedagogical research, sound studies is associated with two of the most well-known listening pedagogues: R. Murray Schafer and Pauline Oliveros. Schafer is recognized largely for his work on soundscapes, but he is also a prolific pedagogical scholar. In publications like *Ear Cleaning: Notes for an Experimental Music Course* and *A Sound Education: 100 Exercises in Listening and Sound Making*, Schafer offers wildly creative ideas and exercises for teaching students about sound. Indeed, a desire to teach the world to listen is a recurring theme in Schafer's sizable body of scholarship.

The late Pauline Oliveros, a composer best known for her stunning experimental art music, was also committed to teaching listening. Like Schafer,

Oliveros's work focused on the notion that listening is ecological—that listening unites humans with the environment. In *Deep Listening*, for instance, Oliveros writes, "If you are too narrow in your awareness of sounds, you are likely to be disconnected from your environment" (xxv). Her concept of deep listening, a kind of bodily training that is aimed at cultivating a heightened awareness of sonic environments, led to the creation of the Deep Listening Institute. The institute offers interdisciplinary classes that incorporate "bodywork, sonic meditations, listening to the sounds of daily life, nature, one's own thoughts, imagination and dreams, and listening to listening itself" (Deep Listening Institute). Oliveros's pedagogical work has motivated generations of students to study their relationships to the sonic world.

Sounding Composition attempts to capture the spirit of Schafer's and Oliveros's pedagogical endeavors. Inspired by these imaginative listening pedagogues, I have tried to develop an enlivening, accessible, and relevant listening pedagogy. I also draw from rhetoric and composition pedagogical scholarship to connect multimodal listening education to multimodal composition—to designing and producing multimodal work. This book's emphasis on listening pedagogy is intended to invigorate how sonic composition is taught in rhetoric and composition, and to provide those who teach sound studies with detailed practices and assignments for listening and sonic composing projects that can be adapted for different situations and courses.

CALLING ALL SOUND STUDENTS

This chapter has introduced multiple areas of scholarly inquiry that can spur rhetoric and composition and sound studies to push each other in new directions—to resonate with, perturb, and provoke one another. My hope is that this partial and preliminary discussion will prompt readers to find more ways to share knowledge and communicate across these fields. Rather than simply isolating and importing ideas from one field to the other, the cross-pollination of ideas from rhetoric and composition and sound studies should leave both fields slightly different than before. *Sounding Composition* is one manifestation of this cross-pollination that I hope sound scholars of all stripes will find thought-provoking and useful.

Though this book is in part a response to specific disciplinary questions and issues—particularly in multimodal composition—the pedagogical principles I offer can be of use to *sound students* broadly construed (Sterne 3). In the introduction to *The Sound Studies Reader*, Sterne describes *sound students* as "practitioners of the field" and notes that "most sound students are also something else: historians, philosophers, musicologists, anthropologists, literary critics" and so on (3). I take Sterne's inclusive notion of *sound students* as an invitation for rhetoric and composition scholars to join the mix. This does not mean that rhetoric and composition scholars need to start calling their work *sound studies*. Rather, the increasing number of sound students in rhetoric and composition can and should engage with sound studies in more robust ways.[7] Sterne welcomes such engagement: "As a field, sound studies should not close in upon itself to protect sound as an object from the encroachment of other fields or to claim it as privileged disciplinary property. Instead, it should seek out points of connection and reflection; it should be the name for a group of people who reflexively *mind sound*" (10). This book is a celebration of the interdisciplinary, porous nature of sound studies and offers "points of connection and reflection" for rhetoric and composition teachers and scholars who already "mind sound," as well as those who are interested in learning more about it. At the same time, it amplifies and makes use of insights from rhetoric and composition, thus offering sound studies teachers and scholars diverse approaches to pedagogy and sonic production. In the next chapter, I begin the work of cross-pollinating ideas from sound studies and rhetoric and composition in an exploration of listening and the body.

TWO

SOUNDING BODIES, COMPOSING EXPERIENCE

(Re)Educating the Senses

*In a certain sense every experience should do something to prepare a person for later experi-
ences of a deeper and more expansive quality. That is the very meaning of growth, continuity,
reconstruction of experience.*

JOHN DEWEY, *EXPERIENCE AND EDUCATION*

WHEN ASKED WHICH BODY PART is associated with listening, most people would point to their ears without a second thought. Despite the deeply
entrenched association between listening and the ears, sound is not experienced exclusively through a single sense; other parts of the body can be
engaged during sonic encounters. Beethoven, for instance, preferred to put a
stick in his mouth to feel the sounds of the piano, and Thomas Edison liked
to chomp on the wood of a gramophone to enhance his listening practices
(Connor "Edison's" 168–169). Of course, bodily experiences with sound are
not just limited to the teeth. Everyone has had the experience of feeling sound
in their chest, throat, legs and other areas of the body—a common occurrence
at concerts where music is amplified, or when walking by an active, jackham-
mer-heavy construction site. It is also possible to see sound as jagged waves
on computer screens, or when vibrations from the bass in your car rattle the

loose change in the cup holder. As these examples suggest, identifying the ear as the body part that enables listening does not capture all that is involved in experiencing a sonic event. Listening is multisensory.

Yet, listening is rarely treated as a practice that requires more than the ears. If listening is taught at all, it is usually discussed as the act of hearing and attending to words or sounds in order to make meaning of them. Students are taught to approach sound as audible content that is to be analyzed and interpreted. In addition to teaching students what sound *means*, however, it is critical to teach them how sound *works* and *affects*. Engaging and composing with sound in a holistic way requires listeners to attend to how sound intersects with other sensory modes to shape their embodied experiences in specific contexts. In this chapter, I examine how multimodal listening pedagogy can prepare teachers and students to become sensitive participants in and designers of sonic experiences. As I will show, learning to attend to the multisensory aspects of sonic encounters can provide information about how sound operates as a mode of composition to create particular effects and affects—intentional or unintentional. We can, then, use this information to become more thoughtful consumers and producers of sound. Generally, the multimodal listening pedagogy I outline will demonstrate how anyone might retrain their bodies to be more aware, attentive, and attuned to sonic events in all of their complexity.

To illustrate the fundamental role of bodily experience in multimodal listening pedagogy, I have chosen to examine the listening practices of deaf solo percussionist Dame Evelyn Glennie. Glennie is a renowned musician who performs more than one hundred concerts a year worldwide. While she often plays with orchestras, she has worked on collaborative projects with a diverse range of musicians—from DJ Yoda to Bela Fleck—and, in 2012, was a featured performer at the opening ceremony of the London Olympics (Glennie "Official Website"). Glennie's experiences provide a valuable model for understanding listening as a multimodal event because they augment the expansive nature of sonic experience that most people, particularly people with fully functioning auditory systems, tend to ignore. For Glennie, what I call *ear-ing* is not an option.[1] In fact, she has received as much media attention for her deafness as for her music. The media's consistent highlighting of Glennie's deafness has depicted her as somewhat of an anomaly—as if the full-bodied listening practices she has developed apply only to her because she cannot hear. Rather than treating Glennie as a specialized case, I maintain that her multimodal listening practices are learned bodily habits that can be reproduced in any individual regardless of where they fall on the hearing continuum.

Glennie's multimodal listening practices exemplify a capacious, inclusive form of listening that has the potential to change how people think about and interact with sound. These practices, as well as her documented bodily interactions with sound, can help anybody (and any body) learn to expand their listening practices and become more critical consumers of sound in their everyday lives. Further, Glennie's full-bodied listening techniques offer a useful framework for teaching multimodal listening in relation to composing and can guide instructors in reimagining the role of listening in the multimodal composition classroom.

THE MATERIALITY OF SOUND

I want to begin by situating my examination of Evelyn Glennie's listening practices within a larger body of sound studies work that focuses on the materiality of sound. Sound is not often thought of as material. Words like ephemeral and fleeting seem to be more apt descriptions of sonic interactions. In *Sinister Resonance*, for example, David Toop emphasizes the spectral qualities of sounds, stating that sounds are "difficult to control or subdue, signals that may seem to come from nowhere, or [from] an unknown source, then fade and die . . . sound seems disturbingly intangible, indescribable or inexplicable by comparison to what we can see, touch, and hold" (xii). This statement depicts a certain ghost-like quality of sound. However, sonic experience is also physical and multisensory—it can be heard, seen, and felt. Our ability to sense sound in multiple ways has to do with vibration, a phenomenon that has captured the interest of a number of sound studies scholars.

Indeed, sound is an exceptional medium for exploring sensory interconnections because of its vibratory nature. In *Senses of Vibration*, author Shelley Trower notes that "vibration crosses sensory thresholds in so far as it can be simultaneously palpable and audible, visible and audible" (5). The palpability of sound—sound's ability to "touch" bodies—has to do with frequency. James Cowan explains, "Frequencies below 20 Hz are known as *infrasonic*. These frequencies, although not audible to most people, can be felt as vibrations. This is due to the fact that our internal organs resonate at frequencies between 5 and 15 Hz. Each physical entity has a resonance frequency associated with it, depending on its density. Exposure to sounds near the resonance frequency of a material causes it to vibrate more than it would when exposed to other frequencies" (5). As this passage makes clear, we do not simply observe sound from a position of remove. Our bodies, which produce their own vibrations, resonate with sound in physical and material ways. Infrasonic experiences— especially the intense sonic experiences associated with trauma and war that have been examined by scholars like Steve Goodman and J. Martin Daughtry— make sound's materiality apparent because these experiences are felt.[2] But it is important to remember that even subtle sonic encounters, like hearing water running out of a faucet, produce bodily effects: vibrations physically move fluid and hair cells in the ear to create neural signals that register as sound, if one's auditory system is functioning, that is. Put simply, sound affects and transforms bodies in a wide range of conscious and unconscious ways. Due to sound's vibrational nature, we are always "incorporated into the sonic event itself" (Daughtry 165).

Vibration also makes it possible to see sound.[3] Deaf artist Christine Sun Kim is known for experimenting with the visible qualities of sound in her work. One of her projects, for example, features minimalist paintings created by "placing coated paintbrushes and inked quills on wooden boards atop subwoofers and speakers pulsing with ambient noise" (Packard n.p.). The sonic vibrations were made visible through the oscillating brushes and quills, and through the traces these tools left on the boards. Kim eventually realized, however, that vibration was only part of how she experienced the visible aspects of sound as a deaf person. Thus, she found other ways to visualize the audible via producing "her own semiotics of sound by piecing together a tangle of overlapping languages and systems, including musical notation, body language, and American Sign Language (ASL)" (Packard n.p.). It is easy for hearing people to forget that sonic encounters involve visual as well as audible information. In her acclaimed work, Kim draws attention to the myriad ways people interact with sound beyond hearing (ear-ing).

While it may seem counterintuitive, deafness is a fruitful area of inquiry when it comes to understanding sound precisely because it does not rely on the ears.[4] In fact, Michele Friedner and Stefan Helmreich argue that "vibration is a crucial plane on which sound studies can intersect with deaf studies and that sound is best taken as 'a vibration of a certain frequency in a material medium, rather than centering vibrations in a hearing ear'" (Sterne "Sonic Imaginations" 7). Friedner and Helmreich are quick to recognize, however, that just because everyone—regardless of hearing capacity—experiences sound as vibration, that does not mean sound is experienced in the same way. Rather, echoing Trower, they contend that vibration "may produce shared experience, but it does not therefore produce identical experience; even within 'one' individual, sense ratios and relations may shift and mix synesthetically. Phenomenologies of vibration are not singular" ("Sound Studies Meets Deaf Studies" 77). The notion that bodily interactions with sound are unique is critical to multimodal listening pedagogy. Thus, I have chosen to feature Glennie in this chapter because she offers a constructive model for sonic engagement that relies on the vibratory, material nature of sound, and because her listening practices provide a flexible framework that can be adapted by individual listeners based on their own distinct experiences and bodily capacities.

The ideas about the materiality of sound I have discussed are vital to helping rhetoric and composition scholars make the shift from treating sound exclusively as an object of meaning—something I elaborate on later in this chapter—to approaching sound as a bodily experience. Sound is an actor in the world that moves and disturbs, that *does things* to bodies that may sometimes be surprising and unpredictable. But, that does not mean we cannot learn to listen and respond to sound, or develop a sensitivity to our bodily responses. While "sounds send our bodies into altered sensuous states," Daughtry reminds us, "under normal circumstances, we listeners have cobbled together a fair amount of agency, however, and so we can train ourselves to react, or not react, to sounds in unique or culturally resonant ways" (4). This point is key to understanding the sensory (re)education I am proposing in this chapter, as well as my conception of multimodal listening pedagogy in general. It is possible and necessary, I argue, to retrain ourselves and our students to stop relying only on our ears and instead learn to attend to the multisensory ways that sound affects our embodied experiences.

COME ON FEEL (AND SEE AND TOUCH) THE NOISE

Dame Evelyn Glennie's listening practices exemplify how sight, touch, and sound work together during sonic interactions, making explicit the multimodal aspects of listening that most people take for granted. For Glennie, listening is a practice that is grounded in the body. In Thomas Riedelsheimer's documentary *Touch the Sound*, for example, Glennie describes sound in visceral terms. She explains, "You feel it through your body, and sometimes it almost hits you in your face" (*Touch*). The next scene is a close up shot of Glennie striking a gong with mallets. After reaching a crescendo, she stops making contact with the instrument but continues to stand directly in front of it. By lingering there, she indicates to the viewer that she can still feel the power—the material force—of the sonic vibrations after she has finished playing. As Glennie demonstrates in this scene, and as the synesthetic title of the film insists, interacting with sound can be a form of touch.

The tactile, bodily interaction with sound depicted in this scene is something that Glennie has emphasized repeatedly in interviews and public talks, and *touching sound* seems to be a salient part of her multimodal listening practices. During my interview with Glennie, she characterized her interactions with powerful sounds as physical encounters. She describes sound as a kind of wind: "You almost feel as if your hair is actually moving, and you're almost being sort of kicked back and forth with the force of that sound" (personal interview). Though listening to sound with one's ears also depends on physical movement—as sound vibrations literally move the tympanic membrane (ear drum) to create rhythmic patterns that the brain can detect—Glennie is instead interested in how sound is experienced by the rest of the body.

Her fascination with the physical aspects of sonic interactions is rooted in the fact that the "living sensation" of sound is what has made her own listening education possible (personal interview). Due to her deafness, she was taught to attend to how various sonic vibrations affected her body in different ways. Glennie discusses her early listening training and the importance of learning to detect vibrations in an essay posted to her website. She writes, "I would stand with my hands against the classroom wall . . . I managed to distinguish the rough pitch of notes by associating where on my body I felt the sound" ("Hearing" n.p.). In her autobiography, *Good Vibrations*, she also describes "getting in touch with music" by sitting "with a clattery old portable tape recorder in my lap, one that vibrated as much as possible so I could experience the waves of sound through my body" (159). In this musical context, Glennie's tactile experiences played a significant role in her listening education. She is not reflecting upon the meaning of sound in these passages. Rather, she is thinking about how the force of sound is working—how it is transforming her body in various ways. Glennie's listening experiences demonstrate that the initial encounter, the material point of contact, between sound and body is in part what makes multimodal listening a possibility. Her bodily listening practices provide her with experiential knowledge about how sound works as an affective mode of communication.

In addition to the vibratory, tactile experience of sound, the visual experience of sound is a prominent feature of Glennie's multimodal listening practices. One of the ways that the film *Touch the Sound* attempts to represent the visual aspects of Glennie's listening practices is by exaggerating her sensory interactions with environments. The camera often positions the audience in Glennie's point of view and magnifies the visual details that surround her body. While the sounds associated with certain images are amplified for hearing viewers, the magnification of visual detail makes it clear that Glennie is experiencing those sounds through her eyes. Some of the most subtle rhythms and movements of the life surrounding Glennie are captured by the lens of the camera, and seemingly, by Glennie herself. For instance, the camera zooms in on the details of rattling suitcase zippers, different shoes walking on a hard surface, and people bobbing their heads to the music of their MP3 players. Attending to rhythm and movement in these visual encounters is a way for Glennie to listen to the sonic environment that she inhabits. It gives her a sense of the soundscape without having to depend on auditory information.

The visual aspects of Glennie's multimodal listening practices figure into her sonic performances as well. For instance, Glennie often experiments with the relationship between sound and visible movement. As she told me during our interview, "if I want to play something quietly, sometimes I move my mallets but I'm not actually touching the instrument. So, the audience feels I'm playing extremely quietly, and they really do believe they're hearing something even though nothing is coming out. It's because they're seeing the movement . . . that automatically gives them the feeling that sound is there" (personal interview). By deliberately attracting attention to the movements of her mallets, Glennie tricks her audience into believing that those movements resulted in audible sound. Playing with the audience's perception of sound enables Glennie to give the audience a glimpse into her own visual listening practices. Her anecdote also highlights the strong connection between sound and vision that most people unconsciously rely on when listening. Indeed, when Glennie performs her sonic compositions, the visual aspects of her performance are an important part of the audience's listening experience. The speed or slowness with which she moves her body as she plays, her facial gestures, and the way that she physically handles the instruments all contribute to how sound is being experienced by the audience.

Glennie's experiences show that multimodal listening involves attending to both the bodily affects of sound and to the multiple sensory modes that can be used to participate in a sonic event. Though I have separated the tactile and visual ways of listening in the above discussion in order to emphasize how each sensory mode can be employed, they do not occur in isolation. On the contrary, sounds, sights, and tactile feelings are often experienced simultaneously during sonic interactions. While Glennie has developed multimodal listening techniques in part to compensate for her diminished auditory capacity, paying attention to the sensory convergences that happen during sonic events is a practice that can help anyone cultivate more reflective, sensitive listening habits.

I realize that multimodal listening practices may seem unnecessary for people with functioning ears. If one can hear, then what is the point of using additional sensory modes to attend to sound? I would argue that the multimodal listening practices Glennie uses are necessary and purposeful to everyone because, unlike ear-ing, these practices allow listeners to achieve expansive sonic experiences that can lead to rich, meaningful sensory encounters. When listeners attend to a sonic event via multiple senses, mundane experiences can be transformed into aesthetic experiences. As John McCarthy and Peter Wright note, "In aesthetic experience, the lively integration of means and ends, meaning and movement, involving all our sensory and intellectual faculties is emotionally satisfying and fulfilling. Each act relates meaningfully to the total action and is felt by the experiencer to have a unity or a wholeness that is fulfilling" (58). Multimodal listening practices help listeners develop a heightened awareness of sound as an *ecological* event in which they are participating, or what McCarthy and Wright refer to as "a lively integration" (58).

In universalizing Glennie's multimodal listening practices, I do not mean to downplay the physiological or social struggles faced by people with disabilities. I am in no way suggesting that the point of multimodal listening pedagogy is to "step into Glennie's shoes" or somehow replicate her particular bodily experience. Rather, I am drawing on Glennie's experiences to provide a general listening framework that can be taken up by a range of listeners and modified to suit their individual needs and abilities. Multimodal listening is not a one-size-fits-all practice. Thus, multimodal listening pedagogy offers flexible listening strategies that account for diverse bodies instead of proposing that all listeners should (or can) listen in the same way. Put otherwise, multimodal listening provides multiple points of entry for participating in sonic experiences as opposed to listening with the ears only. Because of differences in bodily capacities and learning abilities, every listener will inevitably practice their own unique version of multimodal listening.

It is also important to underscore that the "unity" or "wholeness" involved in aesthetic experiences does not require a fully or normatively functioning sensorium (McCarthy and Wright 58). Participating in such experiences simply requires people to be aware of how the senses *that they have access to* work together in particular moments. This distinction is key because, as Melanie Yergeau has argued, a multimodal pedagogy "built for only those whose senses are 'intact' is a pedagogy that centers able-bodiedness" ("Shiny"). Unlike scholarship about multimodality that celebrates able-bodied sensory experiences (i.e., presumes that everyone has access to all senses all of the time), multimodal listening pedagogy offers situation-specific practices that can be tailored according to listeners' distinctive bodily experiences ("Shiny").[5]

I designed this supple pedagogy so that no student is excluded from a multimodal education. Rather than using multimodal listening pedagogy selectively for a special unit on disability studies or to respond to a student with disabilities, multimodal listening can and should be adopted widely in courses that deal with sound and listening.[6] This is not to say that disabled and able-bodied students will participate in classroom activities in the same way. I want to be clear that the assignments and pedagogical suggestions in this book will not meet the needs of every student in every context. Such a task would be impossible. What multimodal listening pedagogy does offer, though, is an array of ways to take part in assignments and experiments involving sound and listening. It is a pedagogy that acknowledges the body and makes room for students' bodily capacities and limitations from the start, not as an afterthought.

The purpose of multimodal listening pedagogy is to challenge students to break the sensory habits on which they have come to rely and become open to a wider range of ways that their bodies might participate in sonic interactions. Multimodal listening is valuable because it can invigorate listeners' sensitivity to their distinctive bodily relationships with the sonic world. As I will demonstrate, this heightened sensitivity can deepen students' understandings of how sound works and affects people in different contexts, thus enhancing students' abilities to use sound strategically during the composing process. Before describing how multimodal listening can augment multimodal composition pedagogy, however, it is necessary to examine the sensory (re)education that is an essential part of cultivating multimodal listening practices.

BODILY LEARNING AND UNLEARNING

Past experiences with sound shape listening practices whether listeners are conscious of it or not, and the accumulation of these experiences results in the formation of listening habits. A crucial aspect of multimodal listening instruction, then, is helping students unlearn the listening habits they have developed over time. Unlearning is an indispensable part of the learning process. In fact, learning, Cathy Davidson stresses, "is the constant disruption of an old pattern, a breakthrough that substitutes something new for something old. And then the process starts again" (5). Teaching students to listen multimodally involves undoing their usual sensory habits—which might include a dependence on the ears, eyes, or any singular sensory mode—and amplifying the multiple senses that they can use to attend to sonic interactions. Multimodal listening instruction requires a feedback loop of teaching students to develop new listening habits while also helping them unlearn old listening habits that have come to feel natural.

Understanding how bodies can be taught to unlearn calls for some general knowledge about how sensory habits are formed. Though the ways that we engage with the world through our senses may seem like a strictly biological matter, sensory interactions are learned and refined through experience. "Our senses require education," states Henri Bergson (48). Without bodily knowledge of how the senses work in different contexts, life would be utterly chaotic. Every interaction with the world would be unexpected, confusing, and potentially dangerous without prior knowledge. Imagine, for example, if your body never remembered how it feels to touch a hot stove. Luckily, bodies have a tremendous capacity for memory because they do learn from past sensory interactions. Bergson explains that "bodily memory" is "made up of the sum of the sensorimotor systems organized by habit" (152). Bodily memory is reinforced during every sensory encounter one experiences. After enough sensory experiences, bodies acquire knowledge about how these encounters affect them, which in turn informs how those bodies will respond to new sensory experiences. In this sense, the very act of living—of being a body interacting with the world—is an ongoing series of educational events.

However, the accumulation or quantity of experiences is not the only factor involved in bodily learning. The *quality* of experiences also facilitates or stunts growth and learning in subsequent experiences (Dewey 47). For example, if a body is persistently assaulted with the same low quality experiences, its sensory interactions with the world will become blunted. During our interview, Glennie expressed concern about the low quality experiences that are associated with sonic excess. Because I find her description so relevant to the topic at hand, I include a lengthy segment here:

> It is just a case of seeing our senses as food. You know, we wouldn't eat 24–7
> and expect to be healthy. . . . If we put something in our mouth every single

second of the day we would be extremely ill. And yet, we're prepared to do that with sound. We're prepared to feed our system with sound upon sound upon sound upon sound. If we sit on an airplane, we have a huge amount of vibration coming from the engine of an airplane. What do we do? We try to cancel that out by putting something in our ears, and listening to music or watching a movie or whatever. So that there is more sound. And there are other announcements and distractions on the plane, which is more sound. And it just sort of clumps itself up just like that. And you know in a way the jet lag thing, I wonder if it's not so much based on the time differences and all that kind of thing but really just based on the huge overload to our senses that we have, that we feel we have to have. So, you know, it's the same with what we see. It's the same with what we smell, but I think we're much more choosy with how we use our sense of smell. We're slightly more choosy with our sense of taste. But yet with our sense of hearing, and the sound sense, it's making no sense, because it just seems to be on overload. (personal interview)

Glennie emphasizes that the accumulation of low quality experiences, or experiences that do not result in learning or growth, dulls one's conscious sensory awareness. Through repetition, these experiences train bodies to become numb—to tune out—and eventually desensitization to particular sonic stimuli becomes the norm. As Glennie mentions, most listeners' reaction to overstimulation from the sonic environment is to ignore it by streaming more sound through their ears. Her example highlights how bodily experiences with sound can lead to the formation of specific listening habits. In this case, a bombardment of environmental sound results in a low quality experience that encourages ear-centric listening.

Throughout the interview, Glennie implied that the best way to unlearn sensory numbness or change the listening habits that have resulted from sonic overstimulation is to expose the body to a range of diverse sensory experiences. For instance, she speaks of her own listening training as a kind of restrictive diet: "what I am aware of is making sure that my sort of daily sound diet, as it were—that there is a huge amount of time where there is no sound. Everything that doesn't exist—but I mean consciously, you know, switching the TV off and just sitting for a few moments with nothing" (personal interview). By spending long periods of time in low-noise environments, Glennie claims that her body is more attuned to sound in other environments. In contrast, another method she employs to heighten her sensory awareness is to experience as many different sounds as possible. Glennie makes "a point of trying to get a range of frequencies" in her "sound diet" (personal interview). One effective way of doing this is to seek out "organic sounds, sound that can reproduce itself, or sounds that are just observed from the surroundings," as opposed to recorded sound (personal interview).

While Glennie's synesthetic sound diet analogy is compelling, it is worth problematizing a bit further. This analogy holds up in situations where listeners can freely choose the sounds with which they would like to engage—just as they might choose a salad over potato chips if those are the options. In other words, dieters make choices, which give them at least some control over their bodies. However, listeners do not always have control over what sounds they encounter or how they will be affected by those sounds. It is not possible to close our ears the way we can our eyes or mouth, and even if we could, it would not matter in cases when sound is felt in other parts of the body. We do not always have the luxury of choosing to "eat" the sounds we want. It is important to recognize, then, that there are occasions when sound's agential power takes hold of our bodies in ways that cannot be controlled or predicted.

That said, when Glennie refers to her own "sound diet," it is in the context of training, of deliberately educating her body to become more sensitive to sound. In part, this training is an effort to recover from the effects and affects of the uncontrollable sonic encounters she experiences in everyday life, such as the desensitizing sonic excess of air travel. Though she may not be able to predict what happens in a given listening environment, she can make conscious decisions about which sounds she wants to expose herself to in situations that she can control. This is something we all do. In fact, because Glennie considers one's "sound diet" to be an integral part of cultivating critical listening habits, she expressed disappointment about many listeners' obliviousness to and conscious evasion of "organic sounds." She explained that "a lot of the younger generation, because they've been brought up with technology," tend to be unaware of and/or underexposed to a full range of organic sounds (personal interview). Glennie is concerned because more and more people choose to be plugged into their computers, smartphones, and other electronic devices. Consequently, they regularly consume reproduced sounds with frequencies that vary in the higher register but not much in the lower register. Sound becomes tactile, or felt, in parts of the body other than the ears in the lower register (below 20 Hz). Thus, exposure to mostly high frequency sounds conditions hearing listeners to depend on their ears. A high frequency sound diet that consists mainly of prerecorded sound trains people to be less sensitive to the fuller sensory experience of sound or how the rest of the body experiences and engages with sound.[7]

The main challenge of multimodal listening instruction, as I see it, is for teachers to design productive, *quality* sonic experiences that will continue to build on and expand students' past sonic experiences. For multimodal listening instruction to be effective, it is necessary to design activities that can resensitize students, who are most likely unaware of their desensitization from repetitive, low-quality sonic interactions. As John Dewey notes, "Wholly independent of desire or intent, every experience lives on in further experiences. Hence the central problem of an education based upon experience is to select the kind of present experiences that live fruitfully and creatively in subsequent experiences" (27–28). To teach multimodal listening involves creating assignments that encourage the kind of heightened awareness that enables students to learn and grow with every new sonic experience. Students need to unlearn the listening practices that they have become accustomed to in their everyday lives, and so teachers must find ways to defamiliarize these habitual practices to make them strange again.

In a way, then, multimodal listening pedagogy is similar to the defamiliarization strategies that are used in textual composition. For example, take into consideration the perspective of Viktor Shkolovsky, who coined the term *defamiliarization*. According to Don Bialostosky, "He [Shkolovsky] saw poetic devices as counteracting the tendency of our minds to get used to everything, including ways of speaking and writing, and no longer to notice anything—a condition of deadened perception and response that produces dead conventional language" (n.p.). To defamiliarize and reinvigorate readers, poets had to come up with innovative ways to break language conventions or to use language in an unexpected manner. Bialostosky continues, "poets had to keep finding new ways to make their language strange, to make it unfamiliar and therefore noticeable" (n.p.). Just as poets and writers use defamiliarization techniques to heighten readers' awareness of language, teachers must plan occasions that give listeners a chance to experience sound in new and surprising ways. The heightened awareness gained from multimodal listening practices can help students become more savvy consumers and composers of sound.

MULTIMODAL LISTENING
AND MULTIMODAL COMPOSING

Drawing inspiration from Glennie's approach to listening, below I propose four ways that multimodal composition pedagogy can benefit from multimodal listening practices. Before elaborating on how multimodal listening practices expand and enrich students' composing practices, though, I want to briefly consider why it is necessary to supplement the sound and listening projects that are already well-known features of many multimodal composition curricula. Podcasts, voice-overs, and audio essays are among the most familiar assignments that deal specifically with sound in the multimodal composition classroom.[8] While I find value in such projects and continue to use versions of them in my own teaching, the listening and sonic composing practices that they require can be limiting in a number of ways. For example, creating an audio essay is often approached like writing a textual essay: Students write a script, record themselves reading it using audio editing software, and sometimes incorporate music or sound effects. Consider the process of composing with sound that Cynthia Selfe, Stephanie Owen Fleischer, and Susan Wright outline in *Multimodal Composition*: "thinking about purpose, audience, and form," "planning and brainstorming various concepts for an audio essay in a word-processing program," "trying out different approaches to arranging and organizing audio material in various versions/drafts of essay," and "peer review of—and response to—drafts" (15). The authors make specific connections between sonic and textual composing. Highlighting the similarities between sound and text is a common move in multimodal composition scholarship. As Bump Halbritter writes, "In soundful compositions, sound is text" (216).

I agree that it is important to stress the parallels between composing with sound and composing with alphabetic text to show students how the writing techniques that are already familiar to them relate to other modes. But sound is also a distinct mode with distinct affordances, and we can leverage those affordances further in multimodal composition. Too often, when the affordances of sound are discussed in scholarship about audio composing genres, sound's most celebrated affordance tends to be its ability to enhance narrative meaning and content. This is something that Selfe touches upon in "The Movement of Air, the Breath of Meaning," an excellent overview of the history of aural composing modalities—speech, music, and sound. She states that in the past several decades "compositionists have continued to experiment with assignments that encouraged students to create meaning in and through audio compositions" (640). Sound is portrayed as separate from text in multimodal composition scholarship. Yet it also seems to serve the same purpose as text— to heighten or convey meaning.

When sound is dealt with as an exclusively semiotic resource in multimodal composing assignments, students miss out on learning how the bodily, material, and contextual aspects of sonic experience figure into the composing process. Assignments that treat sound as a text diminish the full range of sound's compositional and rhetorical affordances. Additionally, what I refer to as sound-as-text multimodal composing assignments seldom require students to reflect on their listening experiences. Rather than asking students to reflect on how their listening practices affect their composing processes, we tend to take listening for granted as something that students just "do" when composing with sound. This assumption is problematic because it perpetuates the idea that listening is a natural, as opposed to a learned, practice, which implies that everybody (i.e., every body) can hear and listen to sonic compositions in the same way. In other words, these ear-centric assignments do not account for an embodied listening audience, nor do they ask students to consider their own or others' bodily capacities or learning needs.

There are, of course, nuances and exceptions to sound-as-text approaches in multimodal composition scholarship on sound. Notably, in "Glenn Gould and the Rhetorics of Sound," Jonathan Alexander examines the experimental work of pianist and recording artist Glenn Gould to argue for more capacious approaches to sonic production in multimodal composition pedagogy. Michelle Comstock and Mary Hocks's "Voice in the Cultural Soundscape" and Kati Fargo Ahern's "Tuning the Sonic Playing Field" offer astute observations and suggestions about listening as a practice. I also find Jody Shipka's theory of *multimodal soundness*, which "resists attempts to bracket off the individual senses and the uptake of required/assigned semiotic resources," to be a fresh take on sound in multimodal composition pedagogy ("Sound" 371). Building upon this work, I want to suggest that approaches to sonic composition can be further enriched by asking students to take their own bodies and senses into account in more explicit ways, to consider the limitations of the digital context in which they are composing, and to think critically about their own listening practices.

Alongside assignments that treat sound as text, the multimodal composition classroom is in need of practices that can sharpen students' knowledge about the distinct ways that sound works as a mode of composition and an affective force. Here I offer some initial suggestions about how multimodal listening practices can respond to this need.

> Multimodal listening practices enable composers to cultivate experiential knowledge that can help them make strategic decisions about how to design sonic compositions for embodied audiences.

Attending to how the body figures into sonic interactions via multimodal listening can help composers take advantage of sound's affective possibilities. While it is a standard practice for composers to think about how audiences will intellectually and emotionally respond to their compositions, multimodal listening requires composers to consider how their sonic compositions will affect *embodied* audiences. By *embodied*, I am not only referring to the representational categories that have become staples of discussions of embodiment in the humanities and social sciences—categories such as race, gender, class, disability, sexual orientation—but to the fact that an embodied audience comprises sensing, nerve-filled, responsive bodies.[9] If composers can develop a critical awareness of how different sounds affect their own bodies via multimodal listening, they will be more attuned to how sound works as an affective mode, and to how their own sonic compositions might affect different audiences in different ways.

I am not suggesting that there is a one-to-one correlation between a particular sound and a particular bodily affect. A sound does not necessarily affect all bodies in the same way every time (or at all), and not all bodies experience sound similarly either. Rather, the point of teaching students to attend to how sound affects bodies is to make them more aware of the *various* affective possibilities and limitations of sonic interactions. To treat sound as a complex, dynamic mode of composition, it is necessary to consider how the affects of sound may vary from person to person, context to context. Multimodal listening practices can be used to highlight the fact that bodies are not uniform—that the audiences for which students compose, as well as the students themselves, have a variety of bodily capacities and needs that will influence how they respond to sound. Experiencing and experimenting with sounds and their affective potential can help composers address questions such as: What kind of sound would be most persuasive—most effective *and* affective—given the embodied audience I am composing for? How are the technologies with which

I am composing enabling me or preventing me from manipulating sound to achieve these desired effects and affects? How will context affect my sonic composition and/or the embodied audience's response to it?

To encourage engagement with such questions, teachers might create assignments that ask students to design sonic compositions that allow audiences with different preferences or bodily capacities to interact with their work. For example, in a more advanced multimodal composition course, students might be asked to create an audio narrative that includes visual and textual options that could be turned on or off by the user, which would be ideal for deaf and hard of hearing audiences. The composition might include a textual narrative that scrolls below the audio file that could consist of brief descriptions of the nonverbal sounds that appear on the screen, perhaps in colors that correspond to the intensity of the sound, and then fade away. Such a design would give users more flexibility and more ways to engage with this sonic composition via multiple sensory and communicative modes. Indeed, echoing Stephanie Kerschbaum, I want to stress that "those who design and produce multimodal texts and environments need to incorporate redundancy across multiple channels in order to make digital texts more—not less—flexible, and they should enable customization and manipulation of these texts" (n.p.). Having students create sonic work that includes visual and/or textual options can be accomplished in a variety of activities. Regardless of the specific assignment, the key is to get students thinking about how an audience could interact with a sonic composition via multiple modes.[10]

By attending to their bodily experiences with sound in digital environments, composers can develop a sharper sense of the affordances and limitations of sound as a compositional mode. Additionally, multimodal listening practices can expand the ways that sensing bodies are figured into the composing process. As McCarthy and Wright contend, "it is only by seeing technology as participating in felt experience that we can understand the fullness of its potential" (x). The heightened awareness of bodily experience in multimodal listening provides an opportunity for composers to design flexible sonic compositions that can be interacted with in multiple ways instead of only through the ears. Thus, to my mind, multimodal listening practices serve as a way to promote *universal design*—to prompt composers to come up with creative strategies for developing sonic compositions that offer more inclusive and accessible experiences. The concept of universal design "holds that one should design spaces and learning environments for the broadest possible access" (Dolmage and Lewiecki-Wilson 26). Adopting universal design should be a fundamental practice in multimodal composing, and I would argue that it is a necessary and critical step toward the production of more inclusive sound-based work in digital environments.[11]

> Multimodal listening practices allow composers to develop a nuanced understanding of how sound works and affects bodies in particular contexts.

While ear-centric listening practices often focus narrowly on the meaning and interpretation of audible words, multimodal listening practices take into account the dynamics of the sonic composition as a whole. This holistic approach to sonic composition requires composers to consider how sound is integrated (or not) with other elements in a multimodal composition (e.g., images, video, text, etc.), as well how those elements and the composing environment in general may affect different audiences' experiences.[12] However, it is important to note that if sonic composing and listening practices are restricted to the screen of a digital audio editor, or any one context, then listener-composers are not experiencing a full enough range of sonic environments to get a sense of how different materials and contexts shape sonic experiences. Isolating multimodal listening and composing practices to a singular sonic environment not only gives students limited knowledge about the affordances of sonic contexts, it sets up a disconnection between sonic interactions in composing environments and sonic interactions in students' lives outside of the classroom. Multimodal listening pedagogy provides opportunities for students to attend to how sound is working in a range of environments, thus making listening instruction a way for students to better understand the relationship between the sonic compositions they create and interact with in the classroom and the sonic spaces they move through every day.

One way that I try to expand students' engagement with sound in my own classroom is to have them compose soundscapes. For instance, in the Sounding Pittsburgh Project, which inspired the "Mapping Sound" assignment I discuss in the Reverberation for Chapter 3, I asked students to work in teams to compose a digital soundscape of the Pittsburgh neighborhood of their choice. Teams conducted field research in neighborhoods by listening, taking notes and photos, and capturing sounds with digital audio recorders and smartphones. Then they assessed their large collection of sonic material and chose the sounds that they felt best represented the neighborhood. Once we synthesized everyone's material to compose a collaborative soundscape of

Pittsburgh, we talked about what information or meaning could be gleaned from the sounds—what stories the sounds told about Pittsburgh or particular neighborhoods. For example, students pointed out that the loud construction sounds in the East Liberty neighborhood occurred more frequently than in any other part of the city we recorded. They ended up making an argument (supported by photo documentation) that sound recordings made it possible to trace the gentrification occurring in different areas of that neighborhood.

Students also compared their embodied listening experiences in the city to their experiences with our digital sonic representation of the city. They reported that their immersive and ephemeral encounters with sound in Pittsburgh neighborhoods were more intense, affective, and dynamic compared to experiencing those sounds through tiny computer speakers. At the same time, the digital soundscape offered a more controlled listening experience since the ability to listen repeatedly in this setting made it easier to analyze and find patterns among the sounds. Having students return to a digital environment after their sonic encounters in Pittsburgh seemed to bring the constraints and possibilities of sound in each setting into sharp relief. As I learned from this pedagogical experiment, teaching students about the complexity of sonic experience and multimodality requires moving beyond exclusively digital contexts to include a wider variety of listening experiences, which I discuss at length in Chapter 3.

> Multimodal listening is an inquiry-based practice that encourages composers to explore and experiment with all of the available effects, affects, and meanings of sound in different environments.

Multimodal listening practices require composers to approach sound not as static and stable but as a highly contextual experience that changes from one setting to the next. That is, multimodal listeners consider the ever-changing possibilities and limitations of sound rather than coming to hasty conclusions about what a sound means or represents. The key to multimodal listening is sonic play and experimentation. Instead of seeking specific sounds to achieve specific affects (i.e., searching for and downloading a sound effect and immediately inserting it into a composition), multimodal listening practices involve tinkering with different versions of sounds before determining which one is most effective and/or affective. Trying out different versions of similar sounds is a standard practice for professional sound designers. In an interview with Trevor Cox, for instance, critically acclaimed sound mixer and

designer Myron Netinga talks about the importance of creating and choosing appropriate sounds: "Myron explained that for a scene about a lazy, calm
night in the country, he might pick a soothing cricket, 'but hey man, if a guy is
creeping around the back of the house looking to jump some people, then all
of a sudden there's a cricket and he's agitated and he's a little nervous, and he's
stopping and starting.' Myron's choice depends on the rhythm of the cricket
chirps and the abruptness with which each sound starts" (Cox 91). This careful
attention to the nuances of sound in a particular context is a crucial aspect
of multimodal listening pedagogy. By encouraging listeners to think about
the full range of a sound's possibilities, multimodal listening practices help
students develop a more sophisticated and reflective approach to integrating
sound into their own compositions.

Teachers might also prompt students to try out the same version of a sound
in different settings. Rather than asking students to make a sonic composition
that will be posted on a blog or a website, for example, teachers could ask
them to design a single sonic composition that will be performed in two places
such as a park and a gymnasium, or a small room with low ceilings and a large
space with high ceilings. Comparing the experience of sound in the two performances would make the significance of the contextual, ecological aspects of
the sonic composition more apparent. Through discovery and play, students
will have a better sense of the available sonic possibilities and limitations in a
specific environment.

I want to be clear that my emphasis on the body as a mode of inquiry in
multimodal listening practices is not any less intellectually rigorous than listening practices that focus solely on the meaning of sound or alphabetic language. Instead, I understand multimodal listening to be what Debra Hawhee
refers to as "a mind-body complex" (10). In her account of the linked practices of rhetoric and athletics in ancient Greece, Hawhee writes, "rhetoric's
relation to athletics hinges on a kind of knowledge production that occurs
on the level of the body . . . This is not to say that 'mind' or thought, is not
important, but rather that it is part of a complex—a mind-body complex—that
learns and moves in response to a situation rather than through the applica-
tion of abstract principles" (10). While Hawhee discusses the role of the body
in relation to ancient rhetorical practices, her comments about bodily pedagogies apply to the multimodal listening education I have been describing.
Unlike ear-centric listening practices that often depend on the interpretation of abstract knowledge (words, ideas, etc.), the cultivation of multimodal
listening practices "hinges on a kind of knowledge production that occurs

on the level of the body" (10). Multimodal listening requires undoing ear-centric habits and developing a holistic approach to sonic encounters through embodied experience in particular contexts.

The bodily pedagogy that Hawhee articulates also resonates powerfully with multimodal listening in that it does not have a fixed aim or goal. She writes, "the 'end result' of such pedagogy is not a finished product, but a disposi-tional capacity for iteration—the ability to continually repeat, transform, and respond" (151). Like the sophistic pedagogy Hawhee discusses, multimodal listening pedagogy is not based on a set formula or universal goal. Rather, through experimentation and repetition students of multimodal listening learn to attend to the bodily and contextual aspects of sonic encounters. With practice, they will be able to translate that acute attention and method of inquiry to bodily interactions with sound in a range of situations. In other words, the multimodal listening habits that students cultivate are meant to provide a foundation for helping them respond to, explore, and compose with sound in a variety of contexts. Multimodal listening does not require master-ing a particular corpus of knowledge. Rather, it is an ongoing, experiential, inquiry-based practice.

> Multimodal listening practices require composers
> to approach sonic composition as a means of
> designing immersive, holistic experiences.

Multimodal listening invites composers to approach sonic compositions not as mere texts, but as total sensory experiences. By attending to one's bodily reaction to sound, the context in which a sound is being experienced, and how sound is working with or against other modes and materials, composers can make more informed decisions about how to ultimately design their sonic compositions to create holistic multimodal experiences. As Graham Pullin eloquently puts it, "the best way to design the experience is to experience the design" (139). Learning to create sensorially engaging experiences is an especially relevant form of composition because it is fundamental to contem-porary design. Sound, in particular, is becoming an increasingly vital design element. One of the primary goals for designers of everything from baseball stadiums to museums to video games is to create pleasurable sensory experi-ences. Designers have to think through the overall experience of a product, a place, or an activity—its sound, look, taste, touch, smell. As I mentioned previously, immersive bodily experiences tend to be more meaningful and memorable than low quality experiences. Teaching students to design holistic experiences via multimodal listening practices can help them compose more enlivening sonic compositions, as well as deepen their understanding of sound as an integral part of the texts, products, and environments that they interact with every day.

It is important to note that digital composing environments have limitations in terms of producing immersive sonic experiences. They cannot replicate the three-dimensional experience of sound or the full range of different frequencies that can be felt in the body. I see these limitations as opportunities for teachers of multimodal composition to ask students to compose and/or perform their sonic compositions outside digital contexts. Consider, for example, a sonic project about the importance of bass in hip-hop culture. The felt experience of bass is part of what makes it a compelling and meaningful sound. Since it is not yet possible in most digital sound environments for listeners to experience the low-frequency sounds that can be felt in the body,[13] this project might best be executed in a space where audiences can feel the bass for themselves, such as in a parking lot where the composer could incorporate the bass sounds from a car, or a space where loud speakers could blast felt vibrations. This is just one of many possibilities for incorporating more experimental sonic composing experiences into the classroom, and I offer additional examples throughout the book. Whatever projects or activities teachers might decide to try, turning to sonic experiences and spaces beyond the computer screen is a great way to help students create multimodal compositions that engage audiences in more powerful, bodily ways.

TOWARD PEDAGOGIES OF LIVED EXPERIENCE

In this chapter I have tried to illustrate that it is more productive to think of listening in terms of sensory possibilities than organ-specific binaries where you either have the capacity to listen or you do not. The fact that bodies can be retrained to experience listening via multiple modes—that listening is an adaptable, dynamic practice that can be learned and unlearned—provides teachers with an opportunity to explore how a broad spectrum of listening practices and sonic experiences might inform their pedagogies. Multimodal listening can lead to unfamiliar, surprising, and imaginative approaches to listening and sonic composing. Perhaps most significantly, multimodal listening pedagogy has the potential to invigorate the role of the body, of *lived experience*, in multimodal engagement and production. The listening pedagogy outlined in this chapter and elaborated on throughout the book strives to give students a fuller, more complex understanding of the role of the body in listening and sonic composing activities.

It is worth repeating that, by underscoring bodily experience, I am not suggesting that we should teach students to stop making meaning of and with sound. Rather, I am arguing that in the pedagogical work we do, it is necessary to emphasize that meaning-making is always embodied. "Embodiment," Anne Wysocki asserts, "has to be acknowledged as both active and passive, felt by us as well as produced by us" (Arola and Wysocki 19). Multimodal listening pedagogy helps students understand that their felt experiences are inextricably linked to the ways they listen to and make sense of sound. At the same time, cultivating multimodal listening practices can raise students' awareness of how the sonic compositions they produce always enable particular bodily experiences and prevent others. Multimodal listening supplements listening practices that focus solely on the meaning and interpretation of sound by offering various ways for students to experience and reflect on what it means to be an *embodied* listener, composer, thinker, and learner. To that end, in the Reverberation that follows this chapter, I offer an assignment that invites students to design a multimodal composition or performance based on a past sonic experience that made them more aware of their bodies. Building on my discussion of Glennie and multimodal listening, this project asks students to think expansively about what is involved in participating in a sonic interaction instead of approaching sound as something that is accessed or understood through the ears only.

REVERBERATION
MY LISTENING BODY

THE INTERCHAPTERS, OR REVERBERATIONS, IN this book are intended to present teachers with possible openings and pathways for implementing multimodal listening pedagogy. While I write from the perspective of my own teaching experience in a particular context, I encourage readers to tailor, adapt, and transform the materials and classroom practices I discuss for their own situations and purposes. The following assignment—based on the bodily listening practices explored in Chapter 2—asks students to consider the ways that sound affects different aspects of their embodied experiences. In addition to the general assignment guidelines, I provide commentary about the project's purpose and design, my pedagogical practice, and student examples. I also include a list of resources for teachers and students.

MY LISTENING BODY

Goal

The aim of this assignment is to gain a critical awareness of how sound shapes and affects embodied experience.

Choose an Experience

This project asks you to design a piece of autobiographical digital media or a performance about a memorable sonic interaction that made you aware of your body. Start by making a list of some of the most the memorable sonic experiences you have had in your life—from childhood to the present. These experiences need not be extraordinary; seemingly mundane experiences with sound can be just as interesting as epic sonic events. Here is an example list to give you a sense of some of the possibilities for this project:

- traveling on a plane for the first time
- going to a hip-hop concert and recognizing how the bass sounds and how moving bodies around me seemed to exaggerate my embodied difference—my whiteness
- standing near the church organ at a crowded Mass
- getting a cavity filled
- irritating my teachers by being "too loud" and "unladylike" in class
- cruising in my friend's car after he installed subwoofers
- riding an old wooden roller-coaster

Once you have a sizeable list, choose the top three experiences that you think might work best for this assignment. Then, take some time to write about each of them—about why these particular bodily experiences are memorable, about how the sound made you think, feel, behave, etc. Go into as much detail as possible. After you have exhausted your ideas, pick the experience that caused you to produce the most substantive, evocative material.

Compose Your Experience

You will need to figure out how to best represent your chosen sonic experience in a multimodal composition. You might decide to do a sonic project using a digital audio editor. Or, you might want to make a video with a voiceover, or with just a soundtrack, or with no sound at all. Alternatively, you may decide that a series of still images with accompanying sounds (and/or text) would work best. You might even choose to do a live performance piece that recreates some aspect of the sonic experience you want to amplify.

The way in which you construct your experience is up to you, but you need to consider *why* you are choosing to use a particular mode(s) of composition: Is it important for audiences to actually *see* your body in this project (why or why not)? How does using video enable you to capture your experience—or the *feeling* of your experience—in a way that sound alone cannot? Or, why would sound, without visuals, be the best choice? (For example, your experience may have taken place in the dark or may have caused you to block out or ignore what was happening around you.)

∿

Once you have decided on the compositional modes that you want to use in your project, you need to figure out how to present your sonic, textual, and/or visual material. You might want to create an experimental, abstract piece that is meant to evoke the feeling of the experience itself; or perhaps it would make the most sense to show your sonic experience in some way. Again, the ultimate form that your project assumes will depend on what, specifically, you are trying to convey about your sonic experience.

∿

Finally, you need to account for a *diverse embodied audience*. That is, you must consider and plan for how a range of people with different preferences or bodily capacities will be able to access your work. If you have a video with a voiceover, for instance, you should include subtitles and/or provide a written transcript of the work to accommodate deaf or hard of hearing listeners (and to provide all listeners with an additional way to access the spoken language in the video). You should also describe all of the nonverbal sounds and images in vivid detail in an accompanying document or in the actual media. We will be reading articles on composing accessible multimedia to help you design a flexible, inclusive project.

Artist Statement

Give your project an appropriate title and write an "artist statement" (1000 words) that addresses the following:

- a description of your project, including your thoughts about what makes your particular sonic experience a valuable/interesting/significant topic to explore
- a discussion of how and why working on this project has expanded or pushed your thinking about sound and embodied experience; you might also want to discuss what your project could offer or teach your peers about sound and embodied experience; cite at least two course readings to enrich this discussion
- a detailed explanation of the various choices you made as a listener-composer throughout the process of working on this project; consider form, material/content, space/place, editing choices, intended effects/affects, what features contributed to accessibility, and any readings or other media that served as influences for your project or your compositional process

You should begin drafting this document as soon as you start planning your project and continue adding to and tweaking it until the due date. In other words, do not wait to start writing until after you have finished everything. Your statement should reflect how your thinking evolved throughout the entire process of designing your project.

Presentation

You will introduce and present your media and/or performance in class on the day that the project is due. This informal presentation should be five minutes or less and will be followed by questions and discussion.

MY LISTENING BODY COMMENTARY

Design and Purpose

The prompt for this project is intentionally broad to give students room to experiment with imaginative ways to represent and perform their experiences. The project emphasizes embodied experience, which I am defining capaciously. That is, embodied experience in this assignment might refer to a particular physical (felt) sonic encounter and how it affected one's emotions, behaviors, and/or thoughts; it could also refer to a sonic experience that caused a student to be hyperaware of their race, class, gender, sexuality, disability, or another part of their embodied identities. Regardless of the specific bodily experience or circumstance that students choose as their focus, this assignment asks them to think expansively about what is involved in participating in a sonic interaction instead of approaching sound as something that is accessed or understood through the ears only.

It is important to stress that students are not required to produce a linear or narrative-based project, though their project may have some linear or narrative elements. Rather, I encourage students to compose media that can stand alone as invigorating encounters in and of themselves—to compose *experiences* as opposed to *texts*. I do ask them to produce a more familiar alphabetic text in the form of an artist statement, but I want to be clear that this reflective work is not separate from their embodied experiences. My choice to name this part of the assignment *artist statement* is meant to highlight the fact that thinking and making, reflecting and experiencing, are always entwined. To put this idea into practice, I ask students to work on their artist statements as they are developing their projects instead of waiting until after they have finished. As Casey Boyle observes, the metacognitive writing (often called *reflections* or *responses*), that has become central to composition courses, gives students the false impression that they need to separate or remove themselves from their embodied, material experiences of composing to do the work of thinking and writing. Boyle instead argues for an approach that situates "writing activities within an expansive media ecology" (547). Riffing on this notion, I believe that *artist statement* is an apt name for the work I am asking students to do because such statements document the thinking that emerges with and from the embodied experience of designing, making, doing, listening, etc. That is, artist statements require students to address how their thoughts and actions relate to a constellation of materials, people, technologies, knowledge, environments, and more (Micciche). The writing practices associated with the My Listening Body Project are embodied, embedded, and ecological.

It is also important to note that, from the start, this project accounts for students who may not have access to audible sound. For example, deaf or hard of hearing students could choose to represent their sonic experiences visually or tactilely without feeling that they had to do so because of their disability. Since all students are required to consider multiple and diverse ways of representing their unique sonic experiences, all ways of interacting with sound and representing sonic experiences are equally valid. Designing accessible experiences is a mandatory part of the project as well. One of the assignment's challenges is for students to produce inclusive media and/or live performances, meaning that they need to ensure that an audience can understand and engage with their projects via multiple sensory and communicative pathways. Students are asked to think about their own embodied experiences and about what embodied experiences their projects make possible. Put differently, the My Listening Body Project is both an occasion for students to perform their own bodily relationships with sound and to consider how the compositions they produce enable or prevent particular embodied experiences.

Context, Attunement, Challenges

While the My Listening Body Project could be useful to a wide selection of courses that deal with sound, multimodality, and embodiment, I designed this project specifically for an upper-level English (rhetoric and composition) seminar called "Sound, Composition, and Culture." Drawing on scholarship from rhetoric and composition, sound studies, and sound art and design, this course explored the communicative and affective aspects of sound in a variety of texts, genres, objects, environments, and experiences. Most of the students in the class had never been asked to think critically about sound before, so, for them, taking an entire course devoted to sound was a new, strange endeavor. Unsurprisingly, students were initially resistant and confused. Why were they learning about sound in an English department or in the humanities in general? What did this have to do with their lives? The first few weeks of the semester were challenging. I was constantly trying to reframe and redirect the students' resistance into something more productive—to turn their skepticism and pointed questions into inquiries that we might examine in more depth. And the students were wrestling with unfamiliar ideas, trying to find a way to enter into the conversations I was attempting to have with them.

In hindsight, our collective frustration during these early weeks turned out to be a good thing because it led to conversations about what was necessary and valuable about sonic education; it prompted us, as a group, to define the exigencies of the course. For instance, at the beginning of the class, I noticed that students often struggled or got completely stuck when trying to describe or analyze a sonic experience. When I shared this observation with them, I mentioned that they did not seem to have issues describing or analyzing the visual experiences we had been discussing. As we began to talk about this disparity, it became clear that the difficulty was in part due to their lack of practice discussing sound. The students explained that, in educational settings, they had rarely (or never) been asked to pay attention to sound, at least not in the same ways that they had been taught to pay attention to textual or visual media. In other words, due to the general absence of sound-related topics and projects in their respective educations, they had been trained unknowingly to *not* notice or place value on sonic experiences. Sound—and by extension, listening—had not been flagged as something that was worthy of their sustained thought or attention. This conversation was a significant turning point for the class because it heightened students' awareness that they—and in fact, all of us—had been conditioned to attend to some senses and modes more than others. This realization resulted in a larger discussion about the hierarchy of the senses (Classen and Howes; Erlmann), and it became apparent that we had some *unlearning* to do.

However, claiming that the need for sonic education is due to its relative absence in schooling or to the fact that sound has been devalued in Western culture is not sufficient. Indeed, my students were not convinced: "OK, we have not been taught to think about sound, but why do we need to? Why should we care?" Two course readings were particularly helpful in terms of responding to and exploring these questions: Cynthia Selfe's "The Movement of Air, the Breath of Meaning: Aurality and Multimodal Composing" and Jonathan Sterne's "Sonic Imaginations," the introduction to the *Sound Studies Reader*. Selfe's essay illustrates the many ways that "aurality has *persisted* in English classrooms in the midst of a culture saturated by the written word" (618–19). This article gave my students a more thorough understanding of how and why sound has figured into the history of rhetoric and composition (and of education more broadly), and thus helped them position the course and themselves—mostly English majors interested in multimodality—in a specific conversation within the field. Sterne's piece, on the other hand, provided a robust overview of the explosion of work on sound in the past several decades and addressed many of the ways that scholars and students from across the disciplines have begun to engage in sound studies. His introduction broadened my students' sense of how and why critical engagements with sound mattered in the academy and beyond. Together, these two readings served to locate students within an ongoing transdisciplinary conversation and gave us a scholarly foundation from which our course could continue to build upon.

Additionally, because bodily experience is fundamental to any sonic encounter, the body seemed to me an obvious starting point for guiding students toward a deeper understanding of how sound affects their everyday interactions and experiences. Thus, in the weeks leading up to the My Listening Body Project, we focused our attention on sound, listening, and the body (see Selected Resources). For example, we watched Evelyn Glennie's Ted Talk on listening, as well as clips from *Touch the Sound*. In these videos, Glennie models for viewers how senses other than the ears can be used to listen to and engage with sound. The multimodal listening practices Glennie demonstrates defamiliarized the typical ways that my hearing students thought about listening and prompted them to think more about how multiple senses figure into their own sonic interactions—something that they had not considered before.

Another resource that was especially effective in terms of attuning students to their own bodily relationships with sound was the *Sounding Out* forum on "Gendered Voices." This forum includes short, illuminating pieces that explore the intersections of sound, identity, power, embodiment, and difference. In a post on cultural conceptions of gender and loudness, for example, forum editor and contributor Liana Silva reflects on how her own "loudness" is tied to her identity as a Puerto Rican woman in complicated ways. In addition to being self-conscious about "loud Latina" stereotypes, she connects comments about her loudness to entrenched assumptions about gender. She writes, "It's no coincidence then that describing a woman as loud is almost never said as a compliment. Although a man can be loud—he might even be expected to have a deep, booming, commanding voice . . . when a woman is described as loud, it's almost never in a good light" ("As Loud" n.p.). Similarly, contributor Art Blake discusses how learning to shift his voice from feminine to masculine as a transgendered man affected his embodied experience of authority. Blake explains, "All those images of authoritative, sonorous, academic masculinity flooded me with panic. Testosterone wasn't going to make me any taller, give me an Adam's apple, or bigger hands and feet. I was going to be a small guy, standing at the front of the classroom with years of academic expertise, but a mismatched voice might undermine that basic authority" (n.p.). The writers in this forum modeled an acute sensitivity to and thoughtfulness about their embodied experiences with sound. Additionally, this forum illustrated how even something as "natural" as the sound of our voices is learned, and can also be manipulated or unlearned for a variety of reasons that are related to our embodied identities. These and other readings about sound and the body helped my students begin to see their own embodied experiences with sound—their own ways of listening and acting in the world—in richer, more complex ways.

In conjunction with the course material I provided, students' past experiences with sound were crucial to the learning and unlearning that took place in the class. I tried to initiate a conversation with students about their lived experiences with sound—to design occasions that could help them find a way into the conversation—and to offer them a mix of resources, materials, and projects that might encourage them to further question their past experiences and cultivate curiosity about their relationship with the sonic world (Hawk 253). My goal was to attune students to how their own experiences figured into broader discussions about sound and embodiment, but it was my students who pushed the course into interesting, unpredictable directions by bringing their unique bodily experiences with sound into the class. As the student examples in the next section demonstrate, I could not have anticipated the surprising ways that students responded to the My Listening Body Project. Indeed, the knowledge that resulted from this project was co-constructed and coproduced: it continuously emerged from, changed with, and circulated among myself, the students, and all of the readings, media, materials, activities, projects, and spaces with which we engaged. This ecological approach to learning was vital to modifying and enriching our bodily practices in relation to listening and composing.

Student Work

With the permission of my students, I share here a few examples of the My Listening Body Project. If you would like to view or listen to the media associated with these examples, they are available at www.stephceraso.com/reverberations. While the student work I discuss represents only a small slice of the range of experiences my students enacted and examined in this assignment, I chose these two examples because of their highly creative, experimental qualities. These projects demonstrate clearly how the My Listening Body Project differs from more linear, text-like sonic composing projects such as audio essays. Quoting text from students' artist statements where appropriate, the following is a description of what I found to be the most striking features of these projects.

Marco Polo

Meghan decided to focus her project on one of the most memorable sonic experiences of her childhood—playing Marco Polo. Marco Polo is a tag-like swimming pool game. The player who is "it" closes their eyes and yells "Marco," to which all of the other players swimming around must respond "Polo." The shouts of "Polo" serve to orient the "it" player, providing an auditory map of the other bodies' locations within the pool. The goal is for the "it" player to swim towards these calls and tag another swimmer, making that swimmer the new "it" player. Inspired by our course readings on the multisensory nature of sound, Meghan thought this game would be an interesting sonic experience to examine because it was about more than just hearing (*ear-ing*). That is, while the game is dependent upon audible sound, or hearing the voices of people yelling, it also relies on the "it" player's sense of space and direction—where the sounds are located within the space of the pool—on feeling the movement of bodies in the water to gauge their proximity, and on the felt splashes of the players who are swirling around the pool trying not to get caught.

Initially, Meghan wanted to represent the experience of playing Marco Polo by capturing a live game on video. She ultimately decided against this idea, however, because she felt it was too limiting; it did not enable her to recreate the experience in the way that she desired: "I wanted them [her classmates] to feel like they were immersed in the sounds of the game." Meghan was frustrated because watching a video on a screen cannot replicate the experience of being surrounded by sounds coming from different directions; the digital space of the video flattens sound and space and is therefore less immersive. Instead of a video, she decided to produce a live performance with sonic media. Consequently, Meghan organized a game of Marco Polo with her friends in the campus pool to create material for this performance. Each player wore a GoPro, which was used to record the sounds of their individual experiences during the game. Afterwards, Meghan extracted the audio from the GoPro videos and edited this recorded sonic material into six separate audio tracks that included the players' voices, as well as the sounds of swimmers moving and splashing in the water.

On the day of her presentation, Meghan came into the computer lab where our class was located and set up her tracks to be played on computers throughout the space. She turned off the main lights so that only the blue glow of the computer screens and the light from the projector illuminated the room. Then, on her cue, she asked her peers, sitting at the computer stations with audio tracks on them, to press Play at the same time. The tracks were staggered to sound at different times to make us feel like we were floating in the midst of a Marco Polo game being played by our computers. A computer on one side of the room would call out "Marco" and distinct voices from multiple computers spread throughout the room responded with "Polo." On the overhead projector speakers, Meghan played a track of ambient water sounds and splashing, which further served to emulate the atmosphere of a pool environment.

The space of our computer lab—and our experience within it—was completely transformed.

There are several things I find striking about Meghan's approach to this project. First, this assignment compelled her to experiment with the possibilities and limitations of different modes, materials, and spaces. Because her initial idea to use a video did not allow for the directional and spatial qualities she desired, she had to come up with a creative way to work with the material space of our classroom (e.g., the arrangement of computer stations, audio tracks on computers, speakers, lights, etc.). This experimental process required a lot of trial and error—of repeatedly testing out ideas and digital content in the physical spaces of the pool and our computer lab. Meghan was also acutely aware of how the materiality of the technologies she used influenced her composition. For example, when recording audio for this project, she stated, [I] "ran into an issue and could not hear the audio associated with my video due to the waterproof camera case." Because the cases prevented the GoPros from picking up particular sounds during the Marco Polo game, some of the ambient water sounds were lost. To compensate, Meghan used MP3 files of water sounds from a free digital sound effects website (https://freesound.org/) to supplement her live recordings. She noted, "I merged these individual sound tracks [the recorded and downloaded tracks] to create an experience. It is amazing how separate and distinct sounds can be perceived as random noises, but together they give context and can provide a listener with a setting." By recreating and rethinking her past sonic experience (in this case, playing Marco Polo), Meghan was able to think differently—more expansively—about her own relationship to sound and about sonic composition. As she demonstrated during the various stages of her project's development, she became more aware of and sensitive to the embodied, spatial, material, and contextual aspects of sonic experience. In other words, this project prompted her to practice multimodal listening. She had to attend to how the different modes and senses involved in the embodied sonic experience she was recreating was affecting both her own body and the embodied audience of her peers. Through the (re)performance of her Marco Polo experience, she incited her peers to think in fresh ways about listening, sonic interactions, and multimodal composition.

It is worth mentioning that Meghan struggled most with the part of the project having to do with accessibility. She attempted to make her live performance more inclusive by creating a visual aid—a map-like image that indicated which computers were calling out specific audio tracks. While this visual

worked generally as a way to show what was happening during the performance, in her artist statement, Meghan acknowledged that it fell short. This
image did not (and could not) recreate the *enlivening* experience of her performance. We talked more about this in the discussion following her presentation
and the class offered some possibilities for how Meghan might make this performance more inclusive for deaf and hard of hearing persons. Some suggestions included visual cues such as the use of lights to indicate when a computer
was calling out and flashing the words "Marco" and "Polo" on the computer
screens that were making sound. Although Meghan's accessibility features were
not as successful as she had hoped, I would argue that she—and her peers—
still gained practice thinking about how a range of hearing and non-hearing
bodies might engage with her project, and this heightened awareness has the
potential to translate to other projects and situations.

Rhythm

While Meghan attempted to recreate the experience of an immersive sonic
environment for her project, David focused on his experience of using sound
as a rhythmic coping mechanism to deal with anxiety. When he gets nervous,
David writes, "I end up tapping my feet quickly, tapping my teeth together,
or drumming with my fingers against tables, books, or my own collarbone."
David was interested in the soothing bodily effect and affect caused by this self-
made sonic experience. As a musician, he is always listening for rhythm. "My
tapping corresponds to musical elements in my head," he said, which calms
him down and helps him to concentrate. At the same time, he realizes that,
for people around him, the sounds he is making with his body are heard and/
or viewed as annoying distractions—as noisy, bodily tics.

For his My Listening Body Project, then, David decided to compose a video
that contrasted his own experience of using sound as a coping mechanism with
how his tapping and other bodily tics might be perceived by others. He played
himself in the film, which portrayed a situation that made him especially nervous: taking a timed test. The film takes place in a large lecture hall. David is
sitting in the middle of the room, alone, and the instructor giving the exam is
sitting at a desk in the front of the room. Like Meghan, David thought about
the relationship between the spatial environment and embodied experience.
The space in which he chose to shoot the video allowed him to visually reinforce the uncomfortable quietness of his classroom experience: "By using a
large lecture room, I was able to capture how unnaturally quiet test-taking

spaces can be. Taking tests is already nerve-racking, and in a near silent space, it becomes difficult for me to focus. The classroom was intentionally empty to amplify the fact that it was so awkward and anxiety-inducing." The film shows David's tics getting more pronounced the longer he sits with the test, and the instructor periodically "shhhhhes" him for being noisy. David also uses a rhythmic track that sounds like an exaggerated ticking clock to heighten anxiety in his listening audience.

To give viewers and listeners a sense of his embodied experience, David used the sound of drums to correspond with his tapping and increased anxiety. As his anxiety worsens, the drums get louder and more aggressive. He felt that recording a live drumming session would be more intense than using a prerecorded track, so he recorded one of his friends playing the drums in a separate location. Near the end of his video—at the height of the intensity—the drummer is shown on a TV screen that is meant to be a representation of what is happening inside David's head. David also used filmic techniques (e.g., close-ups, distortion) to visually represent what the sonic experience felt like for him. To achieve the effects and affects he desired, David had to experiment with the technologies that were available to him. He mentions, for instance, that he spent a long time learning to use different lenses and apps on the camera of his iPhone to achieve various special effects.

David's artist statement also cites course materials and other media he was exposed to outside of class as influences for his project. He was especially inspired by the footage of Evelyn Glennie that we examined in class. Glennie's discussion of sonic experience as multisensory resonated with David, and he attempted to demonstrate his own multisensory experience in the video through the use of filmic techniques. He also discusses Stephanie Kerschbaum's essay, "Modality," which explains how using multiple modes to express the same things can make multimodal texts more accessible. David tried to enact Kerschbaum's suggestions by including a detailed transcript for his video, and by using visual techniques that corresponded with the intensity of the sound. Even if viewers watch his video with no volume, they can still get a sense of when and how the sound is affecting him via the visual distortions, cuts, and close-ups. In addition to our course materials, David noted that two movies, Birdman and Whiplash, provided inspiration for his use of sound in the video. He writes, "both films use erratic drumming to elicit anxiety in the audience." When making his video, he tried to imitate particular audio and visual effects from these films. In short, David used his project as a vehicle for exploring listening experiences from his own life, as well as new ideas he was

exposed to in class. Throughout the process of composing his video, he practiced multimodal listening by attending to how the material, spatial, and sensory aspects of his past sonic experience could be recreated for his audience
via visual, textual, and sonic information. David's project demonstrates—and
models for his peers—a capacious approach to listening and embodied experience.

Meghan and David's examples encapsulate the inventive student work that
the My Listening Body Project generated. However, I do not want to suggest
that all of the student work, or even the featured student work above, was
excellent in every way. As is the case with any assignment, there was a spectrum of quality within the body of student work that was submitted. Some
students spent more time, thought, and care than others in terms of coming up with creative ways to (re)perform their embodied experiences. In
addition, despite the fact that we discussed sonic experiences in relation to
race, gender, sexuality, and other aspects of embodied identity, none of my
students decided to focus on identity in their projects. This may have been
because more of the course readings were centered around sensory experiences, which, in retrospect, was due to my own research interests and biases,
or because students were not comfortable representing certain parts of their
identities. The next time I teach this project, however, I intend to do a better job emphasizing that physical experience and embodied identity are not
separate. This idea is taken up by Jennifer Stoever in a concept she calls the
"embodied ear." She explains, "I use 'embodied ear' to represent how individuals' listening practices are shaped by the totality of their experiences, historical context, and physicality, as well as intersecting subject positions and
particular interactions with power" (*The Sonic Color Line* 15). Including more
readings and discussions about the "totality" of embodied experience is a
necessary revision that I plan to make in the next iteration of this project,
and I hope that others will consider making identity a salient part of this
assignment from the start.

What I hope is clear from my discussion of the My Listening Body Project
is that this assignment can engage students in invigorating, defamiliarizing,
and challenging ways. It invites and carves out space for students to begin to
make connections among scholarly readings, media, and personal experiences
to enrich and extend their understanding of sound and listening. Combined
with a series of other projects and activities that ask students to repeat similar
bodily practices—some of which I discuss in later Reverberations—projects like

My Listening Body have the potential to help students expand their capacities as listeners and composers.

Evaluation

I am always reluctant to give advice on evaluating student work because evaluation, like multimodal listening, is not a one-size-fits-all practice. Evaluation methods can and should vary widely based on institutional and departmental context, student population, the particular goals of courses, assignments, teachers, etc. However, due to the experimental nature of the assignment I have presented, I understand that providing some explanation of how one might respond to such work could be useful. What I offer is not intended to be a formula for evaluating the My Listening Body Project but a description of the way that I approached evaluation in this specific class.

First and foremost, I want to stress that evaluation did not occur only after students turned in their final work. Rather, it was an ongoing practice that played a role at each stage of project development. For example, we began the My Listening Body Project with a "pitch meeting." Students were asked to share and explain their composing ideas for two experiences that might be the focus of their projects, and their peers provided detailed feedback about the possibilities and limitations of each of these proposed ideas. Students were also responsible for presenting their in-progress work during several peer revision sessions—working both with partners and in small groups. This peer evaluation was a chance for students to get feedback that could lead to productive revisions, and a chance to collaboratively think through and experiment with the ideas and media under consideration. In addition to being a form of early evaluation, peer feedback was an opportunity for students to push each other's thinking about sound, listening, and their own notions of multimodal composition. Being exposed to a range of ideas and approaches to the My Listening Body Project during these feedback sessions enriched my students' and my own understanding of the various ways that sound figures into embodied experiences in particular situations. In a sense, then, evaluating the My Listening Body Project was a collaborative endeavor with my students. Throughout the process students were simultaneously experiencing and articulating what they were learning about sound, embodiment, and multimodal composition.

Of course, I did eventually have to give these projects a grade. Below I include a list of general criteria that proved helpful in guiding my response to student work. With these criteria in mind, I tried to treat each student's project as an individual case that demonstrated—to varying degrees—the thought, inventiveness, and bodily attunement that the My Listening Body Project demanded. I responded to each of the following statements with "definitely yes" (A), "mostly yes" (B), "somewhat" (C), or "no" (F), and assigned a grade based on the accumulative responses. I kept these criteria basic on purpose. Rather than assigning them a specific point value, I wanted the criteria to serve as a tool for me to estimate a holistic grade that might be appropriate for a student's project. Then, to determine the final grade, I weighed this holistic grade against my own response, taking into account the unique qualities of each student's work. I also explained my assessment and response in written comments to the student. Again, this is not intended to be a magic formula that will work for everyone. In my experience, however, this method allowed me to hold students to the same general standards and gave me the flexibility to assess their distinctive approaches to the project.

1. Media and/or Performance
   - takes full advantage of the affordances of the various modes, materials, media, and spaces used in the project
   - demonstrates a thoughtful consideration of the student's bodily relationship with and understanding of sonic experience
   - challenges and expands peers' notions of listening and sonic experience by representing the experience in a creative, defamiliarizing way
   - meets all assignment requirements
2. Accessibility
   - demonstrates that an audience of people with diverse bodily capacities and preferences are able to engage or interact with the project in both media/performance and artist statement
   - reflects "best practices" in terms of the disability studies scholarship we read in class
3. Artist Statement
   - addresses thoughtfully and thoroughly the prompts included in the assignment guidelines
   - explains in detail how and why sound and other media, materials, spaces, etc. were designed or manipulated in specific ways to reflect the purposes and/or goals of the project
   - incorporates relevant sources from the course to enrich the discussion of the project

Selected Resources

SOUND, LISTENING, AND THE BODY

Daughtry, J. Martin. *Listening to War: Sound, Music, Trauma, and Survival in Wartime Iraq*. Oxford: Oxford UP, 2015.

Glennie, Evelyn. "How to Truly Listen." *TED*. Feb. 2003. Web. 8 Mar. 2003. http://www.ted.com/talks/evelyn_glennie_shows_how_to_listen ?language=en.

Ross, Alex. "When Music Is Violence." *New Yorker*. 4 July 2016. Web. 5 July 2016. http://www.newyorker.com/magazine/2016/07/04/when-music-is-violence.

Silva, Liana. "As Loud as I Want to Be: Gender, Loudness, and Respectability Politics." *Sounding Out: The Sound Studies Blog*. 9 Feb. 2015. Web. 10 Feb. 2015. https://soundstudies blog.com/2015/02/09/as-loud-as-i-want-to-be-gender-loudness-and-respect ability-politics/.

Stoever, Jennifer Lynn. *The Sonic Color Line: Race and the Cultural Politics of Listening*. New York: New York UP, 2016.

"Todd Selby x Christine Sun Kim." *Nowness*. Nov. 2011. Web. 7 Oct. 2013. https://www.nowness.com/story/todd-selby-x-christine-sun-kim.

Touch the Sound: A Sound Journey with Evelyn Glennie. Dir. Thomas Riedelsheimer. Docudrama, 2005. DVD.

ACCESSIBILITY AND DESIGN

"Composing Access." Committee on Disability Issues in College Composition and Computers and Composition Digital P. n.d. Web. 11 Oct. 2014. https://u.osu.edu/composingaccess/.

"Disability Rhetoric." Disability Studies SIG. 2009. Web. 11 Oct. 2014. http://disabil ityrhetoric.com/.

Kerschbaum, Stephanie. "Modality." *Kairos: A Journal of Rhetoric, Technology, and Pedagogy*. "Multimodality in Motion: Disability in Kairotic Spaces." Eds. Melanie Yergeau et al. 18.1 (2013): n. pag. Web. 7 Nov. 2014.

THREE
SOUNDING SPACE, DESIGNING EXPERIENCE
The Ecological Practice of Sonic Composition

If we had a keen vision and feeling of all ordinary human life, it would be like hearing the grass grow and the squirrel's heart beat, and we should die of that roar which lies on the other side of silence. As it is, the quickest of us walk about well wadded with stupidity.

GEORGE ELIOT

Our sense of sound includes the embrace of our body by the environment.

MICHAEL STOCKER

THE CATHEDRAL OF LEARNING IS an iconic forty-two story building that juts out of the University of Pittsburgh's main campus. The multiple first floor entrances of the Cathedral lead into a massive space—three stories high, one hundred feet wide, and two hundred feet long—known as the Commons Room (Toker 327). This room features ornate Gothic architecture, including arches with ribbed vaulting, stone shafts, and decorative statues. Wooden tables and benches are scattered throughout, making it a popular study area for students despite the fact that it is heavily trafficked by those passing through the Cathedral. I am always struck by how quiet the Commons Room is even when it is full of activity. When sounds of muted footsteps or murmuring voices become audible, they float through the air almost unnoticed. The tranquility of the room seems odd for a bustling university space.

I completed much of the writing for this chapter in the Commons Room. As a ritual, I would spread my research notes across the same wooden table day after day, then sit and listen for a few moments before writing. One of the first things I noticed while occupying this space was the immediate change in behavior as people transitioned from the outside to the inside of the building. Through the turnstile doors, I saw several groups of students having animated conversations—gesturing and speaking loudly enough for me to hear muffled versions of what they were saying. As they walked into the Commons Room, though, they became subdued and the volume of their voices diminished. Perhaps the room's scale and elaborate ornamentation encourages inhabitants to act as if they were entering a sacred building. It is named the *Cathedral* of Learning, after all. Even when a sudden burst of laughter or the thud of a dropped book disrupted the room's unspoken code of conduct, the sound bounced off of the high ceiling, reverberated briefly, and got swallowed up by the massive space.

It turns out that the Commons Room's aesthetic features were designed to promote the silent reverence I had been observing. John Bowman, the University Chancellor who oversaw the building of the Cathedral, wanted the church-like space to incite respect and admiration for higher learning in its visitors. The Cathedral was considered to be a manifestation of the colossal importance of education in the region (Toker 327). However, the awe-inspiring aesthetics are not the only reason for the Commons Room's near soundlessness. Pittsburgh historian Franklin Toker notes, "The Commons Room is always quiet despite its use by thousands of students every day, because the 'stones' between the ribs are actually Guastavino[1] acoustical tiles" (327). Acoustical tiles are made with sound-absorbing materials like mineral fiber pulp and fiberglass, which reduce noise and prevent excessive reverberation. Sound gets soaked up by the architecture before it has the chance to produce any significant effects. Both the aesthetic and architectural features of the Commons Room play a role in composing its sonic environment, and its sonic environment seems to influence the ways in which people listen to, interact with, and move through space.

I begin with this meditation on the sonic space of the Commons Room to accentuate the fact that sound is part of a larger material, aesthetic, and spatial ecology. While the main focus of the last chapter was on the bodily experience of multimodal listening, this chapter situates multimodal listening practices within a broader system of relationships among sounds, bodies, and environments. I argue that training listeners to become attuned to site-specific sonic experiences will heighten their sensitivity to the functions, effects, affects, constraints, and possibilities of sound in a variety of settings. In turn, this heightened sensitivity can lead to more informed decisions about how to compose with sound in particular contexts, and to a richer understanding of how sound works as a rhetorical force in everyday spaces.

To identify useful practices for teaching students about site-specific listening and composing experiences, I first embed my argument within larger disciplinary and interdisciplinary conversations by discussing relevant scholarship on soundscapes, ecology, and composition. I then explore the field of acoustic design—the professional practice of designing sound for buildings and outdoor spaces. Drawing from a mix of acoustic design scholarship and personal interviews with acoustic designers, I suggest various ways that acoustic design practices can enhance multimodal composition pedagogy. By examining several spaces with strategically designed soundscapes, I also show how adopting acoustic design practices can teach students how sound works as a rhetorical force in a variety of places—from office buildings to shopping malls. Ultimately, my aim is to pinpoint listening and composing practices that can help people become attuned to how soundscapes affect their embodied experiences in a range of settings.

SOUNDSCAPES, ECOLOGIES, AND MULTIMODAL COMPOSITION

Throughout this chapter I rely on key ideas from interdisciplinary soundscape studies to develop an ecological approach to listening in rhetoric and composition. The term *soundscape*, coined by Canadian scholar and composer R. Murray Schafer,[2] refers to any acoustic environment (e.g., city, forest, building, auditorium). Schafer's work on soundscapes is especially relevant to multimodal listening pedagogy because it underscores the ecological relationship among sound, bodies, and environments as an essential part of the process of listening to and composing soundscapes. In *The Soundscape*, for instance, he contends that the artful design and manipulation of sonic environments requires knowledge of acoustic ecology, which is defined as "the study of sounds in relationship to life and society" (205). According to Schafer, sonic composing practices must account for how humans experience, interact with, and contribute to the soundscapes they inhabit.[3]

While Schafer's scholarship provides a strong foundation for understanding the ecological aspects of soundscapes, I find Emily Thompson's more material approach to soundscapes to be an indispensable supplement to Schafer's work. In *The Soundscape of Modernity*, Thompson writes, "The physical aspects of a soundscape consist not only of the sounds themselves, the waves of acoustical energy permeating the atmosphere in which people live, but also the material objects that create, and sometimes destroy those sounds" (2). Whereas Schafer discusses soundscapes and their effects in rather broad terms (i.e., using general categories like "The Natural Soundscape," and "The Industrial Revolution"), Thompson is precise in identifying how the specific material features of environments, such as the tile or brick used to construct buildings, can influence soundscapes and the experiences of their inhabitants. Blending Schafer's and Thompson's definitions, I use the term *soundscape* (or alternatively, *sonic environment*) to refer to the ecological network of sounds, bodies, aesthetics, materials, technologies, and spatial features that make up an environment. Indeed, the experience of a sonic environment is not dependent upon sound alone; rather, it is shaped by the entire ecological system of which sound is a part. Or, as Steven Connor argues, "Soundscapes are more than sounds—they are sounds joined by relations . . . for a soundscape is a sound plus relation, and that relation need not be fully and in itself sonorous" ("Rustications" 18).[4]

Ecology is already a familiar concept in rhetoric and composition. Ecological perspectives have been informing approaches to writing for years (Cooper; Syverson; J. Rice 2005; Dobrin and Weisser).[5] As Sidney Dobrin maintains, "Writing, of course, is an ecological phenomenon. It is spatial, relational, and complex, and thus requires that writing specialists develop complex theories in order to attempt to understand its intricacies, functions, and possibilities" (*Ecology* 2). While ecological approaches to writing are by no means new to the field, such approaches have not been applied with the same rigor in the teaching of multimodal composition—particularly with regard to sound.[6] Developing more complex theories of listening and sonic composing can lead to a deeper and nuanced understanding of sound's "intricacies, functions, and possibilities" (2). What I want to suggest is that teaching students to attend to soundscapes can contribute to a dynamic, ecological understanding of what it means to listen to and compose with sound in multimodal composition. As I will show, heightening students' awareness of sound as part of a larger ecology is a vital step toward helping them develop and expand their listening and composing practices.

Teaching students to cultivate a sensitivity to the ecological nature of sound will first require defamiliarizing the digital sonic environments they have become accustomed to interacting with in multimodal composition courses. Rather than limiting students' sonic interactions to digital spaces, we need to give them opportunities to engage with a wider range of soundscapes in both digital *and* nondigital contexts. Like Geoffrey Sirc, I believe that "the spaces of our classrooms should offer compelling environments in which to inhabit situations of writing instruction, helping intensify the consciousness in the people who use them" (1–2). Offering such compelling environments means extending the space of the classroom to include the world at large. Jody Shipka also stresses that it is crucial for teachers of rhetoric and composition to search for new scenes of composition pedagogy—"to recognize that the classroom is just one of many spaces through which they [students] move, learn, act, communicate, and compose" (*Toward* 36). I see turning to soundscapes as new (sonic) "scenes" in rhetoric and composition as one way of implementing the capacious multimodal pedagogies that Sirc and Shipka promote.

While it is necessary to expose students to an array of soundscapes, it is also important to teach them to approach digital spaces as listening environments. In the words of Thomas Rickert: "We should begin to consider media not simply the medium by which we interact and communicate with others but more literally a place" (*Ambient* 44). Just as the high ceilings and Guastavino tiles contribute to the experiences of listeners in the Commons Room, the material, aesthetic, and spatial features of a digital environment—the size and quality of computer speakers, volume control, two-dimensional space, visual layout—contribute to a user's listening experience. Listening experiences in both digital and nondigital environments are similarly shaped by an ecological network, and learning to practice multimodal listening in relation to both types of soundscapes can sharpen students' sensitivity to how sound works and affects people in diverse contexts.

AN ECOLOGICAL APPROACH: ACOUSTIC DESIGN

Acoustic designers are sound professionals who create or manipulate sonic environments to achieve specific effects.[7] The field of acoustic design is often associated with the use of math and physics to eradicate acoustic problems, or prevent unwanted noise in a space. There is an enormous body of dense, jargon-laden acoustic design texts that are based on the science of noise reduction, such as *Active Noise Control: Fundamentals for Acoustic Design* (Rosenhouse) and *Applied Acoustics: Concepts, Absorbers, and Silencers for Acoustical Comfort and Noise Control* (Fuchs). For readers who lack specialized knowledge of acoustic design, these texts do not provide much information about what acoustic designers actually do on a daily basis. To get a fuller sense of what acoustic design involves as a practice, I conducted in-depth interviews with two experienced acoustic designers.[8]

Though acoustic design is thought of primarily as a technical practice, here I explore acoustic design as an imaginative mode of sonic composition. As my interviews reveal, acoustic design is not simply the elimination or suppression of sound, but rather an inventive, process-based composing practice. When I interviewed Greg Coudriet, an acoustical consultant and designer, he described "acoustical enhancement" as a fundamental yet challenging part of his job: "Acoustical enhancement is more interesting and creative [than noise reduction]. It involves changing the shape, finishes, and construction of a space to achieve a specific acoustical environment" (personal interview). The creative compositional practices acoustic designers employ in their work make acoustic design an especially generative area to explore in relation to rhetoric and composition. In what follows, I identify salient acoustic design practices that can serve as heuristics for developing more expansive and complex approaches to sound in multimodal composition pedagogy.

Acoustic designers attend to the aesthetic, material, and spatial characteristics of an environment.

Paying attention to sound as part of a larger aesthetic, material, and spatial ecology is a central practice in acoustic design work. Music halls, for instance, require a material structure that enables the production of sonic qualities such as musical clarity, warmth, and reverberance. To arrive at such qualities, acoustic designers must consider how various features in the physical environment affect the ways that sound is experienced by a listening audience. Due to their sound-absorbing qualities (or lack thereof), the materials used to construct an environment have a major influence on what that environment sounds like. Adding wood paneling to a music hall would create a different sound than concrete; incorporating carpet into the design would affect the soundscape much differently than marble flooring. The height of the ceilings and shape of the space (e.g., rectangular or rounded) can have significant effects on the sound as well (Cavanaugh, Tocci, and Wilkes 147).[9] Attending to and sometimes changing these features is a critical part of composing the sound for a particular space.

In contrast to the common sound-as-text approach to multimodal composing I discussed in Chapter 2, learning to listen and compose like acoustic designers would require students to treat sound as part of an ecology. In a nondigital setting, students might be asked to compose site-specific compositions that take advantage of the aesthetic, material, and spatial qualities of a room to achieve different sonic effects. To produce feelings of isolation, for instance, a student could perform a sonic composition in a large, reverberant space with a high ceiling that would sonically draw attention to the vastness or emptiness of the environment. Designing site-specific assignments can help students understand sonic compositions as holistic experiences that are dependent upon more than sound alone.

Treating sound as part of an ecology is a valuable practice for sonic composing in digital spaces as well. A student who is creating sound for a website that is intended to be experienced as a warm and intimate digital space—like a music hall—would need to consider how the sound could be effectively integrated with other aesthetic elements of the website (i.e., color palette, textures, visual layout, etc.) to create a feeling of warmth and intimacy. Even if the sound has an inviting effect, if the colors do not convey the same warmth, then the composer's overall design, including the sound, will be less potent. As Coudriet stated in his interview, "Aesthetics are very important. Oftentimes an interior designer has a very specific vision for a space. The goal in that case is to develop acoustical solutions that essentially disappear into or complement that vision. Other times, the interior designer is looking for the acoustical design to drive the aesthetic of the space" (personal interview). The same principle applies to composing with sound in digital spaces. Whether sound is the driving component of a digital environment or more of an ambient presence, the space's aesthetics are essential to making that sound more effective and affective. In addition, the material and technological resources involved in composing a website (e.g., the computer, software, and type of code used to build the website) will directly influence its aesthetic design; and the affordances and limitations that determine the aesthetic design will ultimately influence how the website is sonically experienced by users. For these reasons, teaching students to attend to sound as an element that is connected to and shaped by its environment should play a salient role in multimodal composition pedagogy.

Acoustic designers experiment throughout the composing process.

Acoustic design work is full of trial and error. To compose sound for spaces in need of acoustical enhancement, acoustic designers experiment with manipulating the physical environment until the desired effects are achieved. As Coudriet told me, "It's an iterative process" (personal interview). Like other forms of sonic composition (e.g., creating music or audio editing), acoustic design requires a repetitive cycle of composing, listening, revising, relistening, recomposing, and so on. To use a specific example, consider the experimentation that was necessary in the acoustic transformation of a neoclassical courthouse in New Jersey. The courthouse's domed ceilings, spaciousness, and curved surfaces were causing excessive reverberation, making it difficult to understand what people were saying when court was in session. Acoustical consultant James Cowan explains in his book *Architectural Acoustics Design Guide*, "The management wanted the historic look of the courthouse to be preserved, but the acoustics of the facility had to be improved for speech intelligibility" (59). To preserve the aesthetics, acoustic designers had to manipulate the existing architecture without making any drastic visual changes. The compositional process required manipulating some features of the material construction (i.e., the texture, surface, and/or shape of the material features in the environment), listening to how that material change affected the sound, changing it again, listening again, etc. This process continued until the desired sonic effects were accomplished. The experiment that worked best involved applying "a spray-on mineral-based absorptive material" on the domed ceiling to soak up the majority of the sound "with the result of lowering the reverberation time to an acceptable level (59). In this successful example, the experimentation process ended with a solution that enhanced the soundscape of the courthouse without changing its aesthetics.

The experimentation that is integral to acoustic designers' listening and composing practices also needs to be emphasized as an essential practice in multimodal composition. Encouraging students to experiment with sound helps them develop a better sense of all of the available sonic possibilities in a specific context and calls attention to how the materials and technologies that they have access to shape those possibilities. One way to get students in the habit of experimenting with sound is to build constraints into multimodal composing assignments. For example, if students are asked to compose multiple versions of a single sonic composition according to a particular set of rules (e.g., they can only use seven predetermined sounds to create and recreate their piece; or they can only use a particular technology; or they must produce and present their work in a specific place), then experimentation becomes a fundamental part of the composing process as opposed to a mere requirement; that is, adding constraints encourages creative problem-solving that inevitably leads to tinkering and trying out different possibilities. Regardless of the project details, students need to be given opportunities to play with sounds and consider how a sound's affordances are connected to and shaped by various materials, technologies, and environments. Such experimentation will guide students toward an understanding of listening and composing as ecological practices, as well as enhance their ability to produce dynamic sonic work.

Acoustic designers always consider how people experience sound in a space.

Attending to the embodied experiences and needs of the inhabitants of a space is central to acoustic design. As senior research associate and professor of acoustics David Swanson described to me, the inhabitants of the space have a direct effect on the acoustic—and therefore aesthetic and functional—design choices that need to be made. When Swanson was hired to create a peaceful sonic environment in a hospital, for instance, he encountered design constraints that were linked to the hospital's health needs and concerns for its patients. For sanitary reasons, he could not change any of the hard surfaces in the hospital because "porous surfaces cannot be kept clean and free of dust, mold," which made it difficult to "quiet down" the space (personal interview). Because he did not have much leeway in terms of changing the aesthetics and materials of the environment, he amplified the noise of the ventilation system "to make a significant 'hiss' sound to cover up the noise of private conversations, worker movements, and noise that disrupts sleep" (personal interview). By strategically blending the hissing sound of the ventilation system with other potentially annoying or disruptive sounds, Swanson was able to change the sonic experience of the hospital. The excess noise provided a more private atmosphere so that patients could confidentially discuss sensitive issues with their families and doctors, and the steady hissing of the ventilation system (similar to the gentle "shhhhhhh" sound people make to quiet babies) also served as a way to calm and lull patients that needed to rest. Listening with the communicative needs and bodily experiences of other people in mind, Swanson created the desired sonic environment. His multimodal listening practices, in this case, involved attending to his own bodily experience of sound in the space to better understand the bodily experiences and needs of that space's current and future inhabitants.

Accounting for bodily experiences often requires acoustic designers to create adjustable aesthetic features that can accommodate different listening situations within a single venue. In other words, acoustic designers are frequently asked to compose flexible, multifunctional environments that provide various ways to interact with sound in a space. In acoustic design literature, churches are cited as the most difficult sonic spaces to get acoustically right. Christopher Brooks elaborates: "A church is a concert hall and a lecture hall in one room at the same time. Church music (organs, choirs, and congregational singing) sounds wonderful in very 'live' or reverberant acoustics—the more reverberant, the better. Speech, on the other hand, can be quite difficult to understand in such reverberant acoustics" (76). To deal with these issues, acoustic designers have invented materials that facilitate more accommodating designs. For example, flying panels, or what are sometimes called *sound clouds*, are panels that can be hung from the ceiling (122). Sound clouds are constructed from materials that absorb sound to prevent excessive reverberation. One can adjust the amount of reverberation that occurs in a space by experimenting with the placement of the flying panels until a balanced acoustic environment is achieved—an environment that allows some amount of reverberation to enhance singing while still producing the right amount of clarity for speaking.

Acoustic designers' consideration of how people experience and use a space provides a valuable example for sonic composing practices in multimodal composition. As I mentioned in the previous chapter, it is crucial to teach students to produce inclusive digital work that can be engaged with via multiple sensory and communicative modes. Encouraging students to account for embodied (sensing) audiences would challenge students to devise creative ways to design sonic compositions that could accommodate a range of different listeners and listening situations. One assignment possibility that would promote this flexible sonic composition is to have students produce a sound-based exhibit for an imagined (or real) public art installation. Students might be required to design an exhibit in which sound must be able to be seen, heard, and felt.

They would need to determine how to represent the different sensory experiences of sound to create a unified theme or feeling that could be understood by an audience that may not have access to all of the senses; that is, students would need to find ways to convey the same idea through visible, audible, and tactile iterations of sound. Teaching students to design for embodied audiences in activities like this one would allow them to move beyond ear-centric listening and composing practices. Acoustic designers' approach to composing for the bodily experiences of inhabitants provides an excellent model for moving toward a more accessible approach to multimodal composition.

Acoustic designers compose with purpose.

Acoustic designers attend carefully to how the sonic experience of a space is connected to its purpose and meaning. To continue with the church example, acoustic designers often need to consult with church leaders about the significance of their religion to design a church's soundscape accordingly. As Douglas Jones observes, because a Catholic Mass revolves around the worship of Christ, some reverberation is necessary to reinforce a sense of awe and reverence in the space itself (70). However, the acoustical manipulation should not interfere with the ornate aesthetic design of the church (i.e., stained glass windows, columns, etc.), which is also used to accentuate the majestic ambiance of the space of worship. In short, the visual and acoustical qualities of the Catholic church are equally important to maintaining the meaning and function of the Mass.

Acoustic designers of churches must also consider how church members' sensory experiences of sound are connected to the ways that they make meaning of their religion. While aesthetics and acoustic function are inseparable in the Catholic church, Jones explains that, in other religions, acoustics tend to take precedence over aesthetics. For example, because of the emphasis on preaching in the evangelical religion, acoustical clarity is valued much more than aesthetics in the design of evangelical churches, and so reverberation must be minimized. Jones notes, "In the evangelical style, the preaching of the Word must be supported by the acoustics and the architecture" (159). Evangelical churches are acoustical spaces that are engineered specifically for ear-centric listening experiences.

In contrast, the goal of acoustic design in a Pentecostal church is to affect the entire body. Music is the most prominent feature of a Pentecostal service: "The song service's function was to make people *feel*, which music is readily able to do . . . Part of the technique for accomplishing this had to do with the raw psychological manipulative power that extremely loud rhythmic music has over the nervous system" (161). Experiencing sound as bodily vibration is a means of spiritual connectedness in a Pentecostal service, and, therefore, the space of the church should be constructed with resonant materials, such as wood, gypsum paneling, and glass. Acoustic designers working in evangelical churches listen with their whole bodies to determine when the sonic environment has reached the desired vibrational effect.

Taking a cue from acoustic designers, I want to suggest that it is important to teach students how to compose with sound in ways that support or enact the meaning that they want to convey in their multimodal compositions. For instance, a student who creates a digital composition about the dwindling nature sounds in urban environments could be prompted to come up with creative ways to sonically overpower bird or insect sounds, like gradually decreasing the volume of these sounds to sonically enact their disappearance. In this example, manipulating the volume of wildlife sounds reinforces the meaning of the composition; sound is being used to *perform* the argument of the piece. Attending to the relationship between nondiscursive sounds and spoken words in a sonic composition is also a crucial part of learning how sound can shape or interfere with meaning. In my experiences with assigning sonic projects, for example, students tend to overpower spoken words with background sound or music, even in parts where the words are more important than the other sounds. Teaching students to strike a balance among different sonic elements in a composition can help them learn to use both sound and silence in strategic ways. Lastly, as I have stressed throughout this book, paying attention to how listeners experience a sonic composition at the level of the senses is critical. Bodily experiences undoubtedly affect the ways that people make meaning of sound and therefore need to be a primary consideration during students' composing processes.

Taken together, the acoustic design practices outlined in this section present an experimental, expansive approach to teaching listening and sonic composing in multimodal composition. These practices are intended to offer some initial possibilities for heightening students' sensitivity to the relationships among sound, bodies, and environments and thus have the potential to contribute to more robust multimodal pedagogies for sound and listening. Adopting acoustic design practices can teach students to make informed decisions about how to design sonic experiences for various contexts and embodied audiences. And, as I will discuss in the next section, encouraging such an approach to multimodal composition provides a way to deepen students' understanding of the sonic interactions and listening experiences that occur outside formal educational settings. Learning to listen and compose like acoustic designers can help students develop an acute awareness of how sound affects their experiences in a range of everyday environments.

LISTENING IN AND TO EVERYDAY SOUNDSCAPES

Teaching students to cultivate an acoustic designer-like attention to sound is valuable not only because it can augment their composing practices, but because it can help them understand how sound shapes and affects their experiences. Sound is always influencing listeners' interactions with different environments, whether they are aware of it or not. Salomé Voegelin illustrates this experience beautifully in a passage about moving through a city: "As I walk through a busy urban street I try to ignore the incessant hum of thick traffic, the noisy commotion and vocal drone of people around me. However, the fact that I do not listen to them consciously or willingly does not mean that these sounds do not shape the reality as it presents itself to me. Sound renders the crowd massive and pervasive, becoming ever denser and more intimidating, encroaching on my physical space" (*Listening* 11). As Voeglin's description makes clear, sound is part of an ambient ecology in which humans are embedded and entangled; humans are constantly immersed in sonic environments that have the potential to induce particular thoughts, moods, actions, and interactions. Thomas Rickert underscores this point in *Ambient Rhetoric*. He states, "Rhetorical action is enmeshed within ambient environs, evoking (but not demanding) a rich panoply of attachments, feelings, responses, and possible (inter)actions" (143). In conjunction with the other elements that constitute an environment, sound acts as a rhetorical agent that influences how listeners' experience a space. It is important to remember, then, that the particular effects and affects of sound—even designed sound—"cannot be reduced to the intentions of any party" (145).

While it is vital for students to understand that all soundscapes, intentionally constructed or not, affect their embodied experiences, in the following discussion, I have chosen to focus on *strategically designed* soundscapes. This is because the considerations involved in soundscape design are most directly relevant to the compositional choices that students have to make when using sound in multimodal compositions. In this section, I explore how teaching students about designed soundscapes can provide a bridge between the sonic composing practices they develop in the classroom and the familiar sonic spaces they move through every day.

Before moving on to specific examples of designed soundscapes, I want to provide some context about why students need to be taught to attend to sonic environments in the first place. Listening to an environment may seem like something that simply happens as a result of being there, yet most people do not pay attention to the sounds of the spaces they occupy. In part, this inattention is due to the fact that, over time, design trends have trained listeners to ignore the spatial aspects of sound. For example, reverberation—a sonic quality that calls attention to space—has been largely eliminated since the widespread development of the acoustical technologies industry in the 1930s.[10] Emily Thompson points out that these technologies, which were incorporated into office buildings, apartments, schools, and other commercial spaces, used "unprecedentedly absorptive materials" that "created a sound that was clear and direct" (170). The elimination of "noise" (including reverberation) in city buildings became the new norm, and the success of the acoustical materials industry fundamentally transformed the way the public experienced sound in everyday life. Thompson writes, "When reverberation was reconceived as noise, it lost its traditional meaning as the acoustic signature of a space, and the age-old connection between sound and space—a connection as old as architecture itself—was severed" (172).[11] This newfound sense of control that acoustical technologies made possible affected people's attitudes toward sound, particularly in terms of what was considered to be an "appropriate" noise level in a building.[12] With the absence of reverberation, these "modern" sonic environments prevented the spatial qualities of sound from becoming apparent, thus de-emphasizing the connection between sound and space in everyday architectural experiences.[13]

In addition to modern architecture's role in directing attention away from the sonic qualities of spaces, the pervasiveness of ear-centric listening practices has also contributed to a widespread inattention to sonic environments. In particular, the practice of personal soundscaping, or the use of audio technologies to create a private soundscape, enables people to ignore sound in the spaces through which they move.[14] Interestingly, while personal soundscaping technologies are making it easier than ever for listeners to cut themselves off from sonic environments, soundscape design is becoming an increasingly prevalent feature in public spaces. In this section, I argue that adopting multimodal listening practices like those used by acoustic designers can serve as a way to raise listeners' awareness of how the sound in a space is being used to "attune and inflect" their "bodily inhabitance" (Rickert *Ambient* 155). Specifically, I illustrate why listeners need to become more sensitive to *sonic rhetorics*, or the ways that sound, in conjunction with other elements of an environment or interaction, operates as a material, affective force that influences, but does not determine, listeners' bodily states, moods, thoughts, and actions. Indeed, multimodal listening can facilitate students' reflective participation in and production of personal and shared soundscapes in their everyday lives.

The Sonic Rhetorics of Designed Soundscapes

It is no secret that sound has the power to transform how people experience and interact with a space. This is an idea that designers, architects, and marketing executives have embraced enthusiastically in recent years. Sound has become an essential element in the designed environments of everything from chain restaurants to sporting events (Beckerman). Here I want to focus on three types of spaces—lobbies, music halls, and shopping malls—in which soundscape design is used strategically to shape listeners' experiences. The soundscapes that are created to affect and persuade people in these contexts offer a basic introduction to the ways that sonic rhetorics are employed in familiar commercial and cultural spaces.

The sound of a building's lobby, a common public space in hotels, large office buildings, and museums, may not seem to be especially significant. However, in his interview, Coudriet emphasized the critical role of sound in a lobby—an area that needs to be lively, but not uncomfortably noisy. He explained, "A lively lobby or atrium will encourage users to mingle and socialize. As they move further into the building, a quieter, deader acoustical environment will cue them that they've entered a quiet area of the building and they'll act accordingly" (personal interview). To add some extra noise and life into the space, Coudriet told me, lobbies are often constructed with reverberant materials. Reverberation makes it seem as if there is more sound filling a space than there actually is, giving the space a warm, energetic atmosphere that makes people feel like it is appropriate to talk loudly and be more social. This encouraged socialization is sometimes reinforced by seating areas designed for conversation—couches and chairs grouped in small clusters, for example. As people transition to other spaces in the building, they are "cued" to behave differently. Coudriet's use of the word *cue* is noteworthy because it implies that the acoustics of the space serve as a signal that nudges people to adjust their behavior. Like the Commons Room in the Cathedral of Learning, "a quieter, deader acoustical environment" is designed to persuade people to be less animated and social as they move through a building.[15] This example demonstrates how sound can be used as a subtle but persuasive force that influences how people interact with and travel through a space.

While inhabitants of lobbies may not be aware of how sound is affecting them, some spaces—like music halls—are designed so that inhabitants pay close attention to their listening behaviors. Because sound is obviously the most vital feature of a music hall experience, these buildings are constructed to promote focused listening. In fact, the rhetorical function of acoustics in music halls has a long history. In eighteenth-century Europe, the performance of music in concert halls—an attempt to crystallize music as a serious intellectual art—became popular (Thompson 46). However, because audiences were used to raucous and interactive street performances, this "street" behavior continued in concert halls. Therefore, people began to design concert halls in ways that encouraged more subdued listening practices. As Thompson writes of a Venetian philosopher and expert in music and architecture:

> When Count Francesco Algarotti had petitioned for an acoustically controlled architecture in 1762, he pleaded as vehemently for a new attitude toward listening to accompany the sound. Algarotti longed for a rationally designed theater that would no longer constitute 'a place destined for the reception of a tumultuous assembly, but as the meeting of a solemn audience.' His desire to control the sound was paired with an equally strong desire to control the behavior of the audience. Algarotti himself already constituted such a concerted listener, and he sought an architectural means to engender this attentive way of listening in all concertgoers. (46)

Eventually, concert halls were designed with an intentionally solemn decor and a controlled acoustic environment. The use of soundproofing materials and other acoustical technologies sealed off the hall from outside noises, separating the space of the music hall from street sounds. Large columns and decorative statues also contributed to the building's serious and sophisticated ambiance. Such measures helped to redefine concert halls as hallowed spaces where attentive listening was expected.

In sharp contrast to the rigorous, concentrated listening practices incited by the design of concert halls, many environments have been designed to promote distracted listening practices. For example, in commercial spaces, programmed music—a sonic "wallpaper" of sorts—has become a standard part of soundscape design. In an article about Minnesota's famous Mall of America, Jonathan Sterne argues that the programmed music in the mall is both a form of architecture and a capitalist business strategy: "A store deploys programmed music as part of a fabricated environment aimed at getting visitors to stay longer and buy more" ("Sounds" 5).[16] Stores use particular playlists to increase the amount of time shoppers spend in them. Market research has shown that the longer shoppers are in a store, the more likely it is they will buy something (10). Programmed music encourages a pleasurable state of distraction in shoppers, which often causes them to linger in stores for longer than they may have intended.

Programmed music, or Muzak, usually refers to recognizable songs—like a radio station designed specifically for a store—or to the lyric-less and banal instrumental versions of popular songs.[17] Sterne explains that the musical qualities of programmed music (i.e., volume, rhythm, tone) have an impact on how bodies move through and interact with stores. For example, programmed music is sometimes used to demarcate different spaces of the mall and to influence the behaviors of the bodies in those spaces. While many stores use familiar songs, programmed music is piped into the hallways of the mall.[18] According to Sterne, the hallways' soundtrack is "a transitional space, a space of movement . . . The mall management does not intend the hallways as a destination for Mall visitors" (11). In contrast, the various stores in the mall all have their own brand or genre of music played at different volumes: "If the volume of the store's music is moderate, the placement of the speakers within the store will determine a sonic threshold: on one side the ambiance of the hallway is primary in a listener's auditory field, and on the other side the sounds of the store will be primary in a listener's ear. This sonic threshold, often a discernible physical point, behaves as a store's front wall. Through clear acoustical delineation, the music produces a sense of inside and outside" (12). The music distinguishes the store spatially from the hallways and, depending on the volume, it can also serve as a way to lure people into the store. The distracted listening encouraged by the mall's programmed music is designed to persuade bodies to gravitate toward merchandise. Once shoppers are lured by the sounds, they often get lost in the memories or moods they associate with songs, thereby ignoring aspects of their shopping experience, such as high prices, that might otherwise deter them from buying things.

While the above examples provide an overview of the intended effects of different soundscape designs, I want to emphasize that these soundscapes cannot *control* the bodily movements or feelings of inhabitants. As previously mentioned, the sonic rhetorics employed in soundscape design are part of an ever-shifting, dynamic web of relations that create conditions aimed at persuading and affecting people. Many unpredictable factors contribute to how the sound of an environment will actually be experienced, such as the time of day one encounters a soundscape, the weather, the thoughts, feelings and embodied experiences people bring into a space, and much more. Such examples make it clear that soundscape designers are not the sole agents involved in determining how sonic environments affect people. Sonic composing is not an asymmetrical act; that is, it does not involve only one person who employs sound to affect listeners in a predictable or predetermined way. Rather, it is an act that is embedded within an emergent ecology of space, materials, technologies, aesthetics, bodies, moods, feelings, thoughts, and actions. Agency is dispersed among the humans (designers, inhabitants) and the various inanimate elements (material and aesthetic features of the space, sound technologies, etc.) that constitute a sonic environment. When teachers ask students to notice or design soundscapes, it is imperative that they stress the ecological nature of soundscapes. Exploring how soundscapes work ecologically via the practice of multimodal listening can help students understand how they are enmeshed with and affected by sound in a range of everyday settings. While no one can predict or control exactly how a designed sonic environment will impact its inhabitants, students can be taught to create optimal conditions with sound to persuade and affect people in different contexts.

Because sound plays a central role in the constructed experiences of modern public spaces, a contemporary listening education needs to include opportunities for students to interact with and produce a variety of soundscapes. Adopting acoustic design practices can assist students in becoming more sensitive, thoughtful listeners as they traverse the spaces of everyday life. In addition, learning to pay attention to how sound works relationally in different environments guides students toward an ecological understanding of the process of sonic composition—an understanding that can result in informed decisions about how to use sound (or not) in their own multimodal compositions. The more knowledge students gain about how sound influences listeners' experiences in different environments, the more equipped they will be to design their own sonic experiences.

Personal Soundscaping

While designed soundscapes like the ones discussed above are aimed at influencing listeners' feelings and behaviors, people often use their own strategies to counter this influence. Now more than at any other time in history, new technologies have given listeners the option of producing and controlling their own sonic spaces.[19] Noise-cancelling headphones, for instance, allow travellers in loud, cramped quarters to escape into a quiet and isolating environment. In an article about Bose QuietComfort Acoustic Noise Cancelling Headphones, Mack Hagood observes, "the QuietComfort brand name conjoins the aural and the tactile—not to mention the aural and the psychological—into a single sign, connoting a quiet respite from physical and interpersonal entanglements. This fabrication of physical and psychological space through the aural is what I refer to as soundscaping" (575). In a travelling context, personal soundscaping is a way to avoid coming into contact with sound that might invade one's sonic space in unwelcome ways. Closing one's eyes or zoning in on a computer while cancelling the noise around oneself serves as a way to erase the surrounding environment, sonic or otherwise.

Technologies such as MP3 players and smartphones also allow users to creatively produce and escape into their own sonic worlds.[20] Consider the popular iPod advertisements that feature the black silhouette of a person, equipped with dangling iconic earbuds, against a solid, brightly colored background ("Shadowlock").[21] In the commercials, the iPod-clad silhouettes move as if they were possessed by music, and in the print ads, these silhouettes are frozen in dance poses.[22] The fact that the bodies of these iPod users are blacked out is significant. These images signify that the listeners are in their own interior worlds. Rather than positioning the iPod users in a detailed, visually interesting environment, the monochromatic background is used to depict a kind of joyful intensity—a feeling as opposed to a physical space. iPod listeners in these ads seem to lose themselves and their embodied sense of being (they are merely shadows). In fact, in a 2013 iPod commercial, the bodies of listeners are not included at all. The iPod is instead displayed bouncing and flipping to the music on its own (Deluigi). In this sense, personal soundscaping via the use of MP3 players has an effect that is similar to noise-cancelling headphones. Hagood notes, "by facilitating the shift of attention to the virtual space of a stereophonic soundscape and/or computer screen, soundscaping allows users to disappear their *own* bodies as well, an ontological shift that reconfigures subjects' relations to their surroundings" (583). Like those who sport noise-cancelling headphones, iPod users usually have the option of "disappearing" into their music or employing it to infuse and color the environments in which they are situated.[23]

These personal soundscaping practices are significant because they can empower listeners to take more control over their sonic environments. There are certainly times when people do not want to be attuned to their surroundings, and soundscaping devices can be used strategically to help individuals customize their soundscapes to match their needs and desires. In the case of MP3 players and smartphones, personal soundscaping can also be a creative, compositional act (e.g., constructing musical playlists for different activities or moods) that can transform mundane spaces, as well as a means of providing a sonic continuity that may not exist in the visual landscape—"a seamless web of mediated and privatized experience in their [listeners'] everyday movement through the city" (Bull "The End" 155).

However, the practice of personal soundscaping does have limitations. It should be recognized that personal soundscaping is a privilege that is not available to everyone. Listeners must be able to afford personal soundscaping technologies to control their sonic environments in this way, and the cost of these devices excludes some people.[24] In addition, when people lose themselves in their own personal soundscapes, it means that they are not attending to—or at least not listening in the ecological way I have been advocating—the sonic environments they inhabit. Noise-cancelling headphones may drown out environmental sounds and the people and things that produce them, but blocking out "noise" often means severing oneself from a shared sonic community. Personal soundscaping practices involve ear-centric listening habits that can cause listeners to become sonically disengaged from the soundscapes in which they are situated, and that disengagement has consequences. As Michael Stocker writes, "The sounds of our surroundings enable us to gauge where we are, how safe or exposed we feel, and our position of dominance or deference in our social and spatial settings. The feelings induced by these sounds influence our ability to act; they inform our communication and affect our willingness to speak" (2). Personal soundscapers often miss opportunities to listen to environmental sounds that can provide salient information about the places they are travelling through and potential interactions with the people surrounding them.

While there are certainly advantages to using personal soundscaping devices, I would argue that listening exclusively to self-created, enclosed personal soundscapes impoverishes individuals' knowledge of how sound works as part of a larger ecology. This is not to say that people should stop using personal soundscaping devices. I am simply pointing out that the (sometimes) limiting sonic experiences associated with these popular devices underscore the need for an ecological listening education that encourages students to be more critical participants in the sonic environments they inhabit. Put simply: the pervasiveness of personal soundscaping practices provides an exigence for multimodal listening pedagogy. Teaching students to listen and compose more like acoustic designers can heighten students' sensitivity to the functions, effects, affects, constraints, and possibilities of both the soundscapes that they choose to design or participate in and the soundscapes that are beyond their control.

Social Soundscaping

Though personal soundscaping devices have made it easier to cut oneself off from sonic environments, such technologies also make it possible for listeners to work together to design sonic environments. Recent developments in mobile technology have inspired the emergence of collaborative soundscaping projects. Kati Fargo Ahern and Jordan Frith discuss a rising compositional movement called "social soundscaping" that involves "contributing, geo-locating, sharing, and modifying sounds uploaded and tagged to specific public spaces" (n.p.). Social soundscaping projects allow listeners to be true collaborators and authors of soundscapes by giving them ongoing control over a sonic space. Here I want to suggest that designing occasions for students to attend to the ecological relationship among sound, bodies, and environments can prepare them to become perceptive participants in this novel form of sonic composition, as well as in their encounters with other public sound installations and performances.

A project called Tactical Sound Garden, which Ahern and Frith examine at length, nicely exemplifies how multimodal listening pedagogy can facilitate students' participation in social soundscaping. Inspired by urban community gardens, Tactical Sound Garden is an open-source digital platform that allows users to upload or "plant" sounds into a digital map of a specific urban space. Tactical Sound Garden creator Mark Shepard describes, "These plantings are mapped onto the coordinates of a physical location by a 3D audio engine common to gaming environments—overlaying a publicly constructed soundscape onto a specific urban space" (n.p.). The idea is that people can wear headphones and use their WiFi-connected mobile devices to listen and contribute to location-specific sound gardens in a virtual environment while they are physically drifting through urban spaces.

What is unique about Tactical Sound Garden is the option users have to manipulate or "prune" (delete) sounds that other participants have contributed. Sound gardens—and the experiences listeners have while physically inhabiting them—are always changing. For example, users can plant sounds in environments that do not belong there, transforming the space's ambiance for listeners. Some might choose to make spaces seem strange or surprising (e.g., by adding elephant sounds to a city park), while others may amplify sounds that are already a part of the natural soundscape (e.g., birdsong that would normally be overpowered by city noises). When changes are made to the soundscape, they are automatically mixed in with the previously existing sounds in real time. Therefore, users who occupy the physical space of a sound garden may encounter and/or contribute to several different versions of that sound garden during a single visit.

While social soundscaping is dependent primarily on ear-centric listening experiences, it is a practice that also accounts for how sounds affect bodies moving through and interacting with particular spaces. The ecological multimodal listening and sonic composing practices that students develop in the composition classroom would thus provide them with a foundation for participating in such projects in thoughtful ways. Further, encouraging students to participate in social soundscaping is valuable because it gives listeners a chance to be active producers of everyday soundscapes, enabling them to have more agency over spaces that are becoming increasingly privatized. As Shepard writes, "[Tactical Sound Garden] seeks to reintroduce a form of active participation in the articulation of public space. Conditions for free and open public space in contemporary cities are mitigated by an array of forces. Surveillance and security systems track our moves and transactions. Marketing forces compete for the captivation of our attention in bus stops, subway passages, and public squares. The privatization of broad sectors of urban space to the profit of large, public corporations have resulted in ever more scripted urban experiences for the passers-by" (n.p.).

Introducing the concept of social soundscaping to students in discussions about multimodal listening could at the very least raise their awareness of how sound works in the public spaces they encounter in their personal lives, and perhaps inspire them to participate in or even invent their own sound-driven community projects.[25] Tactical Sound Garden is just one example of the kinds of participatory sonic composing projects that fuse digital and physical sonic experiences for creative and/or political purposes. Interactive sound-based projects in museums, parks, and a broad range of public spaces are cropping up all over the world.[26] Whether students encounter these sonic projects on their own or in a composition classroom, multimodal listening pedagogy will help them develop flexible practices that they can use to participate reflectively in artistic and cultural sonic events.

LISTENING ECOLOGICALLY

Multimodal listening pedagogy aims to sharpen and expand students' awareness of how sound works as part of an aesthetic, material, and spatial ecology to affect their feelings, thoughts, actions, and experiences in particular environments. As I have argued, if students are taught that multimodal composition happens exclusively on computer screens or that listening is an exclusively ear-centric practice, they are given a falsely narrow sense of what it means to be an attuned listener and composer. This is why multimodal listening pedagogy promotes classroom activities that are explicitly connected to students' lived experiences with sound in the world. Echoing Elizabeth Ellsworth, I believe that pedagogy should offer learning experiences that teach students "to come to know the world by acting in it, making something of it, and doing the never-ending work and play of responding to what our actions make occur" (56). To teach students about the richness and complexity of sound, the occasions for learning that teachers design need to move beyond the classroom and into the sonic spaces of everyday life. I offer an example of such an occasion for learning in the Reverberation that follows this chapter, which features an assignment called Mapping Sound that requires students to collaboratively compose and analyze a digital sound map of the physical space of their campus.

REVERBERATION
MAPPING SOUND

THIS INTERCHAPTER STEMS FROM CHAPTER 3'S focus on how sound affects the ways that we experience and make sense of space—something acoustic designers always consider when listening to environments. In addition to asking students to analyze sound maps in digital spaces, I require them to create their own collaborative digital sound map by engaging with the physical space of their university's campus. As with the previous Reverberation, I provide example assignment guidelines, pedagogical commentary, student work, and a list of relevant resources.

MAPPING SOUND

Goal

The aim of this project is to gain a critical awareness of how sound influences our sense of place.

The Project

Working as a group, we will spend several weeks collecting field recordings around campus—in various classrooms, common spaces, outdoor spaces, etc. Each of the recordings will be uploaded to a digital sound map on the Soundcities website (http://www.soundcities.com/), where it will be tagged with the appropriate information (e.g., location, time, description). We will then use the map to discuss what information the sounds reveal about our campus. In addition to recording and tagging sounds during fieldwork, you will be writing about your individual experiences with this form of collaborative composition.

Field Recording

You may use any digital recording device you wish (e.g., smartphone, digital audio recorder, etc.). Once you get to the Soundcities site, click "Baltimore" to locate the map of our campus and follow the instructions for uploading sounds.

Artist Statement

Make sure to take notes during the field recording process. After our collaborative map is completed, continue to take notes as you explore it on your own. Then, based on all of your notes, please write a formal "artist statement" about your experience creating and listening to the map (1000 words). You should address the following questions:

- What information does the digital sound map provide about this physical place?
- How would you describe your field recording process? What made you decide to record some sounds and not others? Why did you think that the sounds you uploaded would be a valuable contribution to the map?
- How did other elements of the environment (think about what you saw, smelled, tasted, touched) affect the ways that you experienced sound in the spaces you recorded?
- In your interactions during fieldwork and with the digital map, how did the soundscape of this place make you feel?
- In what ways has this project made you more aware of or sensitive to the sonic environments you inhabit in your everyday life?

- Based on this experience, what would you say are some of the affordances of digital sound maps? What do digital sound maps make possible that other forms of mapping cannot?
- What are the limitations of experiencing sound in a digital environment? How is experiencing the sounds via the digital map different than experiencing them in their original environment?

Presentation and Discussion

After our digital sound map is completed, we will spend a full class discussing what information it revealed (or not) about our campus, as well as other observations you made during your experience of creating, exploring, and writing about the map.

MAPPING SOUND COMMENTARY

Design and Purpose

"The interactive sound map is a relatively recent invention," writes Gascia Ouzounian, which "emerged at the intersection of soundscape studies, acoustic ecology, and sound art practices in the late 1990s" (165). This project was inspired by my own encounters with various types of elaborate digital sound maps during the past few years. Authors of these maps—usually multiple people and/or communities—record sounds from an environment and upload them to an interactive digital map, where they are sometimes tagged with information. Many digital sound maps also include images of locations and textual descriptions to supplement the sound. While different sound maps have different purposes, generally speaking sound mapping is intended to give users an opportunity to listen to and examine the soundscape of a place to get a better sense of what life is like there; to document changes in the soundscape over time; and, for people who already inhabit those spaces, to amplify sounds that they may not notice anymore due to overexposure.

Interacting with digital sound maps like the ones listed in the resources section at the end of this interchapter raised interesting questions for me about the possibilities and constraints of experiencing digital representations of soundscapes versus experiencing sound as it actually occurs in the world:

What does interacting with a digital sound map enable users to do or understand that might not be possible when moving through physical spaces and vice versa? How might the process of creating a digital sound map give students a fuller sense of the ecological nature of sonic composition? With these questions in mind, I developed the Mapping Sound Project, which I view as an opportunity for students to experience how sound influences the ways that they make sense (figuratively and literally) of different environments. This assignment also promotes an expansive sense of multimodal composing that includes attending to embodied interactions in both physical and digital environments.

In addition to the general assignment guidelines, I provided students with some specific rules to ensure that the fieldwork requirement of the project would be sufficient. For example, I asked each student to upload a minimum of thirty sounds to our digital map. The number of sounds that instructors require will depend on the number of students in the class and the amount of time devoted to the project. Regardless of the specifics, setting a requirement will increase the likelihood that the digital sound map will contain enough material to generate a substantial discussion. Also, for assessment purposes, I required students to keep a running list of every sound they recorded. The list included the date, time, location, and description of the sound. This detailed documentation was useful to students when it came time to upload and tag their sounds, and it provided me with clear evidence that everyone contributed equally to the project.

In terms of the recording technologies needed for fieldwork, I gave students permission to use any digital audio recording device they desired. Most of my students chose to use free recording apps on their personal smartphones. Using Wi-Fi enabled smartphones works especially well with a platform like Soundcities because students can record audio and then immediately upload their recording to the digital map with the same device. For students who do not have access to smartphones, I always keep several digital audio recorders on hand, which I purchased for under twenty dollars each. (Inexpensive digital audio recorders are available online and in most stores that sell electronics). Students do not need to use expensive or high-end technology to participate in sound mapping assignments.

Finally, I want to stress that the "artist statement" is integral to the project's design. The questions I included in the prompt are intended to guide students' thinking as they compose and interact with the sound map. Requiring students to grapple with these questions in writing before the full class discussion of the map will (ideally) lead to a more thoughtful conversation about their experiences. As I mentioned in the assignment guidelines, students should start writing in the form of field notes as soon as they begin the recording process, because asking them to wait until after the map is finished to reflect would imply a binary between experiencing and thinking/writing. On the contrary, writing is always ecological. "Writing moves through space," Nathaniel Rivers observes, "composing connections among people, places, and things" (576). It is important to encourage students to document their in-progress experiences with the Mapping Sound Project to help them understand their writing as part of an ecology that includes their embodied interactions in particular locations, their recording technologies and digital sound files, the time of day and weather conditions during fieldwork, the affordances and constraints of the Soundcities website, and so on. It is this entire ecology that contributes to and informs students' composing processes.

Context, Attunement, Challenges

I have taught different iterations of the Mapping Sound Project in various courses over the past seven years, and I always introduce this project with what is called a "Soundwalk." Soundwalking—a practice that emerged from R. Murray Schafer's World Soundscape Project—refers to taking a meditative walk with the primary intention of listening to the environment (Westerkamp). I spend at least one class session soundwalking with students. Before we embark on this walk, I explain the rules: 1) no one is allowed to talk until we have completed the walk, and 2) all smartphones and digital devices must be turned off during the walk. I also instruct students to pay attention not only to what they are hearing, but to how their bodies are feeling at various points during the walk, and to what they are noticing about the environment. In other words, I invite them to practice multimodal listening. This exercise feels awkward at first. Students are not accustomed to walking in a large group without interacting with people or things (e.g., smartphones, earbuds, each other, etc.), so it usually takes several minutes for them (and me) to focus. After fifteen or twenty minutes, we stop and students write about their soundwalking experience before we have a group discussion. In my experience, students have often been surprised by what they notice during such a simple activity. For instance, here is a selection of comments from students' written reflections of our last soundwalk: "I've never really listened like that before. I almost always have earbuds in when I'm walking on campus, so this was totally different. I felt hyper-sensitive." "I never noticed how the construction noises near the library make my body tense up." "I can't believe how many different bird songs I heard. I didn't think there was that much wildlife on campus." As these comments suggest, soundwalking can attune students to their embodied relationships with the sonic environment, and it also encourages them to think about and question their own listening habits.

Before beginning the field recording part of the project, I also assign a range of material about sound and the environment to provide students with context for this work. There are many excellent sources on sound and the environment, and in the Selected Resources section, I include a list that I have found useful in my teaching. Alongside this material, students explore a variety of digital sound maps. I ask them to consider how each map is composed, how it works, what purpose it serves, and what its limitations and affordances are in terms of using sound to represent a place/space. During our discussion of this exercise, many students expressed that they were surprised by how familiar sounds like traffic, birds, and children playing—sounds that they did not spend much time thinking about in their everyday lives—could provide salient information about places (e.g., information about the health of an environment, human and animal populations, lifestyles of the people who inhabit or live in these places, etc.). Together with the soundwalk, the digital sound map exercise serves as a way to heighten students' sensitivity to environmental sounds and their potential significance before setting out to do their own fieldwork.

Accessibility was one of the biggest challenges of the Mapping Sound Project. While I did not have any students in class who identified as "disabled," I did ask all students to think about how we could make the project more accessible. During this discussion, several students pointed out that there were already various ways for deaf and hard of hearing persons to engage with our digital sound map. For instance, the visual pins in the map and the text used to tag sounds make it possible to get a sense of what sounds are occurring in specific locations on campus without depending upon audible information. To further increase our map's access, however, my students' textual descriptions would need to be more detailed. Unfortunately, the Soundcities platform has particular constraints that curtailed my students' efforts to be descriptive, such as limited word count and no special characters. Uploading images or video is also not an option. Soundcities is a useful, easy-to-use mapping tool that can be employed to construct a digital sound map with hearing students in a short time, but it is not ideal in terms of accessibility for non-hearing users. As I learned from this project, creating more inclusive sound maps would require building customized digital maps. The "How to Make a Sound Map" blog post, located under Selected Resources, contains information about digital map-making platforms that might prove useful in this respect.

In class we also discussed how to make the field recording part of the Mapping Sound Project more inclusive. One way that deaf or hard of hearing students might participate in this project would be to upload detailed textual descriptions, images, and/or videos to the map to document their embodied experiences in specific locations. For example, rather than capturing an audio recording, a student might wander around a specific location and gather tactile or visual evidence of sound. Asking all students to document detailed visual and textual information about their bodily experiences—with the addition of audio recordings uploaded by the hearing students—would make the digital map much more accessible and informative for all users. These are ideas that I hope to test in future iterations of this project. It is also important to account for students with limited mobility by providing a reasonable (and flexible) time frame for collecting field recordings. The design and physical layout of a campus (or any area used as the Mapping Sound site) will affect the amount of time needed for fieldwork, so instructors should be cognizant of how site accessibility might help or hinder students.

Student Work

To view the digital sound map that my students created at the University of Maryland-Baltimore County (UMBC), go to the Soundcities website (http://www.soundcities.com/) and click on "Baltimore." There you will be able to zoom in on particular areas of UMBC's campus, listen to field recordings, and read the tagged textual descriptions of the sounds. The link to our sound map is also available on the "Reverberations" page of my website (www.stephceraso.com/reverberations). With my students' permission, I include in this section excerpts from their "artist statements" to offer a fuller sense of what students thought about and learned from doing this project. I have categorized these comments based on common themes that emerged in my students' writing. I provide brief commentary after each theme.

RECORDING AS COMPOSING

"The sounds we decided to record were ones we thought should represent an area. . .people find different sounds important to represent their environment. This is a personal choice, so when you are listening to the map, you are listening to choices people made about what to record, not necessarily an accurate soundscape of a place."

∿

"One place I liked to go for quiet is the sixth floor of the library which is supposed to be the absolutely quiet floor. Even though it is quiet you can still hear doors closing, computers clicking and papers rustling. I did a recording on this floor just to show that there is always some environmental noise."

∿

"As far as just kind of a personal preference in recording, I noticed on colder days I tended to record indoors much more. This was in part because there were less people outside and therefore less noises to record, but also because I didn't want to stand in the cold and record sounds."

∿

"I also didn't record during bad weather, heavy winds and rain were a major deterrent for me to sit there and record a noise. If I went back and did it again I may try and capture these sounds, but I think I would need a better microphone. My phone's microphone is pretty small, therefore, I don't really get the best fidelity. A wind noise completely trumps all the noises that I would want to be recording."

∿

"How a [recording of a] space sounds depends on how I face my microphones, how I move, wind conditions, my gain level, whether I'm set to stereo or mono, and various other factors. There is not yet a perfect way to replicate the sound of an environment."

∿

The only instruction I gave students about their recording practice was that they should try to record sounds during different days of the week and different times of the day so that our map would capture a fuller range of variation in the campus' soundscape. In general, though, they were free to record any sounds they felt were worth their attention. One of the most important take-aways from this project, as the above comments illustrate, was that the act of recording sound is itself a form of composing. As my students learned, one must choose what to record, and that decision is based on a number of factors such as one's own agenda, the weather conditions, physical comfort, personal preferences, and the capacities and qualities of particular recording technologies. Rather than thinking of this project as merely documenting a soundscape, then, students came to realize that the choices they made about what sounds to include (or not) in the map significantly shaped the meaning of our overall composition—that the sonic story we were telling about UMBC was only one of many possible stories.

AFFORDANCES OF SOUND MAPPING

"Overall, I think someone who is unfamiliar with UMBC's campus could pick up on the fact that various parts of campus are being worked on because of all of the construction sounds . . . Judging by the fact that many of our sounds come from The Commons or Starbucks, a person listening in might conclude that those are the most popular hangout spots on campus, and if they pay attention to the different times of the recordings, they might be able to figure out when these places are the busiest."

~

"As someone who lives on campus, it was interesting to see how my sounds were different from the sounds of the commuter students in the class. While I had a few sounds in the residential areas, like Walker Apartments and Harbor Hall, I noticed that for some of my classmates the sounds were entirely focused in academic buildings and the Commons. I think that shows how different types of students really have different experiences at UMBC."

~

"The first thing I noticed is how rural the campus is . . . Despite how close it is to Baltimore, and that Baltimore is in its name, the nature sounds that are present show us that this is not an urban campus . . . if one listens to the map they can probably tell that this is a learning environment. Many of the sounds, especially in the classrooms, contain noises of desks moving, backpacks being packed, and computer typing."

~

These comments amplify some of the information students were able to glean from our sound map. For example, the map made it easy to locate where construction was happening on campus, which might reveal information about the values of the university (i.e., construction noise in certain parts of campus might indicate that the university is investing money in particular disciplines or departments). Students were also sensitive to what the map could tell them about human activity on campus and to the different experiences of their peers. As one student noted in her "artist statement," commuter students' recordings all occurred in a concentrated area on campus while students who lived on campus captured a much wider range of locations and sonic experiences. This suggests that commuters tend to have a limited experience with the campus environment that is mostly restricted to academic buildings. Additionally, as nearly every single student mentioned in their writing, the most striking thing about our sound map was the sheer number of natural sounds we recorded. In our discussion, students were quick to point out how different our sonic representation of campus was compared to how campus is marketed. One of the ways that the university tries to attract students is by having a Baltimore address, which suggests it is an exciting urban environment. As the university website touts, "there is never a shortage of things to do" ("Visitor's Guide"). Despite UMBC's Baltimore address, however, campus is located in a rather secluded, bucolic area. My students pointed out that most undergraduates do not take advantage of the campus' proximity to the city. In this way, our sound map provided an interesting contrast to other ways that the school is represented to the public. The sounds on our map also exposed something about the embodied experience of campus that textual descriptions or visual maps alone would not have been able to capture in the same way.

LIMITATIONS OF SOUND MAPPING

"Sound is fluid and always changing. New sounds are also being created . . . Unless the map is constantly fed new sounds, it can become outdated really quickly."

~

"Context also seems to matter a lot. While I can easily explain my recordings at The Retriever Weekly [the student newspaper office], an outsider might not be able to pick up on that just from listening. Contextualizing all of the sounds makes them mean so much more, and that seems to be the big flaw in sound maps."

~

"In the map, you can only hear the sound while vision, smell, taste and other senses are not available (at least not in the same way as experiencing live sound), so you have to imagine other senses when listening to the sound."

~

"As a visually-inclined person, this sound map feels sporadic and full of gaps, like I'm not getting the full 'picture,' yet it's the desire to see a picture that might be holding me back."

~

My students observed that digital sound maps cannot represent accurately the experience of a sonic environment because soundscapes are always changing. "Soundscapes," Blesser and Salter remind us, "are alive by definition; they can never be static" (15). Our digital version of the soundscape transformed site-specific sonic moments into something stable that can be experienced repeatedly. While digital sound mapping can make it easier for users to find patterns among the sounds in a particular site, interacting with the digital map is far removed from the embodied, immersive, ever-changing experience of encountering sound in its original environment. As one of my students acknowledged, listening to the digital map is a diminished sensory experience compared to inhabiting the actual soundscape. This project made apparent to students that experiencing sound in the context of its sounding is much more intense and dynamic compared to experiencing the same sounds through tiny computer speakers. It is also worth noting that students were aware of their own sensory habits during this project. The student who writes about being "visually-inclined," for instance, points out that his own visual bias may have prevented him from understanding fully what the sound had to offer. In other words, he was too focused on comparing sonic information to visual information instead of thinking about the distinct affordances of sound. Many of the limitations students wrote about led to conversations about listening habits, as well as embodied experiences in physical and digital spaces. Generally speaking, this project heightened students' sensitivity to the ways that sound shapes their experiences in the environments with which they interact daily and compelled them to examine their own listening practices. Sound mapping can serve as an effective way to introduce students to the ecological nature of both listening and composing practices.

Evaluation

I treat this assignment as more of an exercise than a project, making it worth a small portion of students' overall grades—10 percent or less. In my experience, this low-stakes approach encourages students to worry less about the grade and helps them concentrate more on what they are doing and learning at various stages of the project. My evaluation is based on the quality and degree of students' participation throughout the course of the project, which I determine by reviewing my notes from in-class activities and discussions and by considering the detail and thoughtfulness of their written contributions. Here I provide the general criteria I used to guide my evaluation. As I did with the My Listening Body Project discussed in the previous interchapter, I responded to each of these statements with "definitely yes" (A), "mostly yes" (B), "somewhat" (C), or "no" (F), and assigned a holistic grade based on the accumulative responses. I also explained my responses and additional observations about students' individual contributions in written comments. Instructors should feel free to change the method of evaluation to suit their own needs and goals.

1. Participation
   - demonstrates a high level of engagement during in-class exercises and discussions associated with the project (i.e., student was present for all in-class activities and discussions; listened attentively to peers and contributed ideas to advance the discussions)
   - contributes the required number of field recordings to the project and provides documentation of recordings
2. Artist Statement
   - addresses thoughtfully and thoroughly all questions in assignment guidelines

- contains astute observations and insights about various stages of the composing process—from fieldwork to interaction with the completed digital map

Selected Resources

SOUNDWALKING

O'Keefe, Linda. "(Sound) Walking through Smithfield Square in Dublin." *Sounding Out: The Sound Studies Blog.* 10 Feb. 2014. Web. 7 July 2016. https://soundstudiesblog.com/2014/02/10/soundwalking-through-smithfield-square-in-dublin/.

Silva, Liana. "Park Sounds: A Kansas City Soundwalk for Fall." *Sounding Out: The Sound Studies Blog.* 3 Dec. 2012. Web. 7 July 2016. https://soundstudiesblog.com/2012/12/03/park-sound-a-kansas-city-soundwalk-for-fall/.

Westerkamp, Hildegard. "Soundwalking as Ecological Practice." Proceedings for the International Conference on Acoustic Ecology. Hirosaki University, Japan. 2–4 Nov. 2006. Web. 10 July 2015. http://www.sfu.ca/~westerka/writings%20page/articles%20pages/soundasecology2.html.

SAMPLE SOUND MAPS

British Library UK Soundmap: http://sounds.bl.uk/sound-maps/uk-soundmap.

Glasgow 3D Sound Map: http://www.glasgow3dsoundmap.co.uk/#map.

London Sound Survey: http://www.soundsurvey.org.uk/index.php/survey/soundmaps/.

Montreal Sound Map: http://www.montrealsoundmap.com/.

Open Sound New Orleans: http://www.opensoundneworleans.com/core.

The Roaring Twenties: http://vectors.usc.edu/projects/index.php?project=98.

SOUNDS, ENVIRONMENTS, MAPPING

EchoXIII. "How to Make a Sound Map: Cartographic, Compositional, Performative." *Acoustic Ecology.* University of Hull, Scarborough Campus. 4 Dec. 2013. Web. 7 July 2016. https://acousticecologyuoh.wordpress.com/2013/12/04/how-to-make-a-sound-map/.

Geere, Duncan. "The National Mall: A Location-Aware App Album." *Wired.* 27 May 2011. Web. 13 Mar. 2014. http://www.wired.com/2011/05/national-mall-location-aware-album/.

Jensenius, David. "FoundSounds" 10 Apr. 2015. Web. 17 May 2015. App. https://itunes.apple.com/us/app/found-sounds/id593338411?mt=8.

Krause, Bernie. "The Voice of the Natural World." *TED.* June 2013. Web. 9 July 2013. http://www.ted.com/talks/bernie_krause_the_voice_of_the_natural_world.

Madrigal, Alexis C. "The Quest to Find the First Soundscape." *Atlantic*. 14 Sept. 2010.
    Web. 3 Oct. 2013. http://www.theatlantic.com/technology/archive/2010/09/the-
    quest-to-find-the-first-soundscape/62842/.

Mars, Roman. "99% Noise." *99% Invisible* Podcast. Radiotopia. 3 Sept. 2010. Web. 8
    June 2015. http://99percentinvisible.org/episode/99-invisible-01-99-noise-by-
    roman-mars-this/.

Schafer, R. Murray. *The Soundscape: Our Sonic Environment and the Tuning of the World*. 1977.
    Rochester, VT: Destiny Books, 1994.

Thompson, Emily. *The Soundscape of Modernity: Architectural Acoustics and the Culture of Listening in
    America, 1900–1933*. Cambridge, MA: MIT P, 2002.

Wise, Pascal. "What Will Our Cities Sound Like in the Future." *Guardian*. 13 Mar.
    2014. Web. 4 Apr. 2014. https://www.theguardian.com/cities/2014/mar/13/sounds
    -city-technology-urban-centres-peaceful.

Ximm, Aaron. "Tips for Recording in the Field." *Quiet American*. n.d. Web. 7 June 2015.
    http://www.quietamerican.org/links_diy-rec_tips.html.

FOUR
SOUNDING CARS, SELLING EXPERIENCE
Sound Design in Consumer Products

The car is one of the most powerful listening environments today, as one of the few places where you can listen to whatever you like, without being concerned about disturbing others, and even singing along at the top of your voice—the car is the most ubiquitous concert hall and the "bathroom" of our time.

OLA STOCKFELT

The car becomes a comfortable platform for the boomin' on-board sound system . . . The car emerges from this as a place of listening, an intrepid, scaled-up substitute for the solipsistic world of the personal stereo, a kind of giant armoured bed on wheels that can shout the driver's dwindling claims upon the world into dead public space at ever-increasing volume.

PAUL GILROY

THE GAZE OF THE CAMERA zeroes in on the sleek body of a BMW, the center of attention in what looks to be a lab for research and design. Bright lights shine down upon the glamorous black car; it is surrounded by plush, theatrical red curtains. The camera pans around the vehicle, periodically zooming in on specific features, as a masculine voice announces: "the evolution of beauty and luxury . . . a texture of impeccable design" (Taimi). The narrator continues to emphasize the car's appearance while the scene shifts to a shot of the BMW racing through an anonymous urban landscape. There is a quick glimpse of a woman on the passenger side dancing to music that viewers cannot hear, then the car speeds off into the distance.

Like many car commercials, this 2011 advertisement for the BMW 760LI focuses on the visual. The red curtains provide a striking contrast to the shiny black vehicle, making it pop against the background. Every curve and line shimmers in the dramatic lighting. The BMW is visually stunning and on display for all to admire. Treating cars like eye candy is a standard theme in automotive advertising, and this is especially apparent in the scene with the woman dancing in the passenger seat. It is obvious that her beauty, elegance, and sensuality are being used to persuade viewers to associate the car with these same qualities. More interesting to me, though, is the fact that viewers do not have access to the music she hears—a strategic choice that serves to underscore the exclusivity of owning a BMW. The sense of environmental privacy in this scene implies that the car is a sonic world unto itself. As the epigraphs suggest, the sonic environments of cars significantly influence people's feelings about driving. Cars, Stockfelt declares, are "one of the most powerful listening environments today" (33). They are personalized sonic spaces that drivers can use to escape from the world even as they traverse it. Though sound may not be as celebrated as the visual, it has always been central to automotive experience. As the authors of *Sound and Safe: A History of Listening Behind the Wheel* state, "Sound is hardly a new concern in the automotive industry. Such attention to sound has actually been part and parcel of car design and marketing since the 1920s" (Bijsterveld et al. 21).

This chapter examines sound as an essential feature in the design, production, and experience of cars. I focus specifically on the listening and composing practices of automotive acoustic engineers—audio design professionals who work for car companies—and also discuss sonic practices associated with driving in general. In addition to the level of sonic control that cars afford drivers, there is a key difference between car sound and the other kinds of sonic experiences I have considered throughout this book: the car is a sonically rich experience that is for sale. It is a consumer product, and an extremely popular one at that. According to John Urry, the car is "the major item of individual consumption after housing" (18).[1] Cars are especially unique consumer products because they are both sonically composed and compose-able. That is, automotive acoustic engineers deliberately compose sonic experiences to attract certain buyers, and drivers also have the ability to compose their own sonic experiences by manipulating a car's features, such as the speaker system. The sonic practices associated with cars are multi-layered and complex.

Composing sound for cars involves designing holistic multisensory experiences—a practice that is becoming increasingly common in product design. Eefje Cleophas and Karin Bijsterveld explain, "while manufacturers had long been interested in what *the consumer did with the product*, since the 1970s they have become obsessed by what *the product does to the consumer*" (119). The manipulation of consumers' senses has become a principal strategy in product design. Products are intended not merely to function, but to look, feel, sound, and in some cases taste or smell a particular way. In other words, designers and marketers aim to construct sensory experiences that consumers will find pleasing. Think of Alka-Seltzer's "Plop, plop, fizz, fizz" jingle or the "Once you pop, you can't stop!" catchphrase associated with Pringles. Television commercials for these brands focus not only on how their products look, but on the sounds and feelings one experiences while consuming them.

Product and *experience* have become interchangeable terms in today's economy. Sensory marketing strategies have proven to be so effective, in fact, that sociologist Gerhard Schulze refers to the current manifestation of consumer culture as "experience society" (Cleophas and Bijsterveld 118).[2] Because car companies were among the first to tap into the importance of sound in the consumer experience, they have set the precedent for sonic design trends in a range of consumer products: "The notion that sound 'is well known to enhance or detract from our pleasure in possessing or using a product' (Boulandet et al. 2008, 1) has thus been reinforced by an emerging and growing network of manufacturers, designers, testing companies, marketers, and academics who reciprocally spread the word of sensorial branding and design" (119). Sound is creating a buzz in the product design world that seems to be getting louder every year. As Ellen Byron proclaimed in a 2012 *Wall Street Journal* article, "Sound is emerging as a new branding frontier" (n.p.).

The pervasive practice of using sound to influence consumers' experiences with products further amplifies the need for a more expansive listening education that accounts for our bodily interactions with objects. In this chapter I argue that the emphasis on holistic, multisensory experiences in the sonic design of consumer products—from cars to kitchen appliances—makes these products ideal objects to explore and experiment with in the multimodal composition classroom. Students need to develop practices that will help them become smart consumers and producers of sound; they ought to learn how to become attuned participants in our "experience society" (Cleophas and Bijs-terveld 118). As I will demonstrate, cultivating multimodal listening practices via engaging with and creating objects that use sound strategically can deepen students' understanding of how sonic rhetorics operate in their everyday interactions with a range of things.

I first situate this argument within rhetoric and composition by discussing how a greater emphasis on sound and listening can enrich disciplinary schol-arship on materiality and design. Drawing from a range of sound studies work on automobiles, I then explore automotive acoustic engineering practices to offer a broad, materially driven approach to listening and sonic composing in multimodal composition. I also address the multimodal listening and com-posing practices associated with cars from the perspective of the consumer, illustrating the ways that drivers employ many of the same practices as automo-tive acoustic engineers to construct very specific experiences. Unlike previous chapters, this chapter does not combine discussions of sound professionals' listening and composing practices with explicit suggestions for classroom applications. Rather, the automotive acoustic engineering and product design practices I identify lay the groundwork for a three-part assignment sequence in the accompanying Reverberation. A separate and more substantial ped-agogical example is needed in order to account for the multi-faceted sonic practices covered in this chapter.

MATERIALITY, DESIGN, AND MULTIMODAL COMPOSITION

Automotive acoustic engineers' sonic design practices rely on bodily inter-actions with the material features of cars. While my focus on automotive acoustic engineering may seem foreign to rhetoric and composition scholars, materiality and design are already prominent areas of research in the field. Indeed, materiality has been explored in relation to a wide variety of topics in disciplinary scholarship. In *Writing Technology*, for instance, Christina Haas examines the materiality of literacy, asking "What does it mean for language to become material? That is, what is the effect of writing and other mate-rial literacy technologies on human thinking and culture?" (3). Jody Shipka also addresses the material aspects of her students' multimodal compositions, such as a memorable object-argument project made with pink ballet slippers, in *Toward a Composition Made Whole*. Her more recent work delves into the compositional and affective potential of personal objects, or "unofficial archives," left behind at estate sales ("On Estate Sales"). In an article titled "Evocative Objects," Doug Hesse, Nancy Sommers, and Kathleen Yancey illustrate how ordinary things can "summon a network of associations and evoke cross-disciplinary inquiries, using both visual and verbal resources in an effort to make meaning" (325). Visual rhetorician Laurie Gries uses the vibrant rhetorical life of the Obama Hope image to invite the field to attend to rhetoric as "a process that unfolds and materializes with time and space" (xiv). Taking an especially capacious approach, Thomas Rickert's materialist conception of ambient rhetoric is grounded in the sensory, material, technological, and ecological relations that wed us to and transform our interactions with the world (*Ambient*). And, in their introduction to *Rhetoric, Through Everyday Things*, Scot Barnett and Casey Boyle offer the concept of *"rhetorical ontology*, a relational framework that harnesses the energies of past and present theories of materiality in rhetoric but also anticipates possibilities for new approaches to materiality going forward" (2).

A heightened attention to materiality is also apparent in disciplinary scholarship on design, particularly in multimodal composition and technical writing. The New London Group has had a clear influence on design work in the field, which often deals with making meaning of and creating digital texts or more traditional material documents, such as informational brochures, charts and graphs, posters, etc. In *Writer/Designer*, for example, Kristin Arola, Jennifer Sheppard, and Cheryl Ball rely on foundational concepts from the New London Group in their guidebook on how to analyze, draft, and produce multimodal texts for audiences across the disciplines. Other rhetoric and composition scholars such as Richard Marback, James Purdy, David Sheridan, Kristin Prins, Anne Shivers-McNair, Carrie Leverenz, and Scott Wible have been considering design as an essential part of writing and various kinds of rhetorical work. Their scholarship covers topics from design thinking to the affordances of makerspaces to the fabrication of objects via 3-D printers.

This brief and necessarily selective overview of scholarship barely scratches the surface of the diverse and ever-growing body of research connected to materiality in the field, which includes engagements with new materialism, object-oriented ontology, posthumanism, and other theoretical orientations having to do with the extrahuman turn. Thus far, disciplinary research has led to insights about materiality with respect to language, images, code, different types of multimodal texts and three-dimensional objects, and, to some extent, sound. With the exception of Rickert's ecological treatment of sound as "crucial to our integration into social and material environments," however, sound has played a rather limited role in material understandings of writing and rhetoric (*Ambient* 139). Following Rickert's lead, I want to suggest that a more extensive focus on sound can sustain and enrich research on materiality in the field. I have already discussed the materiality of sound in terms of vibration and the body in Chapter 2, and I provided examples of how the material structure of an environment shapes the ways that we experience sound in Chapter 3. In this chapter, I further develop ideas about sound and materiality via examining sound as a vital design element in many everyday objects.

This chapter and its accompanying Reverberation demonstrate how rhetoric and composition scholars might bring together ideas about materiality, design, and sound in ways that can expand how we think about our interactions with objects. While I concentrate specifically on how the sonic design of cars and other consumer products might inform approaches to multimodal composition pedagogy, my hope is that this discussion will encourage writing and rhetoric scholars to consider the role of sound in explorations of materiality more broadly. As the automotive acoustic engineering practices I elaborate on below make evident, sound is not a superfluous design element, but a fundamental part of our relationships to and experiences with things.

SOUNDING CARS

Cars are expertly designed objects that require a hefty financial investment. For that reason, most people drive the same car for years. Making the financial and temporal commitment to purchase a car is about more than getting from point A to point B; it is an emotional and affective decision. In addition to meeting practical transportation needs, then, cars must be designed to *feel* good to consumers. Indeed, cars today are designed to be an extension of one's home—"a living room on wheels"—and sound is an important feature in the production of "home-like" car environments (Urry 23). As Michael Bull suggests, "The interior 'soundscape' of the automobile can produce feelings of protectedness, security, and confidence in a manner that the physicality of the automobile or the visual aspect of automobility tends not to do on its own" (*Sound Moves* 89). The car seals off, or at least muffles, the sounds of the outside world, thus giving drivers a sense of sonic privacy that is often associated with domestic environments. Additionally, the sounds that cars make—sounds associated with turn signals, horns, stereo systems, etc.—all contribute to drivers' feelings about cars. Automotive manufacturers are conscious of the fundamental role of sound in driving experiences, and thus they dedicate substantial money and resources to ensure that the sonic features of their cars, including their capacity to diminish unwanted sounds, are well designed.

There are a growing number of acoustic engineers in the automotive workforce, and over time these engineers have developed sonic composing and listening practices that are aimed at enhancing driving experiences.[3] Auditory design, Brandon LaBelle states, adds "dynamic input into building cars as experiences, turning driving and the car into a form of lifestyle—to control the stylized aesthetics of being on the road, and the experiences found therein" (145).

In what follows I identify automotive acoustic engineering practices that can serve as useful heuristics for approaches to sound in multimodal composition pedagogy.[4] Some of these practices overlap with concepts that are familiar to composition instructors. For instance, creating the sounds for cars involves considerations of audience, style, rhetorical effects, and revision. What automotive acoustic engineers add to these standard features of the composing process is an explicitly physical, experiential dimension. Their emphasis on embodied interactions with the material features of cars, I contend, can expand the ways we think about listening and sonic composing in multimodal composition.

Automotive acoustic engineers listen to and design sound with target audiences in mind.

Manipulating sounds for target audiences is one of the most basic practices involved in the composition of car sounds. Much like acoustic designers compose environments with specific inhabitants in mind, automotive acoustic engineers go to great lengths to make sure that the sounds they produce are geared toward specific drivers: "Since the late 1990s, leading automobile manufacturers have advertised the sonic qualities and interior tranquility of their vehicles with increasing fervor . . . Indeed, manufacturers have invested considerable time and money in making sure that switches, warning signals, direction indicators, windshield wipers, the opening of car windows, the locking of car doors, or the crackle of the leather upholstery come with the *right* sound" (Cleophas and Bijsterveld 103). "Right" sounds, in this case, are called "target sounds" (103). Automotive acoustic engineers fine-tune sounds to appeal to particular buyers; or, to put it in compositional terms, acoustic designers always consider "target audiences." For example, "sporty" sounds, such as a loud, growling engine, are designed to attract certain demographics—usually young and middle-aged men—while "safe" sounds like seat belts that click loudly into place and door locks that "produce a reassuring solid sound" might be aimed at car buyers with young children (103). As is the case with most forms of composition, understanding the experiences, needs, and desires of target audiences is vital to the process of composing sound for cars.

Automotive acoustic engineers must also develop a precise language when creating "target sounds." For instance, they need to consider questions like: How does one describe or define a "sporty" or "safe" sound? Or, how can such sounds be manipulated to more accurately represent these adjectives? (Cleophas and Bijsterveld 112–117). Inventing a common sonic vocabulary, which might be used in the audio engineering process or for market research, is a difficult but necessary task that promotes a functional communication process. In order to determine whether or not a sound needs to be tweaked to fit a specific adjective, acoustic engineers must perform an iterative cycle of composing, listening, and conversing until they achieve the results they are after. Revision is crucial during every step of design and production.

Automotive acoustic engineers develop a distinct sonic style.

Like musicians or bands that have a signature sonic style, automotive acoustic engineers design distinct sonic styles that represent the overall identity of the company. Cars have a highly stylized sound just as they have a certain "look" or visual style. For instance, though a Ford Explorer may sound slightly different than a Ford Focus, they are merely variations of the same sonic identity that Ford has created for itself. In other words, it is possible to distinguish the sound of Ford vehicles from the sound of BMWs or Audis or Volvos. The practice of styling the sounds of cars and other consumer products is referred to as "sonic branding" (the sonic equivalent to a visual logo)—a technique that the car industry has embraced with enthusiasm. As Bijsterveld muses, "Car makers even believe the sound of engine and exhaust to be critical for their make's image: 'One vrmm is not quite another'" (201).

Interestingly, many car manufacturers are now replacing or masking real engine sounds with artificially designed sounds, a process called "engine-sound enhancement" (Colwell n.p.). For example, to mark the occasion of the fortieth anniversary of the 1968 film *Bullitt,* which featured a Mustang driven by Steve McQueen, Ford wanted to recreate the movie's car for modern audiences. Joel Beckerman explains that sound was essential to this undertaking: "If the car didn't have the right sound to initiate the whole multisensory experience, all of that attention to detail would fall apart—it wouldn't *feel* right" (33). The problem was that the original sound could not be recreated exactly because the car's body and power train had been redesigned with modern materials and technologies. Additionally, the loud engine sound from the movie, which had been manipulated during the film's production, could not be used in a real-life scenario because it would violate contemporary noise ordinances (34). Thus, the engineering team set out to capture the distinct *feel* of the sound rather than the sound itself.

The attention-grabbing—but not too loud—growling sound of the engine that they came up with was a success. Noise and vibration engineer Shawn Carney elaborates on his highly effective compositional process: "'I'm trying to give people a visceral experience. You're making something new, and it's ok to be a little bit different from that historical reference that everyone has in their memory. Blend them together and you have an experience'" (Beckerman 37). The skeuomorphic sonic experience of the new Bullitt Mustang captured both the nostalgia of the original and gave the car a style that was distinctly unique to Ford. At a price of $31,075 each, nearly sixty-four hundred cars were made and all of them sold (35). As this example demonstrates, sonic style contributes to the sonic rhetorics of cars, or the ways that car sounds are designed to affect, attract, and persuade targeted consumers. Not surprisingly, car manufacturers put an extraordinary amount of effort into developing the "right" sounds for their brand.

> Automotive acoustic engineers pay close attention to how
> individual sounds work together to produce an overall effect.

Automotive acoustic engineers' sonic branding practices require attending to how all of the individual sounds work with or against each other. Similar to the process of designing sounds for target audiences, this kind of sonic production involves repetitive and often nonlinear cycles of composing, listening, talking, and revising until the desired sonic experience is achieved. Producing an integrated, holistic sonic experience is necessary because cars are becoming sonically complex. For example, based on an interview with a Ford employee, Bijsterveld suggests that automotive acoustic engineers' holistic sonic composing practices will continue to gain significance, even as future drivers (seemingly) acquire more sonic control: "In the ideal world of this Ford sound engineer, future Ford customers would be able to upload a series of car sounds (for the turn signals, seat-belt warning, windshield wiper, and so on) of their choice, just like uploading a ringtone for a cell phone. Yet, and this was a crucial twist, this option should be available to the customers only after the Ford sound engineers had created a full 'sound composition' in which all of the sounds would be typically Ford and go together extremely well" (116). Though this example focuses on a future possibility for the sonic design of cars, synthesizing car sounds to create cohesion is already an established practice of automotive acoustic engineers. The individual sounds of cars are arranged and manipulated in order to make them flow in a harmonious way. In a process that is both highly technical and creative, engineers integrate sounds to compose a total sonic experience.

> Automotive acoustic engineers attend to how sound works
> together with other material and sensory elements to shape the
> experience of the car.

To create powerful sonic compositions, automotive acoustic engineers must concentrate on more than just the sounds themselves.[5] As Blesser and Salter observe, "The automobile manufacturer, by controlling the properties of the interior, can treat aural design as a complete system—positioning the seats, orienting the windows, selecting the presentation format, mounting the loud-speakers, designing the acoustics, and adding signal processing" (192). How sound functions in a car is contingent upon material features that may seem to have nothing to do with sound, including how much metal or glass is incorporated into the car's design, and even where the seats are positioned in relation to the speakers. All of these things will affect how drivers experience sound.

To figure out how and to what degree material and sensory elements will influence the experience of sound in a car, automotive acoustic engineers rely on multimodal listening practices. Much like Evelyn Glennie and the acoustic designers I discussed in previous chapters, automotive acoustic engineers attend to the ways that multiple sensory modes—particularly sight, sound, and touch—work together during sonic experiences. These multimodal listening practices inform acoustic engineers' decisions about how to manipulate the various material and sensory features of the car during the sonic composing process.

Objective Evaluation of Interior Car Sound (OBELICS), a research project funded by the European Union in the late 1990s, illustrates the role of multimodal listening in the composing processes of automotive acoustic engineers. The goals of the project "were to understand the subjective evaluation of car sound . . . to establish 'methods and tools for an objective evaluation' of automotive sound, and to define 'target sounds for different driving situations'" (Cleophas and Bijsterveld 109). What I find most fascinating about the OBELICS experiments is their reliance on bodily engagement. OBELICS engineers developed car simulation experiments that emphasized sonic experience as a holistic, multisensory event as opposed to merely asking people to listen to isolated sounds and to talk about what they thought of them. According to Cleophas and Bijsterveld, "This [car simulation] system, as the firm claims in its advertising, 'accurately and interactively simulates different driving situations. In a driving simulator it creates not only engine, tire, wind, and other vehicle or background sounds but also structure-borne sound in the form of vibration. Instead of being passive recipients of car sounds, the test subjects were now expected to interact with the setting. The headphones or speakers would produce new sounds only when the test driver acted, such as by shifting gears or putting on a turn signal" (111). Test subjects' experiences involved engaging with the car's interrelated visual, sonic, and tactile features. Subjects' evaluations of the car sounds were based on immersive and interactive experiences. Automotive acoustic engineers then made revisions to the sonic design of the car based on both their own material interactions with the car and the bodily experiences that the test subjects described. As this example makes clear, the task of automotive acoustic engineers is not only to design sounds, but to design multisensory experiences—a practice that relies on multimodal listening.

> Automotive acoustic engineers must consider how to diminish
> the sensory experience of the car.

In addition to using multimodal listening and sonic composing practices to *enhance* the effects of a car's sensory environment, automotive acoustic engineers employ these practices to *diminish* the sensory experience of the car. As Urry points out, "The car is a room in which the senses are necessarily impoverished" (23). If drivers could feel the full impact of the external environment (e.g., the tires making contact with the road) or internal elements (e.g., the engine, brakes, etc.), driving would be a physically uncomfortable experience. Moreover, it would be a tremendously *noisy* experience. During the second half of the 1930s, around the same time that insulation and soundproofing were becoming popular in the field of acoustic design, car manufacturers started using sound-absorbing materials to control internal and external car noise.

Noise was perceived as a social problem associated with the industrial revolution, and so emerged a need to rethink the sonic design of the car.[6] Bijsterveld explains, "protests against urban traffic noise reached such intensity that making cars more silent became a goal in its own right . . . Several engineers knew that the use of leather and felt could absorb car noise, which is generally low frequency and quite easily carried via all the metal and wood in cars" (195).[7] Since the 1930s the materials used to build cars have been a principal factor in the sound design process. If automotive acoustic engineers determine that there is too much vibration, for instance, they might add more sound-absorbing materials to car seats or floors. Even the gears were redesigned to reduce noise by using "flexible materials like rubber or cotton-reinforced Bakelite" (Bijsterveld et al. 30). The degree to which engineers amplify and/or diminish sound by manipulating materials has a considerable effect on drivers' overall sensory experience.

The sounds that are heard (or not) while driving are also worth paying attention to because they can influence how people perceive the car. This is something that Kara Gordon, a noise and vibration performance engineer for General Motors, deals with on a daily basis. Gordon's job is to make sure that the sounds of the car's electrical or mechanical parts are masked (Maly). This masking is necessary because it contributes to drivers' perception of what a safe, functioning car should sound like. When drivers hear "unpleasant" sounds like rattling or clinking, they worry that something is wrong with the car. In an article featuring Gordon, Tim Maly notes, "It's not enough for the car to run well, it needs to sound like it's running well too. Sound is part of the user experience" (n.p.). Though it varies from model to model, diminishing the "unpleasant" noise of cars until the "right" sound is achieved is a primary concern for automobile manufacturers; masking or silencing sounds is just as important as creating strategic sounds for cars. This type of sonic composition depends on a keen sensory awareness of how sound affects and is affected by other sensory and material features of the car.

> Automotive acoustic engineers consider the sensory
> experiences of pedestrians.

While "quietness" is a quality of cars that is valued by many consumers, sometimes diminishing the sounds of a car too much can result in serious problems. The electric car is a case in point: "The United States National Highway Traffic Safety Administration determined that pedestrians are considerably more likely to be hit by hybrid or electric vehicles than by those with an internal-combustion engine" (Norman n.p.). Because they are nearly silent, especially at slow speeds, pedestrians do not hear electric cars approaching. This is a particularly worrisome issue for blind pedestrians who often rely on car noise to know when it is safe to cross the street. To deal with this problem, hybrid and electric car manufacturers are now creating artificial car sounds that will alert pedestrians of their vehicles' presence.

The challenge of this kind of design is to invent sounds that will be noticed without making them irritating. In other words, Don Norman explains, "Because these sounds will be heard frequently even in light traffic and continually in heavy traffic, they must not be annoying. Note the contrast with sirens, horns, and backup signals, all of which are intended to be aggressive warnings. Such sounds are deliberately unpleasant, but because they are infrequent and relatively short in duration, they are acceptable" (n.p.). Though the creation of pleasant sounds must follow some standardization guidelines, car manufacturers have come to see this design challenge as a branding opportunity. Indeed, they have been experimenting with hybrid and electric car engine sounds that range from sporty growls to tweeting birds (Norman). Considering the sensory experiences of pedestrians turned out to be both a practical concern and an opportunity for innovative design. It is essential for automotive acoustic engineers—like the sound professionals I identified in previous chapters—to attend to the bodily, multisensory experiences of those who interact or come into contact with cars, which includes a diverse range of people with different sensory capacities and needs.

The sonic composing and listening practices I have outlined in this section illustrate the dynamic process of designing sound for cars. These examples have shown that automotive acoustic engineers are concerned with much more than sound alone. They must consider how sound works with other sensory and material features of the car, as well as how sound affects the bodily experiences of drivers and pedestrians. Automotive acoustic engineers' attention to the ways that multiple sensory modes intersect during the sonic design process is a practice that is fundamental to multimodal listening pedagogy. Due to the persistent use of sound in consumer products, it is necessary to teach students to be attuned to how sound works in relation to cars and other sonically designed objects. Before moving on to discuss possibilities for incorporating soundful objects into the composition classroom, however, I want to briefly touch on some of the listening and composing practices that drivers share with automotive acoustic engineers. Exploring how drivers interact with and control sound in their vehicles will further demonstrate why cars are valuable sonic objects to consider in relation to multimodal listening pedagogy.

DRIVERS AS ACOUSTIC ENGINEERS

As I stated in the introduction to this chapter, cars are unique consumer products because they are sonically composed and compose-able. Much like automotive acoustic engineers, drivers can manipulate car sound to produce preferable sensory experiences. This is a practice that Bijsterveld calls "techno-cocooning," or "the use of technology for creating sensory privacy, or individual control over the sensory stimuli that enter a particular space" (192).[8] Many drivers use "techno-cocooning" as a creative mode of sonic composition. For example, drivers often employ sound to produce or intensify feelings. Michael Bull points out that "drivers are increasingly able to co-ordinate the soundscape of the automobile to match their mood or their journey. The automobile becomes a perfect listening booth for drivers, who thus deny the contingency involved in their traversal of these routine spaces and times of daily life" (*Sound Moves* 102). Drivers are able to treat their cars as a private sonic escape much like the personal soundscaping devices—iPods, noise-cancelling headphones, etc.—I described in the last chapter. However, the difference in using the car as a personal soundscaping device is the control drivers have over the environment surrounding them. Cars allow drivers to heighten their experiences through both the manipulation of sound and the manipulation of the material, sensory environment of the car. Actions like regulating the temperature, adjusting the position of the seats, and adding decorative seat covers or air fresheners help to synchronize the visual, tactile, and olfactory features of the car with the overall mood/ambiance drivers are attempting to design through sound.

To get a better sense of the car as a highly controlled space for personal soundscaping, consider the relationship between drivers and iPod (or earbudded smartphone) users. Like iPod users, many drivers create playlists before they leave to set the "right" tone for their trip. These songs may be based on the landscapes drivers pass through, the people they will be driving with, or the purpose of the trip itself. In fact, people have described both iPod and car interactions as filmic experiences in which the soundtrack colors and exaggerates their feelings as they move through banal spaces.[9] The major difference between iPod users on foot and drivers who use music to creative ends is that the acoustic cocoon composed by the driver is doubly reinforced by the material structure of the car (Bull *Sound Moves* 101). Whereas iPod users walking along wintry streets cannot control the environmental elements around them, drivers can turn up the heat in a snowstorm, inhale the scent of a tropical air freshener, and listen to songs that remind them of the beach. The car provides listeners with more control of their holistic embodied experience than iPods. Similar to automotive acoustic engineers, drivers develop a bodily awareness of how sound works in conjunction with other sensory and material elements, and then manipulate those elements to create a desirable car experience.

Some drivers enjoy taking full advantage of the tactile affordances of sound in cars, using vibration to heighten their bodily experiences. In *Sound Moves*, Bull recounts how Nathan, one of the interviewees featured in his book, installed a twenty-two speaker sound system in his car because he enjoys feeling sound. The way that Nathan chooses to make use of the speakers during a drive has a noticeable—and severe—effect on his body. When the speakers are at full capacity, he says, "After a time I have to stop the car and get out. I lean against the car, as I can't stand properly. My legs are limp and it takes a few minutes for me to regain the equilibrium of my body" (102). This extreme example amplifies the physical relationship between sound and the body. As Bull notes, "Nathan's body is affected by the volume of and intensity of the sound to such an extent that he can no longer stand. In North America Nathan's automobile would be referred to as a 'boom car,' the interior louder than that of a typical clubbing interior, 130db. Music that loud can be heard up to 100 metres outside the car with its windows shut!" (102). Nathan prefers having intense, tactile interactions with sound, and thus he designs a sonic environment that allows him to achieve this physical experience. He determines when and how to adjust the sound and other material and sensory features of the car by attending to the various ways that his body is affected by sound. That is, he practices multimodal listening. While Nathan recreates a club-like sonic environment[10] in his car to transform his physical experience, this booming sound also transforms the soundscapes through which he drives; his felt beats leak out into the streets. In this way, his car serves as both a compose-able space and a mobile form of sonic composition.

Nathan is clearly concerned with the sound-driven sensory experience he is creating inside of his car. Yet there are other drivers who prefer to direct the sounds from cars at external audiences—people who use car sound, particularly bass systems, to project specific sonic meanings into the spaces around them. Like Nathan, these drivers rely heavily on the tactile affordances of sound. Cars, Brandon LaBelle describes, can have "a deep bass that is more tactile than sonorous: the automobile is a conducting mechanism that, when fitted with 15-inch sub-woofers in its trunk—itself a resonating chamber—may produce frequencies ranging below 20Hz and decibels well above legal limits" (149). In addition to amplifying the felt engagement with sound for their own pleasure, drivers who participate in what LaBelle calls "bass culture" choose to create a meaningful vibratory presence in the neighborhoods through which they cruise (149). For example, in his examination of bass cultures in southern California, LaBelle maintains that projecting the bass from one's vehicle can serve as a mode of attention grabbing, territorial marking, act of aggression, and/or racialized statement that emanates "cultural energy to cohere group identity" (155). He writes, "The rumble of bass and beat, which are mostly felt and heard as surprising vibrations, as sound pressure and oscillating wave, as throb, function as part of the identity of the car and its driver or the crew . . . To drive is to project oneself. Sound and music dramatically support this projected embodiment, marking the street as a space of transformative amplification" (160). To a much greater degree than other consumer products, the car makes it possible to project sound that people can feel through vibration. The visual aspects of the car—like the bouncing lowriders that have become a staple in rap videos—play a role in shaping the sonic experience of onlookers as well. However, the bass of the car is often heard and felt even before it can be seen, thus creating a powerful presence without visual confirmation. Lowriders, or what are called "thumpers" in the Mexican American context Ralph Cintron examines, are "a brilliant extension of the self's ability to occupy space because the special signifier of the thumper [in this neighborhood] was its domination of a plane beyond the visual, that of sound space" (115). Bass serves as a way to fill or occupy space, to project a physical presence, through sound. It is another great example of sound's agential power. While the person employing the bass has agency, those who come into contact with the sound do not. Experiencing bass is not a choice. It affects the body regardless of whether or not a person desires to listen. In bass culture, sonic rhetorics work at the level of the body to encourage people to feel fearful, powerful, angry, connected to a community, etc. The specific feeling(s) that individuals have depends on the relationship between the driver and the audience that the bass is able to reach, as well as the particular location in which the bass is sounded.

Drivers of cars with bass systems, like automotive acoustic engineers, attend to their own and others' embodied experiences with sound and manipulate the material and sensory features of cars according to the effects (and affects) that they want to achieve. Their multimodal listening practices are directly related to their multimodal composing practices. It is also important to acknowledge that the uses and meanings of bass are connected to experiences of and ideas about race, class, gender, and cultural context. The bass blasting from a car full of young Latino men riding around in a low-income neighborhood could be interpreted quite differently than the bass blasting from a car full of young white girls and boys in a middle-class suburb (which, depending on the audience, may be understood as an act of mocking or imitating the uses of bass in other racial and cultural contexts). Stereotypes, in other words, can certainly influence the ways that people use and make sense of bass in different situations. In addition, buying a vehicle and/or supplemental technologies to enhance sound and other features of the car requires a significant amount of money. The various sonic composing practices that cars make available are not accessible or effective for every driver in every context. What I find relevant about the driving experiences I have described, though, is that they all require some amount of attention to the bodily, multisensory aspects of sonic experience. Both the acoustic engineering and driving practices I have explored in this chapter underscore the key role of material interactions in the design of sonic experiences, and thus serve as excellent heuristics for expanding approaches to sound and listening in the multimodal composition classroom.

SONIC OBJECTS AND PEDAGOGY

The sonic practices associated with cars are especially useful for teaching students about sound and listening because these practices are being employed in many other areas of product design that affect students' lives. The success of sound design in the car industry has set the standard for how other product designers can increase the value and sophistication of their products (Özcan and Egmond). Until recently, designers of consumer products were concerned only with how sound could improve the function of a product, such as the beep an oven makes to indicate that it has reached the appropriate temperature (Robare). In contrast to this strictly functional approach to sound design, designers of everything from snack food bags to floor-cleaning robots are now taking a cue from the car industry by treating sound as integral to their design work.

General Electric (GE), for example, is currently revamping the sounds for its entire line of products. Kyle VanHemert reports, "Instead of voicing all its next-gen dryers and dishwashers with the same beeps and boops, GE's trying to distinguish its four appliance brands by giving them each their own unique sonic palette, culled from a fully realized, brand-specific product" (n.p.). A happy and carefree sonic palette might include heavy woodwind sounds targeted at "refined" upper-class consumers, while a fun and energetic palette may incorporate distorted guitar sounds targeted at "hip" young adults. These sounds are designed to appeal to specific demographics, as well as incite feelings that contribute to an overall experience. Visual and tactile features still figure into GE's design in significant ways, too. However, since the visual features of these new GE products are becoming increasingly minimal and modern, designers are relying more on sound to shape consumer experiences. Head designer David Bingham had this to say about a line of GE products that features a soundtrack with "a driving, woodwind-heavy affair": "It's got this nice, bouncing cadence that feels upbeat . . . It gives this sense of someone looking off in profile, with their hair in the wind" (VanHemert n.p.). Bingham explains that his team is trying to evoke "the happy feeling of driving with the windows down, off into a nice sunny day" (n.p.). This meticulously designed sonic experience is intended to create a positive sensory and emotional connection between the appliance and the consumer. To some extent, consumers of appliances will eventually be able to customize the soundscapes in their kitchens as they do in their cars. This is just one example of how sound has become an important concern for product designers. I provide a bank of additional examples, such as sonically designed SunChips bags and Snapple caps, in the Reverberation for this chapter.

Designing sound for cars is, in some ways, different from designing sound for other consumer products, but the shared goal of creating holistic experiences requires the same basic sonic composing and listening practices I have been stressing in this chapter and others—practices that involve attending to audience, style, rhetorical effects, the integration of sound with other sensory modes and materials, the enhancement and diminishment of sensory experience, and most importantly, embodied, multisensory interaction. Adapting these practices for the multimodal composition classroom can invigorate pedagogical approaches to sound and listening. Sensory experience has become a top priority for product designers, manufacturers, and marketing firms, and it is necessary to help students cultivate practices that will enable them to analyze and create the sensory-rich objects they encounter in everyday life. As I have been arguing throughout the book, multimodal listening pedagogy gives students an opportunity to reflect on and learn from their embodied interactions with the world. This reflection and learning needs to include interactions with objects.

To help students learn about the sonic design of everyday objects, we must develop a broader, materially diverse approach to sonic composition. In the Reverberation associated with this chapter, I share an annotated assignment sequence on sonic objects that attempts to incorporate such an approach into the multimodal composition classroom. I define *sonic object* as any object that employs sound strategically to influence users' overall experience. This project invites students to design their own sonic objects by developing a prototype and creating distinct sounds for their object in a digital audio editor. My decision to use the word "object" instead of "product" is deliberate, as the aim of this assignment is not to turn students into entrepreneurs. Instead, the word *object* leaves the project open to interpretation so that students have the option to produce artistic or experimental objects, not necessarily ones "for sale." By reimagining for the classroom the listening and sonic composing practices that are associated with cars and other everyday products, I have created an assignment sequence that asks students to consider sound as a dynamic mode of composition that is part of a larger sensory and material network.

Teaching students to attend to how sound works as part of a holistic multisensory experience is a crucial step in helping them understand and use sonic rhetorics in different contexts. As I have shown, multimodal listening pedagogy offers listening and composing practices that are relevant to a range of everyday sonic experiences—lived, multisensory experiences that are not accounted for in sound-as-text approaches to multimodal composition. A pedagogical focus on bodily interactions with objects is especially timely considering that the design of sensory-rich products has become pervasive in our "experience society" (Cleophas and Bijsterveld 118). The sonic practices I have outlined in this chapter can thus guide students as they learn to move from composing sonic *texts* to composing sonic *experiences*.

REVERBERATION
SONIC OBJECTS

THIS ASSIGNMENT SEQUENCE OFFERS A material approach to sound and listening pedagogy. I developed this sequence as a way to explore how the sonic composing and multimodal listening practices critical to product design—as illustrated by automotive acoustic engineers—might be reimagined and integrated creatively into the multimodal composition classroom. The sequence consists of two projects (Parts 1 and 2) and an accompanying in-class exercise (Part 3). While the multipart structure of this interchapter differs from previous Reverberations, the general content remains the same: assignment guidelines, commentary, student examples, and resources for teaching.

PART 1: EXPERIENTIAL ANALYSIS OF A SONIC OBJECT

Goal

The aim of this assignment is to learn to treat sound as a mode of composition that is always shaped by and connected to other sensory modes and materials.

Choose a Sonic Object

With your team, choose a sonic object found in an everyday context. We will be examining some examples in class to help you generate ideas. Keep in mind that the object you ultimately choose needs to meet the following guidelines:

- Your entire team must be able to physically interact with the object (i.e., everyone must have access to it).
- Because your team will be giving a presentation on the object, you will need to bring it to class to show us how it works. If your object is too large to bring to class—a car, for instance—then you may bring in a video of your team interacting with it. If the object is elsewhere on campus, you could take us on a brief field trip.

Be strategic. If you choose a toy that only makes one kind of sound, it will be difficult to come up with comments to make about it. Try to choose an object that has multiple sonic functions—one in which sound plays an integral role in the overall experience of the object. Your team will need to come up with at least two possibilities for your sonic object by the start of the next class.

Experimentation and Analysis

With your team, spend some time playing with your chosen sonic object outside of class. Pay particular attention to your sensory experience with the object and take notes about your interaction. After discussing your individual and collective experiences, your team will need to collaboratively write an object analysis that is focused on sound. This document should be 800–1000 words. Use the following questions to guide your writing:

- How do the sounds make you feel (emotionally and physically)?
- Do you associate any particular meanings with the sounds?
- If there are multiple sounds, do they work well together? Why or why not?
- How does the sound contribute to the object as an experience?
- What are the affordances, or the various possibilities and uses, of sound in this object? What are the limitations?

- How does the sound complement (or not) other elements of the object (visual, tactile, olfactory, etc.)?
- Does the sensory experience of the object persuade or teach you to behave or interact with it in a particular way?
- What consumers do you think the designers of this object are trying to target? What makes you think so?
- What else did your team experience, observe, and/or conclude about the object's design?

Presentation

After your team completes the written analysis, you will need to prepare a presentation about your sonic object and your findings. Your team's presentation should include a brief demonstration of how the object works and a discussion of what you wrote about in your collaborative analysis. You may divide and structure this information in any way you see fit. The total presentation, including questions, ought to be at least 10 minutes and no longer than 15 minutes.

COMMENTARY

This initial assignment is part of my ongoing effort to provide students with a broad, relevant conception of multimodal composition that includes the design of everyday objects. Before students perform their analysis of a sonic object, it is useful to frame the project by discussing research on sound and product design. In the resources section at the end of this assignment sequence, I have included an annotated bank of example sonic products and a list of readings that I have found useful in my own teaching.

This assignment is first and foremost dependent upon physical interactions with objects. Typically in academic settings, analysis involves taking an objective stance or studying an object (e.g., text, film, photograph, etc.) from an intellectual distance as opposed to interacting or playing with it; thought tends to be separated from sensory experience. Even analyzing a website or a multimodal text that contains audio and video clips results in a diminished sensory interaction. The computer screen acts as a shield—much like the windshield of a car—that prevents a certain level of physical engagement with the objects being analyzed. In other words, there is still a degree of bodily abstraction involved in the interactive analysis associated with digital environments. Rather than having students think about an object in an abstract way, this assignment begins with students' bodily engagement with the object. During these explicitly embodied interactions, students address questions about the object's function and meaning(s). This assignment teaches students to think through and with their bodies, which is fundamental to developing the multimodal listening and sonic composing practices that can help them take an expansive approach to any sonic experience.

Part 1 of the assignment sequence serves several purposes. First, students are asked to attend to how sound works in relation to other sensory modes and materials. That is, they must treat multimodal composition as the practice of designing a total experience. Developing an understanding of the role of sound in holistic experiences, as I have shown throughout this book, can help students become more savvy consumers and producers of sound in various contexts.

Second, this project heightens students' awareness of the sonic objects they encounter every day. Discussing the different ways that sonic objects can affect people presents an opportunity to talk about sonic rhetorics with students—a concept that can be applied to a wide range of sonic texts, spaces, objects, and experiences, not just things for sale. Regardless of the pedagogical activity instructors choose, experiential learning about how sound works as a persuasive and affective force needs to be a primary feature in teaching students to become attuned listeners and composers. Finally, the most practical purpose of this project is that it encourages students to engage in questions and cultivate practices that are essential to the next assignment in the sequence: Design a Sonic Object.

PART 2: DESIGN A SONIC OBJECT

Goal

The aim of this assignment is to invent and design a sonic object by applying the critical listening practices you began to develop in Part 1.

Brainstorm

Conduct a brainstorming session with your team and choose an idea for your sonic object. This object might be a totally new invention, or your team has the option of enhancing a sonic object that is already in existence. The only requirements for your chosen object are:

1. It must target a specific audience (or audiences).
2. It must use sound strategically to enhance or improve user experience.
3. It must include more than just sound, like visual and tactile elements. Or, if you want to get really creative, you could incorporate olfactory and/or gustatory elements as well.

Once your team has decided on an object, draw some initial sketches and write down ideas about the object's function (How does it work?), purpose (What is the point?), audience (To whom is it meant to appeal?), and overall aesthetic design (How do the visual, tactile, sonic, and other elements work both separately and together?).

Prototype and Sound Design

Your team must create a prototype—or initial version—of the object you choose to design. These prototypes do not have to look professional or be fully functional. For example, your team might create something out of Lego pieces, cardboard, or other materials to make the object roughly the right size, shape, and color. Then explain what the actual materials are supposed to look like, feel like, and do at a later phase. The idea is to bring your concept to life in the best way you can given your team's knowledge and resources.

However, the sounds for the object must be fully designed. Your team will need to use Audacity or another digital audio editor to design the sounds for your object. You have the option of creating your sounds from scratch or manipulating found sounds from sites like SoundCloud, Creative Commons, Freesound, and Jamendo Music. If you use the do-it-yourself approach, Epic Sound (http://www.epicsound.com/ sfx/index.php) offers information about how to make sound effects with everyday objects. Like straying from a recipe, feel free to diverge from the formulas given to you. In other words, this resource is meant to provide inspiration rather than specific instructions. The following two-part student documentary might also be useful as you generate ideas about how to create particular sound effects:

Part 1: http://www.youtube.com/watch?v=0h05HpTte3U

Part 2: http://www.youtube.com/watch?v=yOaDzcgSnA&list=UU-LrQfx
c-Y7HaQp68e1LJ8w&index=6&feature=plcp

Sound Vocabulary [see Part 3]

On the day your prototypes are due, we will be conducting an in-class
exercise about sound and language that is aimed at helping your team with
object revisions.

Peer Feedback and Revision

We will have a formal group feedback session in class. Please do not begin
revision on your object until you have received comments from your peers.

Presentations

Presentations must include: 1) a demonstration and detailed tour of your
object that emphasizes its sonic features, 2) a discussion of your object's
target audience(s), 3) an overview of your team's multimodal composing
process, taking us through the steps your team took to arrive at the final prototype, and your team's design choices, and 4) a description of your team's
collaborative process, including each team member's main contributions to
the project. In addition, your team will need to address the following questions at some point during the presentation: What has your team learned
about sonic composing and listening practices from this project? How has
this project informed your ideas about other compositional tasks, such as
composing with text and images? In what ways has this project changed the
way you think about or approach consumer products in everyday life? Your
team's presentation should be 15-20 minutes, including questions.

COMMENTARY

Part 2 of the sequence is based in part on what Jody Shipka calls a theory
of "multimodal soundness" ("Sound" 355). In her own classroom, Shipka

designs assignments that rely on an "activity-based multimodal theory of composing" that "offers students opportunities to engage in highly reflective, rigorous-productive play" (356). Employing a theory of multimodal soundness
involves asking students to experiment with the rhetorical effects of sound
in various contexts, attend to how sound is integrated with other modes and
materials, and consider how their compositional choices influence the design
as a whole. A theory of multimodal soundness, Shipka explains, provides an
approach "that is both inclusive and robust enough to *allow us to examine the complex interplay that exists between the various modes, materials, methods, and technologies* students
choose to take up (or that they may only imagine themselves taking up) in their
work" (371, my emphasis).

Following Shipka, my assignment gives students a chance to experience and
experiment with sound via "rigorous-productive play" (356). By requiring
students to grapple with "the complex interplay that exists between the various
modes, materials, methods, and technologies," this assignment offers a multimodal composing task that is more explicitly embodied than an assignment
that requires students to use a single mode for composing (e.g., only text, only
images, etc.). This is not to say that assignments that rely on a single compositional mode are somehow monomodal. Rather, my point is that assignments
based on "multimodal soundness" generate a greater number of rhetorical and
compositional challenges and questions. Asking students to create a three-
dimensional model of a sonic object requires them to engage physically with
their compositions to figure out how sound's effects, affects, functions, and
meanings are influenced by particular materials, technologies, and design
choices. This level of hands-on interaction is not possible in solely digital
environments. While my students designed rudimentary objects constructed
from found materials, cardboard, etc., teachers with access to 3-D printers,
Arduino products, and/or makerspaces with other technologies could add
more complexity and technical rigor to this project. Regardless of the specific design approach instructors take, the Design a Sonic Object assignment
can provide students with an expansive approach to multimodal composing by
encouraging them to produce experiences that engage the body and senses in
more holistic ways than exclusively digital forms of composition.

Collaboration is also a key feature of this assignment. It is important that
teams work together to develop strategies and practices, so they can work effectively during the multimodal composing process. Additionally, teams give
students a chance to pool their collective knowledge and resources. Because
this project draws on techniques from composition, marketing, design, art,

and engineering, grouping students with different backgrounds and academic concentrations will facilitate collaboration. It may also be beneficial to allow students to stay on the same teams they formed in Part I, since they will have most likely begun to develop ways of working with and talking about sound that can be transferred to this new assignment.

I realize that having students build sonic objects, which might seem odd or unfamiliar to teachers of composition, could be misconstrued as an "unserious" or "unintellectual" exercise. Indeed, Shipka faced similar problems when she implemented the theory of "multimodal soundness" in her own classroom. She writes,

> Given the mixed reactions that my students' work has received, I am cognizant of the challenges faced by those who support the production of texts that do not appear to look, function, or sound like the linear, print-based texts that are often associated with writing courses. In fact, of either of the sound-based texts featured later in this article, one might ask: 'I grant you that the text makes sound, but is it also sound in the sense of being purposeful, rigorously crafted, or soundly constructed?' (Or less tactfully put: 'Is this really rigorous academic work, or are students just playing around? What, if anything, are they learning about writing or composing? Is the theory supporting this work really sound?'). ("Sound" 356)

I want to call attention to the double meaning of *sound* Shipka mentions here because it is something I took into account when designing this assignment. Indeed, the Design a Sonic Object Project is intellectually sound because, like Shipka, I provide opportunities that encourage students to think deeply about their embodied, material composing practices. This assignment enables students to experience firsthand that listening and composing practices are necessarily connected. Students must go through repetitive cycles of composing (literally putting together), listening, and revising to achieve the desired sonic effects and affects for their objects. The assignment's focus on multimodal listening helps students understand listening as a communicative and creative bodily act that is linked to production. In sum, this *sound* assignment invites students to grapple with challenging questions about the consequences of their choices as listener-composers; and, by putting bodily interactions with objects at the center of multimodal inquiry and practice, it can heighten students' sensitivity to how the senses figure more broadly into sonic experiences and multimodal interactions.

PART 3: SOUND VOCABULARY

Goal

The aim of this in-class exercise is to generate a common sound vocabulary or a productive way of talking about sound that will facilitate your collaborative design process during revisions.

Small Group Discussion

Describing sound—especially sound that does not yet exist—can be a difficult task. With your team, discuss some of the challenges you have encountered with language during the process of composing the first draft of your sonic object. For instance, how did you explain to team members what sonic effects and affects you were trying to create? What words did you assign to particular sounds and sonic practices in the invention, composing, and editing phases, and why? Were those words sufficient and effective? Do you think that the meaning of the words you used to describe sounds will be understood by others outside of your group? What is the value of refining the language you use to talk about sonic composition?

Team Vocabulary

Each team should make a list of the key terms and phrases they used to describe sound in the process of composing. Then, write these key terms and phrases on the board and be ready to share what you have been discussing. When appropriate, you can play some of the sounds your team has been talking about to give the class a clearer sense of the issues your team has encountered.

Common Vocabulary

Based on what all of the teams have to say, we will have a conversation about how our collective key terms and phrases might help you all develop a more productive, practical way of discussing sound and sonic composing as your team moves ahead with object revisions.

COMMENTARY

This exercise was born out of my own experience participating in collaborative sonic productions. On several occasions I have worked as part of a small team to produce sonic compositions like podcasts, soundscapes, and other creative projects, and each time we encountered difficulties coming up with an operational language to describe the ways that we wanted sounds to sound. As I was doing research for this book, I realized that describing sound in precise ways was not just an isolated problem I was having with my collaborators. Recurring problems with the relationship between sound and language have been documented in different contexts throughout history. For example, Stefan Krebs' examination of a 1928 automotive journal that published drivers' letters about technical problems revealed a pattern of difficulty when it came to translating sounds into language. These letter writers tried hard to describe sounds specifically, using adjectives such as "knocking, singing, howling, growling, ticking, hissing, and droning" (85). Some drivers relied on other sounds they were familiar with, such as "the chirps of a cricket" to try to be more precise (85). Despite drivers' efforts to find the right language, their letters resulted in failed communication time after time. As Krebs notes, "Often the editors had difficulty making sense of the written accounts because motorists, despite the attempts to codify car sounds in handbooks and journals, shared no standardized vocabulary to describe their auditory experiences" (85). Clearly, creating a common language is an essential part of learning how to communicate effectively about sonic experience.

Knowing that it would be a struggle for students to talk about sound, I designed this activity because it requires them to reflect on and refine the ways that they have been discussing sound during the production process. The main goal of this exercise in describing and evaluating discursive representations of sound is to help students develop a working vocabulary that can make their sonic composing processes more generative and productive. Another beneficial aspect of this exercise is that it will inevitably expose the subjectivity involved in describing sound (e.g., one person's idea of a "bright" or "warm" sound might be much different from another person's). Though students may not agree about the language used to label a sound, being aware of this subjectivity can have a positive impact on the holistic design of their sonic objects. For instance, if a team disagrees about what a "motivational" sound sounds

like, they can negotiate by manipulating the sound until it is close to what people agree upon, and then ensure that the other parts of the sonic object (visual,
tactile, etc.) also reflect the "motivational" theme that they are trying to convey. In other words, disagreements over the language used to describe sounds
could lead to considerations of how all of the modes and materials might
be better balanced and integrated to reflect design goals. Giving students a
chance to practice describing sound can also enhance their ability to produce
accessible sonic work. Developing precise ways of talking about sound, for
example, has the potential to result in more detailed and creative transcripts
and captions in a range of sonic projects. This would allow those who cannot
hear audible sound to access sound through vivid textual descriptions, which
could help them gain a better understanding of what sounds are being used
and why. To create inclusive multimodal compositions, it is necessary to learn
how to articulate via language the qualities and nuances of sounds.

Rather than bringing a "professional" or "expert" sound design vocabulary into the class, I designed this exercise so that students are required to
invent their own vocabulary. My reasoning here has to do with context. As I
have shown repeatedly, sonic experiences are highly contextual. Therefore,
the language used to describe sonic engagement and production should be
highly contextual as well; it needs to be relevant to the situation at hand and
reflect the knowledge base of the composers. This point is illustrated nicely
in Thomas Porcello's research on the training of sound recording engineers
in a musical setting. In his analysis of conversations between a professional
sound engineer and a student in training, Porcello reports that language was
the cause of much confusion and miscommunication during the production
process. Specifically, the professional sound engineer tended to rely on technical language about the instruments and technologies used to manipulate
sound, while the student attempted to describe sounds by referring to artists
and bands that he admired (724).

Porcello's example is striking to me because, in describing sound, both the
student and the engineer grasped for language from contexts that were most
familiar to them. In this case, the different contexts from which the trained
professional and novice student derived their language made it difficult for
them to understand each other. To my mind, this example amplifies the
importance of encouraging students to develop their own vocabulary based on
familiar sonic experiences. This language might be borrowed from different
genres or styles of music, audio techniques (like remixes and mash-ups) from

pop cultural contexts, or even shared sonic experiences that occurred at some point in the assignment sequence. Regardless of the specific language, sharing a common framework for discussing sound can reduce confusion and foster a more productive working vocabulary.

On a larger scale, this exercise amplifies the significance of language in relation to a variety of sensory-rich composing situations. As Porcello points out, "The problem of representing sensorial phenomena through language is not, of course, unique to sound. Wine tasting, for example, raises the problem of how to make taste accessible to others in language, and attempting to describe perfume does much the same for rendering the sense of smell" (734). My hope is that the sonic vocabulary activity I have shared will be useful to various sonic composing projects, as well as other multimodal projects that focus on a wide range of sensory experiences. While multimodal composition is often discussed in contrast to language-based approaches to composition, language can actually enhance our understanding of other modes, and vice versa.

Student Work

The full assignment sequence offered in this Reverberation was designed for this book, though I have taught parts of this sequence at invited workshops and conferences—one of which I wrote about in a piece for *Composition Studies* (Ahern and Ceraso). In my Sound, Composition, and Culture course, students also completed a project that eventually became Part 2 in the above sequence. Based on my teaching experiences with sonic objects, I then tweaked the rest of the sequence to include more scaffolding and opportunities for experimentation during the composing process. Here I discuss some of the collaborative student work associated with my trial run of Part 2, Design a Sonic Object. To view/listen to the media associated with this student work, visit www.stephceraso.com/reverberations.

SONIC JOURNAL

One of the Design a Sonic Object Project teams decided to add sound to an old school notebook to help motivate writers who prefer to write by hand instead of typing on a computer. According to the team's design plan, the notebook (based on the Moleskine brand) would come with a book light and a companion smartphone app. The book light would be equipped with speakers and a digital scanner, and users could control the settings of this book light with the smartphone app (via Bluetooth). For instance, the app would enable writers to set a timer for their daily writing, choose customized sonic notifications for particular activities, or scan digital photos of notebook pages to keep as a backup of the physical copy. The scanner is also what makes it possible for the app to document writing progress in the form of word or page counts.

In their presentation, this team explained that the physical notebook they imagined offers something that strictly computer-based writing productivity applications cannot—a more intense and pleasurable sensory experience. In other words, writing in a notebook involves unique sensory interactions that do not exist in computer-based writing situations—feeling the weight of the notebook in your hands, seeing and touching the texture of the pages, feeling the movement and pressure of a pen or pencil pressing into paper, smelling the paper, etc. The team believed that enhancing this experience with sound would further increase the pleasure of writing.

When designing their sounds, it was important for this team to think about their (admittedly niche) target audience: people who preferred writing with pens and pencils instead of writing with computers. The team explained that they did not want the sounds to sound computerized despite the fact that they were designing them in a digital audio editor. After some experimentation, they ended up composing "warm," "cozy" sounds by recording one of the team member's playing an acoustic guitar. They then created soundbites out of the most appropriate parts of the guitar recording, manipulating them with digital tools to achieve the precise sonic qualities they desired.

The team argued that the guitar sounds elicited positive, comforting feelings that would make writers want to keep coming back to the notebook; after repeated interactions, writers would connect the feel-good effect (and affect) of the sounds to the act of writing itself. This team also wanted writers to feel as if they were participating in a full-blown experience instead of an isolated task. For example, they created sounds that occur when users open and close the notebook, which were meant to frame the writing experience and give it some structure. While this strategy is similar to the one associated with the start-up and shut-down sounds of computers, the team's sound design was intentionally noncomputer-like. As one student claimed, the sound of an acoustic guitar is perceived as an "organic" sound that is more akin to a paper notebook (made of trees) than a computer. All of the sample sounds the team created for their prototype had the same "natural" quality. Much like automotive acoustic engineers, this student team was able to design a collection of sounds that have distinct purposes but also work holistically; all of the sounds sound like they belong together regardless of their specific functions.

There are things that this team could have done to improve upon their project. For instance, they did not design fully the companion app but instead sketched it out in a general way, and some of the technical features could have been more thoroughly explained and researched. They also could have invented a wider variety of sounds for different functions or notifications. These shortcomings were in part due to time constraints and my own inexperience guiding students through this project for the first time. In general, however, I think that the team demonstrated that they were able to think about and practice sonic composition in nuanced, imaginative ways. As they stated in their presentation, "we learned to think about sound contextually and materially—about how to match sound with our goals."

SONIC CAR SEAT

Another student team decided to design a child's car seat that uses sound to amplify its safety features. According to their design plan, the car seat would be built with sensors that would sonically alert the driver when potentially dangerous changes occurred. For example, the team created sonic indicators that let drivers know when the safety belt is unbuckled, when the safety harness is unfastened, when the car seat is unstable, when the temperature of the car is too hot, and when the car is turned off and the child is still strapped in the car seat. To create these sonic indicators, the team identified and manipulated a number of video game-like sound effects from an archive of sound files at Freesound. The students argued that the car seat's sound design is practical because it serves as a way to monitor a child's safety. That is, drivers can keep their eyes on the road while relying on the sounds to let them know what is going on in the back seat. At the same time, their object serves as a pleasurable sonic experience for the child that is intended to feel like a game or amusement park ride. The team mentioned that many children do not like being restrained by a car seat, and so they attempted to design sounds that might help to make this situation a more fun, engaging experience.

In addition to the sounds, they designed physical parts of the car seat such as the Rainbow Lock, a rainbow-shaped harness that lights up when it is secure. According to the team's presentation, the combination of the positive sound that occurs when the harness is secured, which has the same sound and rhythm as someone exclaiming "ta-da," and the color and light emanating from the rainbow will encourage children to leave the harness alone. The sounds and cardboard prototypes of these features are demonstrated in the video that this team made as part of their presentation, which I have made available on the book's website.

In the discussion after this team's presentation, their classmates had some valid criticisms of the Sonic Car Seat. For instance, one student mentioned that, in the prototype video, the last sound, which indicated that the car was turned off, resembled horror film theme music and that the minor notes and dark tone seemed mismatched compared to the other exuberant game-like sounds that the team had created. Further, while this sonic indicator is useful for a rare and serious situation (e.g., when a driver, who is about to leave the car, forgets that there is a sleeping child in the back seat), this sound would be otherwise repetitive and therefore irritating. Other students believed that the sounds associated with the car seat would annoy the adults in the car, and that the sounds might actually encourage children to put themselves in jeopardy. For example, the child might repeatedly buckle and unbuckle the harness to see the rainbow light up and to hear the warning sound.

Clearly, the team had some significant problems with their object's design. Yet, this is what the prototyping phase of a project is for—experimenting, failing, and learning from that failure to improve the next version. The time constraints in this particular class unfortunately did not allow for further revisions or another attempt at the project. In fact, this experience is what led me to revise the above assignment sequence to include more time for peer feedback and revision. Though this team did not execute the project as well as they might have, they still received critical feedback from peers that challenged their initial design ideas and made them think about how they might tweak and enhance the next version. They also gained practice thinking about sound in relation to different contexts, situations, embodied interactions, modes, and materials. Indeed, both projects I have discussed in this section gave students a chance to cultivate their multimodal listening practices and expand their understanding of multimodal composing as a material, ecological practice. Most importantly, the practices that these students began to develop in the Design a Sonic Object Project can help them make sense of a range of sonically enhanced objects in their everyday lives.

Evaluation

While this project involves thinking about the technical and material features of designed objects, the quality of students' prototypes is not my main concern when evaluating this work. In other words, I am not grading students' artistic ability or technical understanding/proficiency. Rather, I am judging how well they are able to articulate and justify their sound design choices. To grade this work, I examine teams' design materials (sketches, notes, prototypes, media, etc.) and evaluate their formal presentation. Because collaboration was a major part of the project, all team members receive the same grade. As in past Reverberations, here I include a list of criteria that I used to grade the trial run of the Design a Sonic Object Project. I responded to each of these statements with "definitely yes" (A), "mostly yes" (B), "somewhat" (C), or "no" (F), and assigned a grade based on the accumulative responses. I also explained my responses, which took into account the unique features of each team's project, in written comments. These guidelines are intended to provide a general sense of how one might begin engaging critically with experimental student work such as this.

Design a Sonic Object Project Criteria

1. Design Strategy

During the presentation, the team is able to explain in detail their sound design choices and process, articulating:

- how and why sound is used to enhance or complement other physical properties of the object
- how and why sound appeals to the identified target audience
- how design choices account for users' embodied interactions with the object, as well as how these choices might encourage particular embodied interactions
- how and why sounds were composed or manipulated in specific ways to reflect the purposes or goals of the object

2. Quality of Design

- the designed sounds contribute to the articulated purposes or goals of the object
- overall design (physical features and sound) is well planned, sensorially engaging, functional, and imaginative
- team's process materials demonstrate evidence of experimentation and consideration of the various possibilities and limitations of their object's design, for example, providing sketches for different versions or features of the sonic object

3. Overall Presentation Performance
- team addresses thoroughly the questions included in the assignment guidelines; meets all project requirements
- all team members contribute to the presentation in significant ways; each explains their role in the design process
- presentation is organized, creative, and persuasive
- team members respond thoughtfully to questions from peers during discussion

Selected Resources

ANNOTATED EXAMPLES OF SONIC PRODUCTS

Snapple Cap

Product designers are especially attuned to the fact that sound increases the quality of consumers' experiences. In *Priceless: Turning Ordinary Products into Extraordinary Experiences*, Diana LaSalle and Terry A. Britton explain, "This ability to give voice to the value of your product is probably the most important role of sound" (93). Consider, for example, the "pop" that occurs when you twist the cap off of a Snapple bottle. As blogger Angela Schumacher notes, "The sound communicates that the product is fresh so effectively that Snapple no longer needs to put the plastic seal around their bottle caps. This sound goes hand in hand with their advertising which talks about Snapple being made from the best stuff on Earth" (n.p.). Savvy sound designers understand that the experience of a product's sound can reinforce ideas about the quality of the product itself. In the case of Snapple, the "pop" that conjures up feelings of freshness persuades consumers to think that the juice is as pure as the advertisements promise. It also assures the consumer that the bottle has not been previously tampered with. The "pop" of the Snapple cap saves money by eliminating packaging fees, and not using extra plastic allows the brand to promote the fact that it is environmentally friendly. It is a highly strategic sound that is intended to voice the message that drinking Snapple—a quality product—will result in a quality experience.

Bosch Dishwasher

Product designers often consider how the sounds of their product will enhance or disturb the larger sonic environments in which they are used. The inspiration behind Bosch's extremely quiet dishwasher—advertised as the "quietest dishwasher in North America"—was to give consumers a more pleasant and practical soundscape in the kitchen and other nearby rooms (Kähler n.p.). As Magnus Kähler states, "In small to midsized kitchens, the noise level can be so overbearing that it's uncomfortable to be in the kitchen when the dishwasher is on. And in many modern homes with open/integrated kitchen-living room layouts, a noisy dishwasher can disturb conversations, watching TV and other activities" (n.p.). Taking into consideration both the sensory experiences of consumers and the open concept trends of contemporary homes, Bosch created a dishwasher so quiet that it is almost unnoticeable. This design enables a more peaceful and functional environment.

Compostable SunChips Bag

Frito-Lay is responsible for one of the most famous and egregious examples of failed sound design. In an attempt to make its SunChips brand more environmentally friendly, Frito-Lay introduced a compostable bag in 2010. Consumers found it noisy and complained. The bag's sound registered one hundred decibels, which is louder than a lawn mower, a motorcycle, and even a subway. The bag had so many haters, in fact, that a Facebook group called "Sorry But I Can't Hear You Over This SunChips Bag" attracted more than 44,000 fans (Beckerman 76). Sales fell, and the financial loss caused Frito-Lay to go back to the environmentally unfriendly bags. A Frito-Lay spokesman acknowledged, "'The packaging of the product is a multisensory experience for our consumers'" (Byron n.p.). Like many chip companies, Frito-Lay is conscious of how the shape, texture, and crunch of their chips contributes to consumers' pleasurable experience with the product. However, overlooking the sound and feel of the bag turned out to be a disastrous mistake that resulted in a decrease in sales. As this example makes clear, the strategic use of sound, which sometimes involves diminishing or eliminating sound, is critical in product design.

Ice Cream Truck

One of the oldest and perhaps most familiar examples of using the emotional nature of sound to sell products is the ice cream truck. According to Daniel Neely, an ethnomusicologist who studies ice cream truck music, even the earliest trucks were meant to trigger specific feelings. As he writes of Henry Burt, who delivered Good Humor bars in the 1920s: "Burt's choice of small bobsled bells for his ice cream trucks was significant because it both recalled the familiar timbre of soda fountain automata and signed a wintry sound that conveyed ice cream's relieving coldness in hot weather" (Beckerman 27). The jingly-jangly sounds associated with early versions of the ice cream truck were supposed to remind consumers of their pleasant memories of hanging out in drugstore soda shops—an activity associated with the youth of that period—and to evoke the cold, refreshing sensation of ice cream on a hot summer's day. Because the sounds could be heard long before the truck could be seen, it also built up a feeling of anticipation and excitement in consumers. Ice cream truck sounds have always been aimed at creating positive feelings that will keep customers coming back for more. The sonic formula used by 1920s ice cream trucks was so successful that it has not changed much even today.

SOUND AND PRODUCT DESIGN

Beckerman, Joel, with Tyler Gray. *The Sonic Boom: How Sound Transforms the Way We Think, Feel, and Buy*. Boston: Houghton Mifflin Harcourt, 2014.

Cleophas, Eefje and Karin Bijsterveld. "Selling Sound: Testing, Designing, and Marketing Sound in the European Car Industry." *Oxford Handbook of Sound Studies*. Eds. Trevor Pinch and Karin Bijsterveld. Oxford: Oxford University Press, 2012: 102–124.

Felton, Emma, Oksana Zelenko, and Suzi Vaughan, eds. *Design and Ethics: Reflections on Practice*. New York: Routledge, 2012.

Siteur, Wouter. "Sonic Branding (3): Examples of Sonic Branding." In *Perfect Pitch* Blog. n.d. Web. 20 July 2016. https://www.inperfectpitch.com/sonic-branding/examples-of-sonic-branding/.

Symanczyk, Anna. "The Sound of Stuff—Archetypical Sound in Product Sound Design." *Journal of Sonic Studies*. 10 (2015): n. pag. Web. 7 Dec. 2016. https://www.researchcatalogue.net/view/221835/221836.

CONCLUSION
MULTIMODAL LISTENING PEDAGOGY
AND THE FUTURE OF SONIC EDUCATION

Listening is an important human activity just because it creates an intimate connection to the dynamic activities of life.

BARRY BLESSER AND LINDA-RUTH SALTER

Pedagogy takes place at the turbulent point of matter crossing into mind, experience into knowledge, stability into potential, knowledge as promise and provocation into bodies in action, doing and making.

ELIZABETH ELLSWORTH

SOUNDING COMPOSITION **HAS EXAMINED THE** listening and composing practices of diverse sound professionals—a deaf percussionist, acoustic
designers, automotive acoustic engineers—and explored everyday sonic spaces
and experiences outside of what is typically thought to be the domain of multimodal composition. Instead of focusing on what the field already knows and
values about sound and listening, I have sought out unfamiliar examples to
enlarge the scope of sonic possibilities in multimodal composition courses.
In providing expansive listening and composing practices that have relevance

in a range of settings, my exploration of multimodal listening pedagogy marks the beginning of what I hope will be a long, nuanced conversation about what a twenty-first century sonic education can and should offer students.

While each of the previous chapters has a distinct focus, consonant ideas about listening and composing practices resonate throughout this book. Together these sonic practices constitute the foundation of multimodal listening pedagogy:

- treating listening as a full-bodied act, as opposed to an ear-centric act
- reflecting on one's own listening habits and embodied relationship to sonic experiences
- considering how a diverse range of bodies with various capacities and needs will experience sound in particular contexts
- designing sonic work with which audiences can interact via multiple modes and pathways
- exploring all of sound's available effects, affects, and meanings in different settings via inquiry and experimentation
- acknowledging listening as part of an ecological interaction between bodies, sounds, and the physical environment
- attending to how sound is connected to the aesthetic, material, technological, and spatial features of listening situations
- developing an awareness of how sound shapes interactions with objects
- producing holistic sonic experiences instead of or alongside sonic "texts"

These foundational practices move beyond ear-centric, sound-as-text methods of sonic engagement and production, which is why I contend that multimodal listening pedagogy can transform approaches to sound and listening in multimodal composition. This claim is not meant to be idealistic or abstract. "Compositionists have been calling for a multimodal transformation of our field for at least forty years," Jason Palmeri reminds us, "and yet, despite these calls, the study and teaching of composition has remained (in many ways) too narrowly focused on alphabetic ways of knowing" (160–61). While I do not expect multimodal listening pedagogy alone to accomplish a "multimodal transformation" in rhetoric and composition, the concrete practices and assignments I have proposed in this book clearly exceed alphabetic ways of knowing. Multimodal listening pedagogy puts bodily experience at the center of learning. Consequently, it can expand how teachers and students actually "do" sound, listening, and multimodality by reawakening and reeducating our senses.

Thus far I have offered many suggestions about how multimodal listening can augment multimodal composition pedagogy. In this conclusion, I turn to a discussion about multimodal listening pedagogy's broader exigence—about what multimodal listening pedagogy can contribute to a twenty-first century sonic education. As I will show, the bodily practices and habits that students develop via multimodal listening are relevant to a range of personal, professional, cultural, and civic activities. Specifically, I consider the value of multimodal listening pedagogy in terms of cultivating listening agility, expanding listeners' capacities as makers or producers of multimodal work, preparing students for relevant careers and everyday encounters with sound-based media and experiences, and providing opportunities to reflect upon one's own and others' identities, experiences, and needs. This chapter aims to attune students and teachers to the myriad ways that sound and listening are connected "to the dynamic activities" of individual and collective life, and to inspire them to make better use of their bodies as vehicles for inquiry and learning within and outside of the classroom (Blesser and Salter 15).

MULTIMODAL LISTENING AND AGILITY

In a recent study of birdsong in San Francisco researchers reported that over a forty-year span white crowned sparrows have raised the pitch of their songs so they can be heard (and hear each other) above the loud urban soundscape (Biello). Similar studies have revealed that birds in cities sing more frequently at night to avoid competing with traffic noise; they even lower the frequency of their song to prevent it from getting distorted by brick and concrete surfaces (Connor "Rustications" 20). Like birds, humans must find effective ways to thrive in soundscapes that are always in flux. As sonic experiences evolve, it is necessary to discover new ways to become more adaptable listeners and sonic composers. Listening must be treated as a practice that, like reading and writing and speaking, transforms over time in response to personal, social, cultural, and technological changes. One of the reasons that multimodal listening pedagogy is critical, then, is because it enables students to cultivate flexible listening practices that help them respond to ever-fluctuating sonic situations. In this sense, the repeated practice of multimodal listening can lead to what might be thought of as listening *agility*.

Multimodal listening pedagogy encourages agility in listeners by emphasizing the radically relational nature of sonic experiences. Listeners are always
embedded in and entangled with the material world. To practice multimodal listening does not mean simply unplugging one's earbuds and paying
attention to the sonic environment as though objectively removed from it.
Rather, it requires a deep awareness of oneself as part of, and as permanently
intertwined with, sonic environments that are in a perpetual state of change.
Multimodal listening pedagogy is hinged on an ecological understanding of
listening as participating in and reacting to everyday soundscapes, and, therefore, it offers practices that help listeners move reflectively among different
sonic contexts: from digital to nondigital environments, from composition
class to other courses, from school to daily life, and vice versa.

To teach students to be attuned listeners in an unstable sonic world, teachers of multimodal composition cannot rely on computer-based sonic experiences alone. Listening and sonic composing activities must include but exceed
digital environments. It is through engaging with sound in a variety of settings
that students are able to learn to become agile listeners. In *Experience and Education*, John Dewey explains, "As an individual passes through one situation
to another, his world, his environment, expands or contracts. He does not
find himself living in another world but in a different part or aspect of one
and the same world. What he has learned in the way of knowledge and skill in
one situation becomes an instrument of understanding and dealing effectively
with the situations that follow" (44). Developing an acute awareness of the
relational, ecological aspects of sound through an exposure to different sonic
interactions enables students to transfer and use that knowledge in subsequent
listening experiences. Multimodal listening pedagogy encourages such agility
by acknowledging the changeability of both sonic environments and listening bodies. It is a pedagogy that accounts for what Elizabeth Ellsworth calls
"a learning self that is in motion" (7). That is, multimodal listening is an
emergent, nimble practice of body and mind—a fluid act of responding to
unpredictable sonic events. Rather than asking students to distance themselves
from sound to make meaning of it, multimodal listening pedagogy provides
students with a flexible set of critical competencies and habits that allow them
to be alert, savvy participants in the sonic world.

Cultivating the agility associated with multimodal listening is important for
twenty-first century learning. Students are exposed to fast-paced, constantly
changing digital media environments and devices in school and everyday life,
so developing flexible competencies and habits is crucial in contemporary

learning experiences. In their book on twenty-first century learning, Douglas Thomas and John Seely Brown state, "We can no longer count on being taught or trained to handle each new change in our tools, the media, or the ways we communicate on a case-by-case basis" (43). In other words, simply giving students instructions about how to perform a digital task is not enough. Instead students today must develop malleable practices, like reflective play and experimentation, that they can use in their efforts to make sense of a variety of different technologies and situations. Through repeated attempts, many of which involve struggle or failure, students learn to build upon their previous experiences and apply that embodied knowledge to subsequent encounters with unfamiliar technologies or digital tasks. While it is true that all learning requires some level of agility, multimodal listening pedagogy's emphasis on experience-based, responsive learning is especially useful for preparing students to thrive in digital contexts.

MULTIMODAL LISTENING AND MAKING

When listening is treated as a receptive practice, as merely receiving audible information through the ears, the rest of the body is ignored. And when the rest of the body is ignored so is the potential for action—for making and doing. This is why multimodal listening pedagogy promotes a body-centric approach to composition in which listeners use bodily experiences to inform their sonic making practices. Indeed, multimodal listening pedagogy provides a robust approach to listening in relation to multimodal production. It is a pedagogy that requires students to *listen as makers*, that challenges them to heighten their awareness of not only what sound means but of how it works to shape experiences.

Unlike "ears only" approaches to listening, multimodal listening pedagogy asks students to think about their own unique bodily experiences and about the unique bodies that might be listening to and interacting with their work. Put differently, multimodal listening pedagogy encourages listener-composers to account for an audience with diverse bodily capacities and needs, which can result in designs that benefit a broad population of people, not just individuals with disabilities (Pullin). Curb cuts or sidewalk ramps that were built to accommodate individuals with wheelchairs are frequently used to illustrate this point. Alongside increasing access for people using wheelchairs, curb cuts have made life easier for bicyclists and skateboarders, and for people pushing strollers or towing suitcases on wheels. This concept also translates to designing sonic projects in digital spaces. For example, providing a transcript that includes detailed descriptions of nondiscursive sound would allow deaf and hard of hearing people to access an otherwise audio-only project. At the same time, that transcript would enable seeing users to scan the text quickly to locate a quote or a description of a specific sound faster than relistening to the audio. Asking students to produce sonic work that can be accessed via multiple modes and senses can also lead to creative and enlivening sonic projects. Multimodal listening pedagogy's emphasis on designing projects for a range of bodily experiences gives rise to more inclusive, inventive, and multisensory listening and composing practices that are relevant to classroom settings and beyond.

Multimodal listening pedagogy can deepen students' understanding of the composing process as well. The bodily experience of making things—of literally combining materials to create something—involves thinking about creative decisions and their intended effects, affects, and meanings. By "going through the thoughtful, physical process of making something," David Gauntlett writes, "an individual is given the opportunity to reflect, and to make their thoughts, feelings or experiences manifest and tangible" (4). As I have shown repeatedly, the embodied experiences of thinking and making are inextricably entwined. Multimodal listening pedagogy makes composers' "mind-body" complex explicit, thus allowing students to see their thinking as part of an ecology instead of something that is detached from their bodily actions (Hawhee 10).

It is especially necessary to expand students' abilities as listener-makers at this moment in time, considering the wide accessibility and rapid development of digital audio technologies—from open source audio editing platforms to DJ apps that allow users to mix and remix audio tracks on their smartphones. Peter Szendy has written at length about how "[digital] equipment opens the possibility, for every listener, of making his own listenings [to others' sounds] recognized: of reproducing them, spreading them, that is to say publishing them, in order to hear them, exchange them, comment on them—in short, to construct a culture of critical listening" (94–95). I agree that the availability of digital technologies has resulted in exciting new possibilities for listening and sonic production. Yet, availability is not enough. Szendy implies that a "culture of critical listening" will emerge from the mere presence of digital audio technologies. To my mind, this suggestion is akin to overblown rhetoric about "digital natives," or narratives that perpetuate the idea that young people who grew up with computers "inherently have the knowledge or skills to make the most of their online experiences" (Boyd 176). Any teacher who uses digital technologies in the classroom can attest to the fact that the concept of "digital natives" oversimplifies the realities of students' lived experiences with digital tools and platforms, which vary widely in terms of knowledge and facility. Similarly, the presence of digital audio technologies will not automatically make students critical listeners or authors. Students need to be presented with occasions to experiment with sound and to reflect on their listening and composing practices in relation to different technologies, settings, and situations. The guided experiential education that multimodal listening pedagogy offers can help students become smart, capable listeners and authors of sonic work—listener-makers who understand how to take advantage of the technical, affective, and semiotic affordances of sound.

MULTIMODAL LISTENING AND RELEVANCE

The listening agility and reflective production practices that multimodal listening pedagogy encourages can impact students' lives long after they leave college. Sound is becoming an increasingly significant medium in a number of professional fields—journalism, art, design, marketing, performing arts, business, computer science, architecture, and publishing, among others. In their future jobs, for example, students may be tasked with integrating sound into websites, apps, videos, audiobooks, video games, presentations, performances, or events. Or they may be tasked with analyzing and creating sonic brands, soundtracks, voice-overs, or soundscapes. Having the ability—and flexibility—to use sound strategically for different situations and purposes is a valuable and valued twenty-first century skill. I do not mean to suggest that the sole purpose of multimodal listening pedagogy is to train students for the workforce. Rather, the adaptable sonic practices that students learn via multimodal listening pedagogy are relevant to a range of contemporary jobs in addition to many other parts of their lives.

Multimodal listening pedagogy can also prepare students to participate in and contribute to sonic culture through activities such as podcasting. In the past several years, there has been a drastic boost in podcast consumption and production. In 2014, the first season of Serial—a week-by-week investigation of a 1999 Baltimore murder case—broke an iTunes record for being the fastest podcast ever to be downloaded and streamed by 5 million listeners (Dredge). The following year, then president Barack Obama agreed to hang out in a California garage to be a guest on Marc Maron's podcast, *WTF*. Obama told Maron during his interview that he was interested in being on the show because he would be able to reach a large, diverse audience. He was right. Podcast listenership has almost doubled since 2008 and continues to surge (Vogt).[1]

While in some ways the boom in podcast consumption perpetuates an "ears-only," "sound-as-text" approach to listening, podcasts are more complex than they seem. In addition to narrative content, podcasts include features like ambient sounds to emplace listeners, music for transitions and to emphasize particular themes or to elicit moods, and a mix of audible language and nondiscursive sound to take listeners on a journey. In other words, good podcasts create *experiences* for listeners.[2] In *Out on the Wire*, a graphic novel that offers a behind-the-scenes look at some of the most successful podcast production teams, author Jessica Abel underscores the experiential qualities of podcasts (8). In a series of panels depicting a workshop with the staff of the popular podcast *Radiolab*, Abel quotes co-host Jad Abumrad talking about podcast production as a kind of "movie making": "We talk about close-ups, distance. And one of the things that we talk about a lot is point of view. When you're working with the characters, you don't want to stand across the street from them and hold your nose. You get really smelly up close and smell the heat of their breath. You want to be inside their head" (83). Memorable podcasts are able to engage listeners' imaginations, senses, and emotions, which is why they can open up possibilities for audio storytelling that go beyond language alone. By treating podcasts as *more than* audio texts or essays, multimodal listening pedagogy can be used to prime students to become discerning listeners of podcasts and other sonic media that they encounter in their daily lives, as well as provide them with the kind of listening and composing practices that are needed to create experiential sonic media.[3]

Additionally, multimodal listening pedagogy can help students become knowledgeable consumers and producers of digital experiences more broadly. Digital storytelling is an essential twenty-first century practice: "Storytelling is at the cusp of a revolution. New media is relentlessly heading toward a future that is completely immersive, interactive and—most exciting of all—designed to please all five senses" (Chibana n.p.). Sensorially engaging storytelling methods are already being employed by many mainstream media outlets whose readers now access most of their news on digital devices, and sound design is a key ingredient in shaping and enhancing people's experiences with these digital texts. For example, *The New York Times* has been experimenting with the use of sound in interactive features such as "Dear Architects: Sound Matters," an article that uses text, video, and three-dimensional audio to give listeners a realistic sense of the acoustic experience of designed buildings and spaces such as a library, an office, a subway, a church, and a bar (Kimmelman).[4] Readers are encouraged to put on headphones, which emulate the experience of directional sound, to feel what it is like to inhabit these sonic spaces. Likewise, a compelling *Washington Post* story called "After the Storm" uses sound to draw listeners into an immersive atmosphere (Grace). This piece features the narrative of a filmmaker who lived through a deadly tornado in Tuscaloosa, Alabama in 2011. Its poignant mix of audio narration, ambient soundscapes, music, videos, text, and animation make it feel as if users are traveling through environments and situations along with the narrator. These are just a few examples of the engrossing, interactive storytelling that is becoming more common in everyday "texts."[5] Multimodal listening pedagogy's emphasis on how sound relates to other material, sensory, technological, and aesthetic features of an environment can prepare students to engage thoughtfully with the multimedia experiences they encounter, and to produce their own multisensory, soundful digital stories.

MULTIMODAL LISTENING AND REFLECTION

On a more personal level, multimodal listening pedagogy provides students with opportunities to reflect upon their own listening habits and embodied relationships with sound. The bodily knowledge students gain from multimodal listening practices can help them make strategic choices about how to use sound in everyday situations. For instance, multimodal listening could help students make decisions about when to use sound—or silence—to change or regulate their moods and behaviors. It could make them more aware of when to plug in earbuds or when it might be wise to attend to the sonic environments they are moving through. Students could employ multimodal listening to design their own sonic environments by constructing appropriate playlists or soundscapes for various occasions—from dinner parties to working out to doing homework. It is true that students can still do these things without any formal listening education. I would argue, however, that multimodal listening pedagogy gives students a more dynamic, nuanced understanding of their own interactions with sound, which has the potential to enhance many facets of their lives.

By cultivating a heightened sensitivity to their own embodied experiences with sound, students become attuned to others' embodied experiences as well. In some ways, then, multimodal listening builds on Krista Ratcliffe's notion of "rhetorical listening," which is defined as "a stance of openness that a person may choose to assume in relation to any person, text, or culture" (1). Rhetorical listening requires attending to "intersecting gender and race identifications" to "promote cross-cultural communication" (34–35). Multimodal listening pedagogy expands Ratcliffe's concept of rhetorical listening by taking a more explicitly sensory approach to the body that includes but exceeds identity categories (race, gender, etc.). For example, while Ratcliffe focuses primarily on listening in relation to spoken or written language and often uses listening in a metaphorical sense, multimodal listening involves considerations of nondiscursive sound in relation to embodied experience. Multimodal listening invites listeners to take "a stance of openness" by imagining how bodies different from their own might interpret or experience particular sonic situations—how a young woman walking home alone from a bar at night might experience the sound of footsteps behind her; how a black man driving on the highway might experience the sound of police sirens; how immigrant families might experience the cheers and roars of a crowd in response to a politician's speech about building walls and travel bans; how individuals' responses to any of these examples would vary depending upon the specific space or place in which a sound occurs, or the person's intersectional embodied identity (i.e., their interconnected experience of race, class, gender, sexuality, ethnicity, disability, etc.), or the person's past experiences with similar sounds (1). Like rhetorical listening, multimodal listening's emphasis on highly contextual embodied sonic experiences provides a reflective approach to listening to and for difference, which has the potential to lead to a sonic education that promotes empathy and understanding.

The reflective listening practices that multimodal listening requires can also facilitate students' participation in "a sonically informed community engagement praxis" (Zwhalen). Sound-based community projects—from collaborative soundscaping initiatives to public sound art installations—are becoming popular among teachers and researchers associated with the field of sound studies, and reflective listening practices are critical to this work.[6] In her discussion of sound and civic engagement, Jennifer Stoever argues that "any act of intervention must necessarily begin with self-reflexivity and examination of how one listens" ("Toward" n.p.). Participating in community work in meaningful ways entails thinking about how and why we listen to communities: Whose embodied experiences do we choose to acknowledge or not in the places we live, and what might this reveal about our own biases? What might our embodied listening experiences help us understand about a community or about our own relationship with that community? What can our experience with the soundscape of a neighborhood or town or city tell us about its needs? Or, as Christie Zwhalen asks: "What does 'need' sound like?" ("Listening" n.p.).

With its attention to embodied, contextual, and ecological listening practices, multimodal listening pedagogy can prepare students and teachers to participate sensitively in community life. Considering the long history of service learning and civic engagement in the field of rhetoric and composition—a history that is well documented in disciplinary publications like *Reflections: A Journal of Public Rhetoric, Civic Writing, and Service Learning*—I believe that teachers of writing and rhetoric have much to offer in terms of forwarding a "sonically informed community engagement praxis" (Zwhalen). Multimodal listening pedagogy can contribute to this important work by providing civically minded teachers and students with a strong foundation for developing community-based sonic activities and projects—many of which I hope will stem from the concrete examples presented in this book.

TOWARD A MULTISENSORY SONIC FUTURE

While listening has always involved multiple senses, now more than ever we need to pay attention to sound as a fundamental part of our "experience society" (Cleophas and Bijsterveld 118). We need listening practices that will reinvigorate our etiolated sensory relationship to sound in digital contexts. We need listening practices that will deepen our understanding of how designed sound is employed strategically to influence our moods and behaviors, and the ways that we interact with and navigate different spaces. We need listening practices that will help us analyze and produce the sonic experiences that are being marketed and sold to us for consumption. And we need listening practices that will facilitate a more engaged and thoughtful participation in the affectively rich sonic world around us. Multimodal listening is a practice that responds to these needs.

Implementing the pedagogy I have proposed in this book will require teachers to embrace unfamiliar compositional modes and materials in their classrooms. Multimodal listening pedagogy demands a willingness to experiment with new ways for students to interact with sound and other media. It entails taking up more expansive notions of classroom spaces and composing contexts and being open to surprise and unpredictability. I am confident that the risk-taking involved in this pedagogy will lead to a contemporary sonic education that is relevant to students' academic, professional, and personal lives. By building on their past experiences with sound, multimodal listening pedagogy gives students a chance to cultivate flexible, responsive sonic practices that they can continue to use in pursuit of "experiences of a deeper and more expansive quality" (Dewey *Experience* 47).

The body-centric exploration of sound in this book amplifies the complexity and interconnectedness of sensory experience. Unlike multimodal approaches that isolate different modes, multimodal listening practices force listeners to confront the fact that there is always more than one way to engage with a text, person, space, or object. This emphasis on sensory relationships is key to moving beyond strictly semiotic ways of knowing. Multimodal listening pedagogy acknowledges students as sentient beings who move through and physically interact with many environments outside of classrooms, from digital spaces to city sidewalks to mountain trails. Multimodal listening allows students to figuratively and literally make sense of their own and others' lived experiences. My hope is that multimodal listening pedagogy will embolden teachers to encourage sonic play, experimentation, and invention in their classrooms; to think about which communicational and creative practices are most pertinent for students in the twenty-first century; and to continue to reimagine how to take a capacious, multisensory approach to multimodal composition and experience.

NOTES

INTRODUCTION

1. I discuss disciplinary scholarship on sound and listening at length in Chapter 1.
2. My use of the term *affordances* in this book is aligned with James Gibson's definition. Gibson argues that "affordances are relational, ecological, and tendential (not determinative)" (Prior 26).
3. Some sound-based apps do encourage listeners to attend to the environments through which they are moving. For instance, Bluebrain's The National Mall is a free "location-aware" sound app that provides a site-specific listening experience. The app was created by geo-tagging segments of music that were composed for specific zones within The National Mall in Washington, D.C. As smartphone-equipped users traverse the monument-filled park, the music changes according to their location and the direction of their movement. Using this app can transform and enliven one's experience of the park. At the same time, it still encourages listeners to ignore the sounds occurring in the park itself (Richards).
4. In making a distinction between "ear-ing" and multimodal listening, I do not mean to suggest that "ear-ing" is somehow unimportant. Listening to and analyzing audible content can be extremely useful. Rather, I am simply pointing out the differences between these two modes of listening.

5. Jody Shipka has argued repeatedly that equating *multimodal* with the digital gives our students a falsely narrow sense of the complexity of multimodal experience, and her work models fresh possibilities for pedagogies that involve a range of material practices and objects as opposed to just digital ones (*Toward*). In a similar vein, Jason Palmeri identifies an archive of techniques and practices that predate the rise of personal computers and the Internet to draw attention to alternatives to teaching multimodal composition in digital-only contexts (*Remixing*). Jonathan Alexander and Jacqueline Rhodes also challenge the field to take fuller advantage of the rich rhetorical affordances and histories of multimodal practices, as opposed to merely using multimodal projects "to do the work of 'writing'" (*On Multimodality* 17).

6. My project also extends the pedagogical work outlined in *Writing New Media* (Wysocki), which addresses various aspects of materiality and embodiment in the writing classroom.

7. This is not to say that the body and senses are never referred to in scholarship on multimodality. In *Multimodal Discourse*, Gunther Kress and Theo Van Leeuwen do raise questions about the role of the senses in multimodal interactions (28). Elsewhere Kress has used synesthesia as a trope in his descriptions of multimodal interactions ("Design"). However, this line of inquiry has not been developed fully in Kress's and Van Leeuwen's individual or collective work. Joddy Murray's *Non-discursive Rhetoric* also calls attention to the body by addressing "the sensual ways that information reception can be rhetorical" (8). In general, however, discussions of how bodily, sensory experience figures into multimodal engagement and production—particularly in relation to sound—remain largely absent in multimodal composition scholarship.

CHAPTER 1: SOUNDING OUT RHETORIC AND COMPOSITION AND SOUND STUDIES

1. Multiple sound studies anthologies—*The Auditory Culture Reader* (Bull and Back), *The Sound Studies Reader* (Sterne), and *The Oxford Handbook of Sound Studies* (Pinch and Bijsterveld), to name a few—illustrate the extensive range of methods, approaches, and topics that fall under the category of sound studies.

2. As composition studies became more professionalized in the mid-1950s and early 1960s by securing a disciplinary position that was focused around the First-Year Writing course, communication—the fourth "C"—was gradually pushed out of leading journals and scholarship (George and Trimbur). For this reason I do not engage much with communication scholarship on sound and listening in this chapter or elsewhere in the book. However, I do include several

older communication citations—from a time when communication was more integrated with rhetoric and composition—in the "Listening" section of this chapter. Though beyond the scope of my project, it is important to acknowledge that listening has a rich history in communication studies. David Beard and Graham Bodie's "Listening Research in the Communication Discipline" provides an excellent overview of this work.

3. One piece of feminist rhetorical scholarship that does discuss listening as a multisensory act is Andrea Lunsford and Adam Rosenblatt's "'Down a Road and into an Awful Silence': Graphic Listening in Joe Sacco's Comics Journalism"—a chapter in Glenn and Ratcliffe's edited collection *Listening and Silence as Rhetorical Arts* (2011). Lunsford and Rosenblatt's highlighting of Sacco's synesthetic listening practices draws attention to the ways in which the senses collaborate.

4. I do not mean to imply that listening must *always* involve attention. For instance, Anahid Kassabian offers a concept she calls "ubiquitous listening." Kassabian compares ubiquitous listening to ubiquitous computing, a kind of listening that "blends into the environment, taking place without calling conscious attention to itself as an activity in itself. It is, rather, ubiquitous and conditional, following us from room to room, building to building, activity to activity" (10).

5. As Andrew J. Eisenberg notes, Steven Feld (1996) uses the term *acoustemology* as a means to "describe a way of knowing place in and through the sonic environment," Jonathan Sterne (1997) calls his examination of programmed music in commercial spaces "architectonics," Alain Corbin discusses the "'auditory landscape,' which emphasizes sensory experience and its discursive framing," and Emily Thompson (2002) redefines soundscape as "simultaneously a physical environment and a way of perceiving that environment" (Novak and Sakakeeny 198).

6. A few notable exceptions include *Sounding Out* (Stoever), which consistently uses images, sound, and video to enhance authors' posts, and *Provoke! Digital Sound Studies* (Mueller, Lingold, and Trettien), a digital edited collection that features sonic scholarship.

7. There are growing numbers of articles, books, and conference panels on sound and listening in rhetoric and composition every year; there is now a Special Interest Group focused on sound at the Conference on College Composition and Communication (a flagship conference in the field); and sound has been playing a larger role in multimodal composition courses. For example, *Soundwriting Pedagogies* (edited by Kyle Stedman and Courtney Danforth)—a new digital collection that amplifies the diverse ways rhetoric and composition teachers use sound in the classroom—is currently underway.

CHAPTER 2: SOUNDING BODIES, COMPOSING EXPERIENCE

1. Glennie began to lose her hearing around the age of eight and was profoundly deaf by age twelve (*Good Vibrations* 46, 63). As she writes, "I am not totally deaf, I am profoundly deaf. Profound deafness covers a wide range of symptoms, although it is commonly taken to mean the quality of the sound heard is not sufficient to be able to understand the spoken word from sound alone" ("Hearing Essay" n.p.).

2. High frequency sounds have also been exploited for the intense bodily affects they are able to produce. For instance, in *Sonic Warfare* Steve Goodman writes about the "long-range acoustic devices (LRADs)" that the United States Marine Corps used in Iraq, which emitted "targeted high-frequency beams of sound about 2,100 to 3,100 hertz of up to 150 decibels within a range of 100 yards" (21). Though LRADs were developed as an acoustic weapon (their sound causes pain and discomfort in the ears), they have also been used "in the aftermath of Hurricane Katrina" and during large protests to disperse crowds (21). Additionally, Goodman elaborates on how sound was used as a means of inducing extreme discomfort in bodies during the Waco siege of 1993: "The FBI engaged in 'acoustic psycho-correction,' playing high-volume music blended with sound effects into the compound of the Branch Davidians led by David Koresh with a playlist that was accompanied by bagpipes, screeching seagulls, dying rabbits, sirens, dentist drills, and Buddhist chants" (21).

3. It is also possible to use sound to make visible and other nonsonic phenomena audible. For example, *sonification* is a practice that transforms nonsonic data, like yeast cells or weather patterns, into audible sound (Sterne and Akiyama). Such practices reveal sound's plasticity—"its ability to convey data across different sensory registers" (547).

4. The relationship between deafness, including Deaf culture, and sound studies has been taken up by a number of scholars, including Jonathan Sterne (2003), Mara Mills (2010), Trevor Boffone (2015), and Cara Lynne Cardinale (2017). Mara Mills's entry for "deafness" in *Keywords in Sound* (Novak and Sakakeeny) provides an detailed overview of work at the juncture of sound and deafness studies.

5. In 2016 the journal *Kairos* published two pieces of multimodal scholarship that reinforce the idea that listening is a distinctive, embodied practice: Crystal VanKooten's "Singer, Writer: A Choric Exploration of Sound and Writing," and Janine Butler's "Where Access Meets Multimodality: The Case of ASL

Music Videos." These works discuss and enact the inclusive approach to sound I am proposing via multimodal listening pedagogy.

6. One of the biggest challenges for disability studies scholars has been figuring out how to reach a wider audience. Margaret Price asks: "How can this project [of incorporating disability studies into our pedagogies] engage students, not to mention teachers, of all abilities, including those who do not specialize in disability studies or are not themselves disabled?" (55). As an able-bodied person (at least at the time of writing this book), I attempt to address this question via multimodal listening pedagogy, which is designed to help listeners of *all capacities* cultivate critical listening habits. My hope is that a more universal and inclusive approach to listening will bring disability studies to a much larger audience of teachers and students.

7. I want to stress that there are also high-frequency sounds in what Glennie refers to as "organic" sonic environments. For instance, many bird sounds are high frequency. It is not that high frequency sounds are bad in and of themselves. Rather, Glennie is calling attention to the need for a range of sounds in listening training to keep listeners on their toes, so to speak. If one only listens to prerecorded bird sounds (what Glennie would call "inorganic" sounds), then those sounds would never change or fluctuate. Listening to bird sounds live, however, is more demanding because the sounds are not static. They change depending on the time of day, the spatial location of the birds and the listener, the environmental context, etc.

8. By *podcasts*, I am referring to audio content (usually a mix of speech, music, and ambient sound) that is composed as a series with multiple episodes. *Audio essays* are typically stand-alone projects, though they are often conflated with podcasts in multimodal composition.

9. I want to be clear that I am not suggesting that identity markers like race and gender are somehow disconnected from the ways that people make meaning of sound. On the contrary, these identity markers are integral to the process of interpreting sound. Here, though, I have chosen to focus on affective, sensory experiences because they are so rarely mentioned in multimodal composition scholarship.

10. For an outstanding resource on the production of more accessible multimodal work, see *Kairos*'s issue on "Multimodality in Motion: Disability and Kairotic Spaces" (Yergeau et al.).

11. Patricia Dunn's *Talking, Sketching, Moving: Multiple Literacies in the Teaching of Writing* provides another example of how the concept of universal design can be used to create more accessible and flexible opportunities in composition. Dunn pro-

poses the use of multiple modes and pathways—talking, sketching, moving—to broaden writing instruction in ways that engage a wider and more diverse range of learners. Multimodal listening pedagogy aspires to accomplish a similar goal in terms of listening and sonic composing practices.

12. Thomas Rickert's "Music@Microsoft.Windows" offers an important ecological perspective on sound. Rickert argues that it is necessary to develop an understanding of "the mutually conditioning (and not determining) confluence of sound, image, material environment, bodies, and mood" (n.p.). Rickert's attention to how sound works with and against other sensory modes and materials in this article and in his book *Ambient Rhetoric* resonates with my conception of multimodal listening.

13. It is likely that in the coming years there will be a more pronounced emphasis on the tactile affordances of sound in audio technologies, particularly in relation to music and video games. For example, Crusher headphones use speaker technology to produce "vibrations that are perceived as powerful bass notes" via bone conduction (Furchgott n.p.). The point of this device is to enable listeners to physically experience music through vibration.

CHAPTER 3: SOUNDING SPACE, DESIGNING EXPERIENCE

1. "Guastavino" is the brand name.

2. Schafer's research group, World Soundscape Project (WSP), initially focused on the negative impact of noise pollution on the rapidly changing environment in Vancouver during the early 1970s. The WSP's research resulted in several publications that led to the creation of Canadian noise bylaws. However, in his 1973 essay "The Music of the Environment," Schafer decided to concentrate on how to create more positive soundscapes as opposed to focusing exclusively on the elimination of unappealing or harmful sonic environments (World Soundscape Project). This change in approach has had a profound impact on soundscape studies as it is understood today.

3. Barry Truax, a colleague of Schafer's and an original member of the World Soundscape Project, is also a noteworthy scholar of acoustic ecology. Traux's *Handbook for Acoustic Ecology* (1978) and *Acoustic Communication* (1984) are landmark texts in the field.

4. For more on how the term *soundscape* has been taken up by scholars, see Ari Y. Kelman's "Rethinking the Soundscape: A Critical Genealogy of a Key Term in Sound Studies."

5. Sidney Dobrin's edited collection *Ecology, Writing Theory, and New Media* provides a thorough overview of disciplinary scholarship on ecology.

6. One notable exception in visual rhetoric is Laurie Gries' 2015 monograph, *Still Life with Rhetoric*, which offers an ecological framework for understanding the circulation and transformation of images.

7. Designing acoustic environments has been a practice at least since the establishment of architectural studies. The ancient Roman architect Vitruvius is often cited as the first "acoustic designer." Emily Thompson notes, "In what is considered to be the oldest extant architectural treatise in the Western tradition, the Roman architect Vitruvius articulated ideas about how to control sound in theaters" (18).

8. I began this project by interviewing two acoustic designers affiliated with reputable firms/institutions in the State of Pennsylvania where I completed my graduate work. After assessing the material from these interviews, I concluded that there was more than enough information for a chapter—especially since I was able to find an abundance of acoustic design and sound studies research that supplemented and confirmed many of the practices discussed in the interviews.

9. Trevor Cox explains, "Evidence suggests that the size of a room, sensed through reverberation and other audio cues, affects our emotional response to neutral and nice sounds. We tend to perceive small rooms as being calmer, safer, and more pleasant than large spaces" (28).

10. By 1930, the acoustical materials industry was booming. Dozens of corporations began manufacturing new products that promised to change the way people controlled sonic environments. For example, Emily Thompson writes, "There were insulating papers, rigid wallboards, stonelike tiles, plasters, and all sorts of mechanical devices for structurally isolating floors, walls, and ceilings" (170).

11. In this respect, the 1926 construction of the Cathedral of Learning, which incorporated acoustical tiles to prevent excessive reverberation, was rather prescient.

12. In addition to acoustical technologies that are integrated into environments and often go unnoticed, bodies can learn about "appropriate" noise levels in more direct or explicit ways. When I was in elementary school, for instance, our cafeteria had a stoplight. The cafeteria was in a gymnasium with hard surfaces, so it got loud quickly during the lunch hour. When noise levels increased during lunch, the light would move from green (OK), to yellow (warning!), to

red (unacceptable!!). If the red light came on, no one was allowed to talk for the rest of the lunch period, and if you did make any noise you got sent to detention. The problem was that every time the light turned yellow, everyone made a "shush" sound in an attempt to quiet others. Unfortunately, the shushing added additional noise that always made the light turn red. After many silent punishments, we were eventually conditioned to whisper (instead of shushing) as soon as the light turned yellow to keep the noise levels down. Our experience with the stoplight taught us what amount of noise was deemed appropriate by the teachers in charge, and thus, we modified our behavior accordingly.

13. Thompson is pointing out a general pattern rather than making a blanket statement about the lack of reverberation in modern architecture. For instance, to raise noise levels, many modern restaurants and bars are designed to be reverberant, thus making those spaces seem more crowded and exciting even when they may not be. In these cases, the intention of the design is not to call attention to the architecture itself but to enhance patrons' experiences via ambiance.

14. I first encountered the term "soundscaping" in Mack Hagood's article, "Quiet Comfort."

15. Interestingly, the number of human bodies that are expected to occupy a space needs to be taken into account in acoustic design as well. As Swanson explained to me, "Bodies act like sound absorbers in the audience, but they also are sound generators when they talk and move about" (personal interview). Since bodies have the capacity to change a sonic environment, they need to be considered as material parts of an environment.

16. Muzak is not just used as a tactic to get shoppers to consume. Historically, it has been employed to control the speed of production. During World War II, the Muzak corporation invented "stimulus progression" to influence the pace and intensity of workers in factories. Steve Goodman writes, "Stimulus progression tactically organized the day around the pulsing center of gravity of the human heartbeat at roughly seventy-two beats per minute. Increasing and decreasing tempo across the day could therefore produce intensification or disintensification. Alternating between music and quiet would produce alertness by the oscillation between silence and arousal" (144).

17. Muzak is the brand name of a defunct company that produced these types of songs, but Muzak is now used to describe an entire genre of music.

18. While this is true of shopping malls in the 1990s, when Sterne's article was written, it is now more common for the hallways of malls to be music-less. The silent hallways still serve the same function, however. They make the stores piping music seem more attractive and pleasurable than the hallways, thus making

people gravitate toward them. Additionally, since the time of Sterne's article, traditional shopping malls have been on the decline. Many of Sterne's observations still apply to other shopping experiences in physical locations whether they be boutique plazas or strip malls. It is still unclear if online shopping environments will adopt the sonic strategies used in brick-and-mortar stores.

19. Technologies such as doors and insulation, which have obviously been around much longer than noise-cancelling headphones, also enable a degree of control over the soundscape. However, newer technologies have increased that degree of control and made it mobile. Now people can produce their desired sonic environments in their own dwellings and on the go.

20. See Michael Bull's exploration of mobile sonic technologies and urban space in *Sound Moves: iPod Culture and Urban Experience* and *Sounding Out the City: Personal Stereos and the Management of Everyday Life*.

21. While iPods have been largely replaced by smartphones and apps (Apple halted the production of the iPod Classic in 2014), using mobile listening as a creative form of escape remains a pervasive practice (Honan).

22. For a fascinating psychoanalytic reading of the iPod silhouette commercials, see Gunn and Hall's "Stick It in Your Ear: Psychodynamics of iPod Enjoyment."

23. I say "usually" because environmental noises can still invade one's personal soundscape; earbuds are not full-proof external sound-blocking devices.

24. However, as Tyler Bickford points out, MP3 players are now inexpensive enough for most middle schoolers to own (10). Though there are certainly still many people who cannot afford to purchase digital audio devices, they are becoming more affordable every year.

25. One of the biggest problems with social soundscaping is that it excludes non-hearing listeners. However, asking students to improve upon public sound projects by making them more accessible would be a great class activity. Finding ways to use images and text to represent sounds has the potential to make social soundscaping a more inclusive sonic practice.

26. For a wide selection of examples of public sound art and installations, see Dyson's *Sounding New Media*, Munster's *Materializing New Media*, Gibbs's *The Fundamentals of Sonic Art and Sound Design*, and Voeglin's *Sonic Possible Worlds*.

CHAPTER 4: SOUNDING CARS, SELLING EXPERIENCE

1. Of course, there has also been a proliferation of anti-car movements that condemn the environmental effects of cars and their reliance on foreign oil. However, as Mimi Sheller points out, "most practical efforts at promoting more 'ethical' forms of car consumption have been debated and implemented as if

the intense feelings, passions, and embodied experiences associated with auto-mobility were not relevant" (222). To the contrary, these embodied, affective dimensions are a powerful force that has in part enabled car cultures to persist.

2. Sociologist David Howes also refers to the emphasis on sensory experience in product design as the "sensual logic of late capitalism" (293).

3. Cleophas and Bijsterveld note, "BMW employs more than 150 acoustical engi-neers, and Ford has an acoustical department of 200 employees" (103). As cars become more sonically complex, these numbers will increase.

4. I reached out to a number of major car manufacturers to ask if I could interview some of their acoustic engineers. Some of them ignored my request, and others denied it. This is not particularly surprising given the competitive nature of the car industry and the increasing importance of sound design. (Perhaps they did not want to make their strategies or acoustic projects public.) Thus, instead of interviews, in this chapter I draw from a substantial body of sound studies scholarship on automobility and sound design.

5. As Brandon LaBelle points out, there is an entire industry based on the expe-rience of car sounds. For instance, in order to prevent noisy experiences on the road and in the soundscapes that cars pass through, "silent asphalt," or a rubberized material that diminishes "environmental noise created by the car itself," was invented (144–145). LaBelle also mentions the construction of "sound walls" which are used to shield homes and businesses from traffic noises by deflecting sound in the opposite direction (145). As these examples illus-trate, the relationship between cars and sonic experience depends on a dispa-rate network of material and sensory elements, some of which are completely unrelated to the production of the car itself.

6. Changes in sonic design practices are often a result of larger social changes in the perception of sound. For example, in the 1920s and 1930s, cars were much noisier than they are today. However, during that time period, the noise was associated with fun and adventure, as well as masculinity (drivers were mostly male at that time) (Bijsterveld 200). Noise was also a matter of function—par-ticular noises would alert drivers that their car was in need of maintenance. However, by the mid-1960s, Bijsterveld writes, "listening to the car's sounds and noises was no longer seen as functional but as a nuisance . . . motorists, by means of a burgeoning car literature, were taught a new auditory culture. They were supposed to listen to their car radio to keep up their spirits; the various sounds and noises of the car's functioning no longer mattered" (200). Thus, the car radio became the most important car sound of the time, and as a result automotive acoustic engineers had to find ways to quiet the rest of the

car. Clearly, the meaning and perception of particular car sounds change and evolve, which affects sonic design practices in the auto industry.

7. In this sense, driving a car is similar to the impoverished contemporary sonic experiences I have been describing throughout this book (e.g., listening to an MP3 player, listening to or composing with sound on computers, etc.). As John Urry puts it, "Sights, sounds, tastes, temperatures, and smells get reduced to the two-dimensional view through the car windscreen and through the rear mirror, the sensing of the world through the screen being the dominant mode of contemporary dwelling" (23). While drivers have the ability to control sound in this environment, much of the car's sound has been diminished by acoustic engineers. For the driver, the car becomes another computer—a highly controllable interface that makes it impossible to feel the full vibratory impact of sound.

8. It is no coincidence that the purchase of cars started to gain popularity at a time when there was an influx of other technologies that allowed consumers to create private aural experiences for themselves. Michael Bull notes, "Significantly, the beginnings of mass ownership of the automobile in the 1920s were also co-terminus with the growth of many domestic media of cultural reception—the radio, the gramophone, and the telephone" (*Sound Moves* 91).

9. See Michael Bull's *Sound Moves*, Dylan Jones's *iPod, Therefore I Am*, and Steven Levy's *The Perfect Thing*.

10. Though creating a car soundscape that is loud enough to disrupt one's equilibrium may not be appealing to everyone, now more than any other time in history it is possible to design a total sensory experience in one's car. In fact, some cars basically do this for you. The Toyota Pod, for instance, is a car that includes "an elaborate system of IT sensing devices, the Pod operates as a living organism, replete with decorative exterior lighting that registers different 'moods' at a driver's command" (LaBelle 158). Cars, then, are not only a home away from home; they can also be technologies that are used to recreate other kinds of place-based experiences.

CONCLUSION: MULTIMODAL LISTENING PEDAGOGY AND THE FUTURE OF SONIC EDUCATION

1. Significantly, there is a correlation between the rise in podcast listening and the rise in long commutes (Souccar). Technological advancements (e.g., reliable podcast apps, USB ports in cars, etc.) have made it easier to access entertaining audible content, which is appealing to the increasing number of drivers who spend hours in their cars daily. According to the Pew Research Center, "As of

January 2015, more than a third of U.S. adult cellphone owners (35%) have listened to online radio in the car. That is substantially more than the 21% who did so in 2013, and nearly six times the number (6%) who had done so in 2010" (Vogt n.p.). I suspect, however, that the popularity of listening to podcasts while driving is about more than killing time during lengthy commutes. Indeed, part of the allure of listening to podcasts in cars is the controlled sonic experience. Even if you are in a traffic jam with hundreds of others, the acoustic space of your car feels private. In a car, you can make numerous adjustments to create an environment that is physically comfortable, and this holistic bodily experience contributes to the pleasure of listening while driving.

2. Additionally, many podcasts provide detailed transcripts for each episode. Thus, the ability to describe nondiscursive sound—something that students are asked to do in multimodal listening pedagogy—could also prepare students to be capable members of podcast production teams.

3. There are other multisensory aspects of podcast production as well. Many popular podcasts, such as *Serial* and *S-Town*, now have websites that feature extra media (e.g., images, video, original documents or artifacts, etc.). These websites extend the podcast experience by giving listeners a chance to dive deeper into particular stories or interviews. Such websites might serve as productive models for including web-based storytelling practices in student podcasting projects.

4. Three-dimensional audio is a technique that uses binaural recording systems to emulate how humans actually experience sound. As Mona Lalwani explains, "The architecture of our anatomy dictates how we understand the sounds we hear: with an ear on either side of a thick skull and spongy brain, we hear sounds enter our left and right ears at different times. If a dog barks by our left ear, it takes a few extra microseconds for the bark to reach the right ear; the sound will also be louder in one ear than the other. In addition, sound waves interact with the physical constitution of the listener—the pinna (or outer ear), the head, and the torso—and the surrounding space, creating listener-specific variations otherwise known as head-related transfer function. The brain scrutinizes these miniscule interaural differences of time and strength in order to localize sound with immaculate precision" (n.p.). With strategic microphone placement, three-dimensional recordings can capture a realistic auditory experience. When users listen to these recordings via headphones they are able to hear layered, directional sound as if they were experiencing it in the original space it occurred.

5. Other recent, particularly innovative examples of sound design in multi-

media journalism include *The New York Times Magazine*'s "25 Songs That Tell Us Where Music Is Going" edited by Nitsuh Abebe; *The New York Times*' "The Ballad of Geeshie and Elvie" by John Jeremiah Sullivan; and *Pitchfork*'s "Glitter in the Dark" by Laura Snapes.

6. For examples of community-based sound projects, see Jennifer Stoever's "Toward a Civically Engaged Sound Studies, or Resounding Binghamton," Wendy Hsu and Steven Kemper's "LA Listens," and Jon M. Wargo and Cassie J. Brownell's "#hearmyhome."

WORKS CITED

Abebe, Nitsuh, ed. "25 Songs That Tell Us Where Music Is Going: A One-Time Spectacular." *New York Times Magazine*. 3 Mar. 2016. Web. 17 Aug. 2016. http://www.nytimes.com/interactive /2016/03/10/magazine/25-songs-that-tell-us-where-music-is-going.html#/intro.

Abel, Jessica. *Out on the Wire: The Storytelling Secrets of the New Masters of Radio*. New York: Crown/Archetype, 2015.

Ahern, Kati Fargo. "Tuning the Sonic Playing Field: Teaching Ways of Knowing Sound in First Year Writing." *Computers and Composition* 30 (2013): 75–86.

Ahern, Kati Fargo, and Steph Ceraso. "Composing with Sound." *Composition Studies* 43.2 (2015): 13–18.

Ahern, Kati Fargo, and Jordan Frith. "Speaking Back to Our Social Spaces: The Rhetoric of Social Soundscaping." *Sonic Rhetorics*. Eds. Steph Ceraso and Jon Stone. Spec. issue of *Harlot* 9 (2013): n. pag. Web. 7 July 2014.

Alexander, Jonathan. "Glenn Gould and the Rhetorics of Sound." *Computers and Composition* 37 (2015): 73–89.

Alexander, Jonathan, and Jacqueline Rhodes. *On Multimodality: New Media in Composition Studies*. Urbana, IL: CCCC/NCTE, 2014.

Anderson, Erin. "Toward a Resonant Material Vocality for Digital Composition."

Enculturation: A Journal of Rhetoric, Writing, and Culture 18 (2014): n. pag. Web. 15 Sept. 2014.

Arola, Kristin L., Jennifer Sheppard, and Cheryl E. Ball. *Writer/Designer: A Guide to Making Multimodal Projects*. Boston: Bedford/St. Martin's, 2014.

Arola, Kristin L., and Anne Frances Wysocki, eds. *Composing (Media) = Composing (Embodiment): Bodies, Technologies, Writing, the Teaching of Writing*. Logan, UT: Utah State UP, 2012.

Ball, Cheryl, and Byron Hawk, eds. *Sound in/as Compositional Space: A Next Step in Multiliteracies*. Spec. issue of *Computers and Composition* and *Computers and Composition Online* 23.3 (2006).

Barnett, Scot, and Casey Boyle, eds. *Rhetoric, Through Everyday Things*. Tuscaloosa: The U of Alabama P, 2016.

Bates, Mary. "Super Powers for the Blind and Deaf." *Scientific American*. 8 Sept. 2012. Web. 10 July 2015. http://www.scientificamerican.com/article/superpowers-for-the-blind-and-deaf/.

Beard, David, and Graham Bodie. "Listening Research in the Communication Discipline." *A Century of Communication Studies: The Unfinished Conversation*. Eds. Pat J. Gehrke and William M. Keith. New York: Routledge, 2015.

Beckerman, Joel, with Tyler Gray. *The Sonic Boom: How Sound Transforms the Way We Think, Feel, and Buy*. Boston: Houghton Mifflin Harcourt, 2014.

Bergson, Henri. *Matter and Memory*. Trans. N. M. Paul and W. S. Palmer. Brooklyn: Zone Books, 1988.

Bessette, Jean. "Audio, Archives, and the Affordance of Listening in a Pedagogy of 'Difference.'" *Computers and Composition* 39 (2016): 71–82.

Bialostosky, Don. *How to Play a Poem*. n.p. 2013.

Bickford, Tyler. "Earbuds Are Good for Sharing: Children's Headphones as Social Media at a Vermont School." *The Oxford Handbook of Mobile Music Studies*. Eds. Jason Stanyek and Sumanth Gopinath. Oxford: Oxford UP, 2014.

Biello, David. "How City Noise Is Reshaping Birdsong." *Scientific American*. 22 Oct. 2009. Web. 10 Apr. 2013. https://www.scientificamerican.com/podcast/episode/how-city-noise-is-shaping-bird-song-09-10-22/.

Bijsterveld, Karin. "Acoustic Cocooning: How the Car Became a Place to Unwind." *Senses and Society* 5.2 (2010): 189–211.

Bijsterveld, Karin, Eefje Cleophas, Stefan Krebs, and Gijs Mom. *Sound and Safe: A History of Listening Behind the Wheel*. Oxford: Oxford UP, 2014.

Birdman (or The Unexpected Virtue of Ignorance). Dir. Alejandro G. Iñárritu. Perf. Michael Keaton, Zach Galifianakis, Edward Norton. Fox Searchlight, 2014. Film.

Blake, Art. "Finding My Voice While Listening to John Cage." *Sounding Out: The Sound*

Studies Blog. 23 Feb. 2015. Web. 25 Feb. 2015. https://soundstudiesblog.com/2015/02/23/finding-my-voice-while-listening-to-john-cage/.

Blesser, Barry, and Linda-Ruth Salter. *Spaces Speak, Are You Listening?: Experiencing Aural Architecture.* Cambridge, MA: MIT P, 2009.

Boffone, Trevor. "Deaf Latin@ Performance: Listening with the Third Ear." *Sounding Out: The Sound Studies Blog.* 3 Aug. 2015. Web. 8 Aug. 2015. https://soundstudiesblog.com/tag/trevor-boffone/.

Booth, Wayne. *The Rhetoric of Rhetoric: The Quest for Effective Communication.* Malden, MA: Blackwell, 2004.

Bowen, Tracey, and Carl Whithaus, eds. *Multimodal Literacies and Emerging Genres.* Pittsburgh: U of Pittsburgh P, 2013.

Boyd, Danah. *It's Complicated: The Social Lives of Networked Teens.* New Haven: Yale UP, 2014.

Boyle, Casey. "Writing and Rhetoric and/as Posthuman Practice." *College English* 78.6 (2016): 528–50.

"British Library UK Soundmap." British Library Board. 2004. Web. 6 Sept. 2016. http://sounds.bl.uk/sound-maps/uk-soundmap.

Brooks, Christopher N. *Architectural Acoustics.* Jefferson, NC: McFarland, 2003.

Bull, Michael. "The End of *Flânerie*: iPods, Aesthetics, and Urban Experience." *Throughout: Art and Culture Emerging with Ubiquitous Computing.* Ed. Ulrik Ekman. Cambridge: MIT P, 2013: 151–62.

Bull, Michael. *Sound Moves: iPod Culture and Urban Experience.* New York: Routledge, 2007.

Bull, Michael. *Sounding Out the City: Personal Stereos and the Management of Everyday Life.* Oxford: Berg, 2000.

Bull, Michael, and Les Back, eds. *The Auditory Culture Reader.* New York: Berg, 2003.

Butler, Janine. "Where Access Meets Multimodality: The Case of ASL Music Videos." *Kairos: A Journal of Rhetoric, Technology, and Pedagogy* 21.1 (2016): n. pag. Web. 9 Aug. 2017.

Byron, Ellen. "The Search for Sweet Sounds that Sell." *Wall Street Journal.* 24 Oct. 2012. 10 Apr. 2013. http://www.wsj.com/articles/SB10001424052970203406404578074671598804116.

Campbell, Trisha N. "Digital Empathy: A Practice-Based Experiment." *Enculturation: A Journal of Rhetoric, Writing, and Culture* 24 (2017): n. pag. Web. 6 Sept. 2017.

Cardinale, Cara Lynne. "Re-orienting Sound Studies' Aural Fixation: Christine Sun Kim's 'Subjective Loudness.'" *Sounding Out: The Sound Studies Blog.* 5 June 2017. Web. 8 June 2017. https://soundstudiesblog.com/2017/06/05/re-orienting-sound-studies-aural-fixation-christine-sun-kims/.

Carter, Steven. "The Beatles and Freshman English." *College Composition and Communication* 20.3 (1969): 228–32.

Cavanaugh, William J., Gregory C. Tocci, and Joseph A. Wilkes. *Architectural Acoustics: Principles and Practice*. Hoboken, NJ: Wiley, 2009.

Ceraso, Steph, and Jon Stone, eds. *Sonic Rhetorics*. Spec. issue of *Harlot* 9 (2013): n. pag. Web. 4 May 2014.

Chancellor, Paul G. "What Songs Has America?" *The English Journal* 33.2 (1944): 81–88.

Chibana, Nayomi. "10 Mind-Blowing Interactive Stories That Will Change the Way You See the World." *Visme*. 24 July 2015. Web. 15 Aug. 2016. http://blog.visme. co/10-mind-blowing-interactive-stories-that-will-change-the-way-you-see-the-world/.

Chion, Michael. *Audiovision: Sound on Screen*. New York: Columbia UP, 1994.

Cintron, Ralph. *Angel's Town: Chero Ways, Gang Life, and Rhetorics of the Everyday*. Boston: Beacon P, 1997.

Classen, Constance, and David Howes. *Ways of Sensing: Understanding the Senses in Society*. New York: Routledge, 2013.

Cleophas, Eefje, and Karin Bijsterveld. "Selling Sound: Testing, Designing, and Marketing Sound in the European Car Industry." *Oxford Handbook of Sound Studies*. Eds. Trevor Pinch and Karin Bijsterveld. Oxford: Oxford UP, 2012: 102–24.

Colwell, K. C. "Faking It: Engine-Sound Enhancement Explained." *Car and Driver*. Apr. 2012. Web. 10 July 2015. http://www.caranddriver.com/features/faking-it-engine-sound-enhancement-explained-tech-dept.

"Composing Access." Committee on Disability Issues in College Composition and Computers and Composition Digital P. n.d. Web. 11 Oct. 2014. https://u.osu.edu/ composingaccess/.

Comstock, Michelle, and Mary Hocks. "The Sounds of Climate Change: Sonic Rhetoric in the Anthropocene, the Age of Human Impact." *Rhetoric Review* 35.2 (2016): 165–75.

Comstock, Michelle, and Mary Hocks. "Voice in the Cultural Soundscape: Sonic Literacy in Composition Studies." *Computers and Composition Online* 23.3 (2006): n. pag. Web. 5 Oct. 2007.

Connor, Steven. "Edison's Teeth: Touching Hearing." *Hearing Cultures: Essays on Sound, Listening, and Modernity*. Ed. Veit Erlmann. New York: Bloomsbury Academic, 2004: 153–72.

Connor, Steven. "Rustications: Animals in the Urban Mix." *The Acoustic City*. Eds. Matthew Gandy and BJ Nilsen. Berlin: Jovis, 2014.

Cooper, Marilyn. "The Ecology of Writing." *College English* 48.4 (1986): 364–75.

Cope, Bill, and Mary Kalantzis, eds. *Multiliteracies: Literacy Learning and the Design of Social Futures*. New York: Routledge, 2000.

Corbin, Alain. *Village Bells: Sound and Meaning in the Nineteenth-Century French Countryside*. New York: Columbia UP, 1998.

Coudriet, Greg. Personal Interview. 16 Feb. 2012.

Cowan, James. *Architectural Acoustics Design Guide*. Columbus, OH: McGraw-Hill, 2000.

Cox, Trevor. *The Sound Book: The Science of the Sonic Wonders of the World*. New York: Norton, 2014.

Daughtry, J. Martin. *Listening to War: Sound, Music, Trauma, and Survival in Wartime Iraq*. Oxford: Oxford UP, 2015.

Davidson, Cathy. *Now You See It: How Technology and Brain Science Will Transform Schools and Business for the 21st Century*. New York: Penguin, 2011.

Davis, Diane D. *Breaking Up [at] Totality: A Rhetoric of Laughter*. Carbondale: Southern Illinois UP, 2000.

Davis, Diane D., ed. *Writing with Sound*. Spec. issue of *Currents in Electronic Literacy* 14 (2011): n. pag. Web. 13 Sept. 2012.

"Deep Listening Institute." The Center for Deep Listening. n.d. Web. 6 June 2017. http://deeplistening.org/site/.

Deluigi, Sandy. "New Apple iPod Commercial 2013." *YouTube*. 21 Jan. 2013. Web. 3 Apr. 2013. http://www.youtube.com/watch?v=THjJFQLUMWc.

DeNora, Tia. *Music in Everyday Life*. Cambridge: Cambridge UP, 2000.

Dewey, John. *Experience and Education*. 1938. New York: Touchtone, 1997.

Dickinson, Greg, Carole Blair, and Brian L. Ott, eds. *Places of Public Memory: The Rhetoric of Museums and Memorials*. Tuscaloosa: U of Alabama P, 2010.

"Disability Rhetoric." Disability Studies SIG. 2009. Web. 11 Oct. 2014. http://disability rhetoric.com/.

Dobrin, Sidney, ed. *Ecology, Writing Theory, and New Media: Writing Ecology*. New York: Routledge, 2012.

Dobrin, Sidney, and Christina Weisser, eds. *Ecocomposition: Theoretical and Pedagogical Approaches*. Albany: State U of New York P, 2001.

Dolmage, Jay, and Cynthia Lewiecki-Wilson. "Refiguring Rhetorica: Linking Feminist Rhetoric and Disability Studies." *Rhetorica in Motion: Feminist Methods and Methodologies*. Eds. Eileen E. Schell and K. J. Rawson. Pittsburgh: U of Pittsburgh P, 2010: 23–38.

Dredge, Stuart. "Serial Podcast Breaks iTunes Records as It Passes 5m Downloads and Streams." *Guardian*. 18 Nov. 2014. Web. 13 Nov. 2017. https://www.theguardian.com/technology/2014/nov/18/serial-podcast-itunes-apple-downloads-streams.

Dunn, Patricia A. *Talking, Sketching, Moving: Multiple Literacies in the Teaching of Writing*. Portsmouth, NH: Boynton/Cook, 2001.

Dyson, Frances. *Sounding New Media: Immersion and Embodiment in the Arts and Culture.* Berkeley: U of California P, 2009.

EchoXIII. "How to Make a Sound Map: Cartographic, Compositional, Performative." *Acoustic Ecology.* University of Hull, Scarborough Campus. 4 Dec. 2013. Web. 7 July 2016. https://acousticecologyuoh.wordpress.com/2013/12/04/how-to-make-a-sound -map/.

Eliot, George. *Middlemarch.* 1871. New York: Bantam Books, 1985.

Ellsworth, Elizabeth. *Places of Learning: Media, Architecture, Pedagogy.* New York: Routledge, 2005.

Enoch, Jessica. "A Woman's Place Is in the School: Rhetorics of Gendered Space in Nineteenth-Century America." *College English* 70.3 (2008): 275–95.

Erlmann, Veit. *Reason and Resonance: A History of Modern Aurality.* Cambridge: MIT P, 2010.

Farman, Jason. *Mobile Interface Theory: Embodied Space and Locative Media.* New York: Routledge, 2012.

Feld, Steven. *Sound and Sentiment: Birds, Weeping, Poetics, and Song in Kaluli Expression.* 1982. Durham: Duke UP, 2012.

Felton, Emma, Oksana Zelenko, and Suzi Vaughan, eds. *Design and Ethics: Reflections on Practice.* New York: Routledge, 2012.

Fleckenstein, Kristie S. *Embodied Literacies: Imageword and a Poetics of Teaching.* Carbondale: Southern Illinois UP, 2003.

Fleming, David. *City of Rhetoric: Revitalizing the Public Sphere in Metropolitan America.* Albany: State U of New York P, 2008.

Friedner, Michele, and Stefan Helmreich. "Sound Studies Meets Deaf Studies." *Senses and Society* 7.1 (2012): 72–86.

Fuchs, Helmut. *Applied Acoustics: Concepts, Absorbers, and Silencers for Acoustical Comfort and Noise Control.* New York: Springer, 2013.

Furchgott, Roy. "Skullcandy Crushers Vibrate to Boost Bass." *New York Times Gadgetwise Blog.* 12 Mar. 2013. Web. 25 Mar. 2013. http://gadgetwise.blogs.nytimes.com/2013 /03/12/skullcandy-crushers-vibrate-to-boost-bass/.

Gauntlett, David. *Making Is Connecting: The Social Meaning of Creativity, from DIY and Knitting to YouTube and Web 2.0.* Cambridge, UK: Polity P, 2011.

Geere, Duncan. "The National Mall: A Location-Aware App Album." *Wired.* 27 May 2011. Web. 13 Mar. 2014. http://www.wired.com/2011/05/national-mall- location-aware-album/.

George, Diana, and John Trimbur. "The 'Communication Battle,' or Whatever Happened to the 4th C?" *College Composition and Communication* 50.4 (1999): 682–98.

Gibbs, Tony. *The Fundamentals of Sonic Art and Sound Design.* Singapore: Ava, 2007.

Gilroy, Paul. "Driving While Black." *Car Cultures*. Ed. Daniel Miller. Oxford: Berg, 2001.

Glasgow 3D Sound Map. Glasgow Caledonian University. Adam Craig, Don Knox, David More, and Gui Yun Tian. n.d. Web. 6 Sept. 2016. http://www.glasgow3dsoundmap.co.uk/.

Glenn, Cheryl. *Unspoken: A Rhetoric of Silence*. Carbondale: Southern Illinois UP, 2004.

Glenn, Cheryl, and Krista Ratcliffe, eds. *Silence and Listening as Rhetorical Arts*. Carbondale: Southern Illinois UP, 2011.

Glennie, Evelyn. *Good Vibrations*. East Sussex, UK: Arrow, 1991.

Glennie, Evelyn. "Hearing Essay." The Official Website of Dame Evelyn Glennie. 1 Jan. 2015. Web. 27 Mar. 2015. https://www.evelyn.co.uk/hearing-essay/.

Glennie, Evelyn. "How to Truly Listen." *TED*. Feb. 2003. Web. 8 Mar. 2003. http://www.ted.com/talks/evelyn_glennie_shows_how_to_listen.

Glennie, Evelyn. The Official Website of Dame Evelyn Glennie. n.d. Web. 27 Mar. 2011. https://www.evelyn.co.uk/.

Glennie, Evelyn. Personal Interview. 29 July 2011.

Goodman, Steve. *Sonic Warfare: Sound, Affect, and the Ecology of Fear*. Cambridge: MIT P, 2012.

Grace, Andrew Beck. "After the Storm." *Washington Post*. 27 Apr. 2015. Web. 10 July 2016. http://www.pbs.org/independentlens/interactive/after-the-storm/#/dear-fut ure-disaster-survivor?tid=a_inl&tid=a_inl.

Gries, Laurie E. *Still Life with Rhetoric: A New Materialist Approach for Visual Rhetorics*. Boulder: UP of Colorado, 2015.

Gunn, Joshua, Greg Goodale, Mirko M. Hall, and Rosa A. Eberly. "Auscultating Again: Rhetoric and Sound Studies." *Rhetoric Society Quarterly* 43.5 (2013): 475–89.

Gunn, Joshua, and Mirko M. Hall. "Stick It in Your Ear: The Psychodynamics of iPod Enjoyment." *Communication and Critical/Cultural Studies* 5.2 (2008): 135–57.

Haas, Christina. *Writing Technology: Studies on the Materiality of Literacy*. New York: Routledge, 1995.

Hagood, Mack. "Quiet Comfort: Noise, Otherness, and the Mobile Production of Personal Space." *American Quarterly* 63.3 (2011): 573–89.

Halbritter, Bump. "Aural Tools: Who's Listening?" *Digital Tools in Composition Studies: Critical Dimensions and Implications*. Eds. Ollie O. Oviedo, Joyce R. Walker, and Byron Hawk. Cresskill, NJ: Hampton P, 2010: 187–220.

Hawhee, Debra. *Bodily Arts: Rhetoric and Athletics in Ancient Greece*. Austin: U of Texas P, 2004.

Hawk, Byron. *A Counter-History of Composition: Toward Methodologies of Complexity*. Pittsburgh: U of Pittsburgh P, 2007.

Hawk, Byron, and Thomas Rickert. "Writing/Music/Culture." *Enculturation: A Journal of Rhetoric, Writing, and Culture* 2.2 (1999): n. pag. Web. 8 May 2015.

Henriques, Julian. *Sonic Bodies: Reggae Sound Systems, Performance Techniques, and Ways of Knowing*. New York: Bloomsbury Academic, 2011.

Here One. Doppler Labs Inc. n.d. Web. 29 June 2016. https://hereplus.me/.

Hesse, Doug, Nancy Sommers, and Kathleen Blake Yancey. "Evocative Objects: Reflections on Teaching, Learning, and Living in Between." *College English* 74.4 (2012): 325–50.

Hocks, Mary, and Michelle Comstock. "Composing for Sound: Sonic Rhetoric as Resonance." *Computers and Composition* 43 (2017): 135–46.

Honan, Matt. "On Death and iPods: A Requiem." *Wired*. 12 Sept. 2014. Web. 5 June 2015. http://www.wired.com/2014/09/rip-ipod/.

Howes, David. "Hyperesthesia, or, The Sensual Logic of Late Capitalism." *Empire of the Senses: The Sensual Culture Reader*. Ed. David Howes. New York: Berg, 2005: 281–303.

Hsu, Wendy, and Steven Kemper. "LA Listens." n.d. Web. 8 Aug. 2016. http://www.lalistens.org/audio/.

Jensenius, David. "FoundSounds." 10 Apr. 2015. Web. 17 May 2015. https://itunes.apple.com/us/app/found-sounds/id593338411?mt=8.

Jones, Douglas R. *Sound of Worship: A Handbook of Acoustics and Sound System Design for the Church*. New York: Focal, 2011.

Jones, Dylan. *iPod, Therefore I Am*. New York: Bloomsbury, 2005.

Journal of Sonic Studies. Eds. Marcel Cobussen and Vincent Meelberg. 2011. Web. 8 July 2013. http://sonicstudies.org/.

Kähler, Magnus. "Bosch Leads Quiet with the Quietest Dishwasher in North America." *Elevating Sound*. 30 Dec. 2013. Web. 12 June 2015. http://elevatingsound.com/bosch-leads-quiet-with-the-quietest-dishwasher-in-north-america/.

Kassabian, Anahid. *Ubiquitous Listening: Affect, Attention, and Distributed Subjectivity*. Berkeley: U of California P, 2013.

Kelman, Ari Y. "Rethinking the Soundscape: A Critical Genealogy of a Key Term in Sound Studies." *The Senses and Society* 5.2 (2010): 212–34.

Kerschbaum, Stephanie. "Modality." *Kairos: A Journal of Rhetoric, Technology, and Pedagogy*. "Multimodality in Motion: Disability in Kairotic Spaces." Eds. Melanie Yergeau et al. 18.1 (2013): n. pag. Web. 7 Nov. 2014.

Kimmelman, Michael. "Dear Architects: Sound Matters." *New York Times*. 29 Dec. 2015. Web. 15 Aug. 2016. http://www.nytimes.com/interactive/2015/12/29/arts/design/sound-architecture.html.

Kirschenbaum, Matthew. "Digital Humanities As/Is a Tactical Term." *Debates in the*

Digital Humanities. Ed. Matthew Gold. Minneapolis: U of Minnesota P, 2012: 415–28.

Krause, Bernie. "The Voice of the Natural World." *TED*. June 2013. Web. 9 July 2013. http://www.ted.com/talks/bernie_krause_ the_voice_ of_the_natural_world.

Krebs, Stefan. "'Sobbing, Whining, Rumbling': Listening to Automobiles as Social Practice." *The Oxford Handbook of Sound Studies*. Eds. Trevor Pinch and Karin Bijsterveld. Oxford: Oxford UP, 2012: 79–101.

Kress, Gunther. "Design and Transformation: New Theories of Meaning." *Multiliteracies: Literacy Learning and the Design of Social Futures*. Eds. Bill Cope and Mary Kalantzis. New York: Routledge, 2000: 153–61.

Kress, Gunther. *Multimodality: A Social Semiotic Approach to Contemporary Communication*. London: Routledge, 2010.

Kress, Gunther, and Theo Van Leeuwen. *Multimodal Discourse: The Modes and Media of Contemporary Communication*. New York: Arnold, 2001.

LaBelle, Brandon. *Acoustic Territories: Sound Culture and Everyday Life*. New York: Continuum, 2010.

Lalwani, Mona. "Surrounded by Sound: How 3D Audio Hacks Your Brain." *The Verge*. 12 Feb. 2015. Web. 15 Aug. 2016. https://www.theverge.com/2015/2/12/8021733/3d-audio-3dio-binaural-immersive-vr-sound-times-square-new-york.

LaSalle, Diana, and Terry A. Britton. *Priceless: Turning Ordinary Products into Extraordinary Experiences*. Boston: Harvard Business School P, 2003.

Lauer, Claire. "Contending with Terms: 'Multimodal' and 'Multimedia' in the Academic and Public Spheres." *Computers and Composition* 26 (2009): 225–39.

LaVecchia, Christina M. "Toward a Pedagogy of Materially Engaged Listening." *Composition Forum* 35 (2017): n. pag. Web. 20 Aug. 2017.

Leverenz, Carrie S. "Design Thinking and the Wicked Problem of Teaching Writing." *Computers and Composition* 33 (2014): 1–12.

Levy, Steven. *The Perfect Thing: How the iPod Shuffles Commerce, Culture, and Coolness*. New York: Simon and Schuster, 2006.

London Sound Survey. Ian M. Rawes. 2009. Web. 7 Sept. 2012. http://www.soundsurvey.org.uk/index.php/survey/soundmaps/.

Lunsford, Andrea, and Adam Rosenblatt. "'Down a Road and into an Awful Silence': Graphic Listening in Joe Sacco's Comics Journalism." *Silence and Listening as Rhetorical Arts*. Eds. Cheryl Glenn and Krista Ratcliffe. Carbondale: Southern Illinois UP, 2011: 130–47.

Lutkewitte, Claire, ed. *Multimodal Composition: A Critical Sourcebook*. Boston: Bedford/St. Martin's, 2014.

Macrorie, Ken. "Teach Listening?" *College English* 12.4 (1951): 220–23.

Madrigal, Alexis C. "The Quest to Find the First Soundscape." *Atlantic.* 4 Sept. 2010. Web. 3 Oct. 2013. http://www.theatlantic.com/technology/archive/2010/09/the-quest-to-find-the-first-soundscape/62842/.

Maly, Tim. "How GM Makes a Car Sound Like What a Car Is Supposed to Sound Like." *Medium.* 30 July 2013. Web. 8 July 2015. https://medium.com/thoughtful-design/how-gm-makes-a-car-sound-like-what-a-car-is-supposed-to-sound-like-c23c5fb86266.

Marback, Richard. "Embracing Wicked Problems: The Turn to Design in Composition Studies." *College Composition and Communication* 61.2 (2009): 397–413.

Mars, Roman. "99% Noise." *99% Invisible* Podcast. 3 Sept. 2010. Web. 8 June 2015. http://99percentinvisible.org/episode/99-invisible-01-99-noise-by-roman-mars-this/.

McCarthy, John, and Peter Wright. *Technology as Experience.* Cambridge: MIT P, 2004.

McKee, Heidi. "Sound Matters: Notes Toward the Analysis and Design of Sound in Multimodal Webtexts." *Computers and Composition* 23 (2006): 335–54.

Mersand, Joseph. "Why Teach Listening?" *The English Journal* 40.5 (1951): 260–65.

Micciche, Laura R. "Writing Material." *College English* 76.6 (2014): 488–505.

Mills, Mara. "Deafness." *Keywords in Sound.* Eds. David Novak and Matt Sakakeeny. Durham: Duke UP, 2015: 45–54.

Mills, Mara. "Deaf Jam: From Inscription to Reproduction to Information." *Social Text* 28.1 (2010): 35–58.

Montreal Sound Map. Max Stein and Julian Stein. 2000. Web. 7 Sept. 2016. http://www.montrealsoundmap.com/.

Mountford, Roxane. *The Gendered Pulpit: Preaching in American Protestant Spaces.* Carbondale: Southern Illinois UP, 2003.

Mueller, Darren, Mary Caton Lingold, and Whitney Trettien. *Provoke! Digital Sound Studies.* John Hope Franklin Humanities Institute. Duke University. 2015. Web. 15 Jan. 2016. http://soundboxproject.com/index.html.

Munster, Anna. *Materializing New Media: Embodiment in Information Aesthetics.* Hanover, NH: Dartmouth College P, 2006.

Murray, Joddy. *Non-discursive Rhetoric: Image and Affect in Multimodal Composition.* New York: State U of New York P, 2009.

Nauer, Barbara. "Soundscript: A Way to Help Black Students to Write Standard English." *College English* 36.5 (1975): 586–88.

"NCTE Position Statement on Multimodal Literacies." Multimodal Literacies Issue Management Team of the NCTE Executive Committee. Nov. 2005. Web. 8 July 2015. http://www.ncte.org/positions/statements/multimodalliteracies.

Norman, Don. "What Noise Does the Electric Car Make?" *MIT Technology Review*. 7 Feb. 2014. Web. 9 Sept. 2015. http://www.technologyreview.com/view/524241/what-noise-does-the-electric-car-make/.

Novak, David. "2.5 x 6 Metres of Space: Japanese Music Coffeehouses and Experimental Practices of Listening." *Popular Music* 27.1 (2008): 15–34.

Novak, David, and Matt Sakakeeny, eds. *Keywords in Sound*. Durham: Duke UP, 2015.

O'Keefe, Linda. "(Sound) Walking through Smithfield Square in Dublin." *Sounding Out: The Sound Studies Blog*. 10 Feb. 2014. Web. 7 July 2016. https://soundstudiesblog.com/2014/02/10/soundwalking-through-smithfield-square-in-dublin/.

Oleksiak, Timothy, and Raechel Tiffe. "Queering the Ear: A Response to Queer Decorum." *Queer Praxis: Questions for LGBTQ Worldmaking*. Eds. Dustin Goltz and Jason Zingsheim. New York: Lange, 2015. 187–93.

Oliveros, Pauline. *Deep Listening: A Composer's Sound Practice*. Bloomington: iUniverse, 2005.

Open Sound New Orleans: A Collaborative Soundmap of the City. Heather Booth and Jacob Brancasi. 2008. Web. 7 Sept. 2016. http://www.opensoundneworleans.com/core/.

O'Reilly, Francis J. "Listening." *English Journal* 16.7 (1927): 548–50.

Ouzounian, Gascia. "Acoustic Mapping: Notes from the Interface." *Acoustic City*. Eds. Matthew Gandy and BJ Nilsen. Berlin: Jovis, 2014: 164–73.

Özcan, Elif and René Van Egmond. "Product Design: An Interdisciplinary Approach?" Undisciplined! Proceedings of the Design Research Society Conference. Sheffield, UK. 16–19 July 2008. Web. 7 Oct. 2013. http://shura.shu.ac.uk/531/5/fulltext.pdf.

Packard, Cassie. "Deaf Artist Christine Sun Kim Is Reinventing Sound." *Vice*. 4 Apr. 2015. Web. 5 May 2017. https://www.vice.com/en_us/article/8gdwkp/gifted-dynamic-and-deaf-rising-star-christine-sun-kim-creates-art-that-reinvents-sound-679.

Palmeri, Jason. *Remixing Composition: A History of Multimodal Writing Pedagogy*. Carbondale: Southern Illinois UP, 2012.

Pinch, Trevor, and Karin Bijsterveld, eds. *The Oxford Handbook of Sound Studies*. Oxford: Oxford UP, 2013.

Porcello, Thomas. "Speaking of Sound: Language and the Professionalization of Sound-Recording Engineers." *Social Studies of Science* 34 (2004): 733–58.

Price, Margaret. "Disability: A Nondisabled Student Works the Hyphen." *College Composition and Communication* 59.1 (2007): 53–76.

Prins, Kristin. "Crafting New Approaches to Composition." *Composing (Media) = Composing (Embodiment): Bodies, Technologies, Writing, the Teaching of Writing*. Eds. Kristin L. Arola and Anne Frances Wysocki. Logan, UT: Utah State UP, 2012. 145–61.

Prior, Paul. "Moving Multimodality Beyond the Binaries: A Response to Gunther Kress' 'Gains and Losses.'" *Computers and Composition* 22 (2005): 23–30.

Pullin, Graham. *Design Meets Disability*. Cambridge: MIT P, 2009.

Purdy, James P. "What Can Design Thinking Offer Writing Students?" *College Composition and Communication* 65.4 (2014): 612–41.

Ratcliffe, Krista. *Rhetorical Listening: Identification, Gender, Whiteness*. Carbondale: Southern Illinois UP, 2005.

Reflections: A Journal of Public Rhetoric, Civic Writing, and Service Learning. Eds. Deborah Mutnik and Laurie Grobman. 2000.

Reynolds, Nedra. *Geographies of Writing: Inhabiting Places and Encountering Difference*. Carbondale: Southern Illinois UP, 2007.

Rice, Jeff. "The Making of Ka-Knowledge: Digital Aurality." *Computers and Composition* 23 (2006): 266–79.

Rice, Jenny. "Unframing Models of Public Distribution: From Rhetorical Situation to Rhetorical Ecologies." *Rhetoric Society Quarterly* 35.4 (2005): 5–24.

Rice, Tom. *Hearing and the Hospital: Sound, Listening, Knowledge, and Experience*. Canon Pyon, UK: Sean Kingston P, 2013.

Richards, Chris. "Bluebrain's 'The National Mall': The First Location-Aware Album." *Washington Post*. 27 May 2011. Web. 24 Aug. 2016. https://www.washingtonpost.com/lifestyle/style/bluebrains-the-national-mall-the-first-location-aware-album/2011/05/25/AGtTVsCH_story.html?utm_term=.55d771cf40aa.

Rickert, Thomas. *Ambient Rhetoric: The Attunements of Rhetorical Being*. Pittsburgh: U of Pittsburgh P, 2013.

Rickert, Thomas. "Music@Microsoft.Windows: Composing Ambience." *The Writing Instructor*. 2010. Web. 9 June 2011.

Rickert, Thomas, and Michael Salvo. "The Distributed *Gesamptkunstwerk*: Sound, Worlding, and New Media Culture." *Computers and Composition* 23 (2006): 296–316.

Rivers, Nathaniel. "Geocomposition in Public Rhetoric and Writing Pedagogy." *College Composition and Communication* 67.4 (2016): 576–606.

The Roaring Twenties: An Interactive Exploration of the Historical Soundscape of New York City. Emily Thompson. Design by Scott Mahoy. *Vectors Journal* (2013): n. pag. Web. 5 Jan. 2014. http://vectors.usc.edu/projects/index.php?project=98.

Robare, Paul. "Sound in Product Design." MA Thesis. Carnegie Mellon U School of Design. 2009.

Rockwell, Leo L. "The Fourth R Is an L." *College English* 1.1 (1939): 61–67.

Rosenhouse, G. *Active Noise Control: Fundamentals for Acoustic Design*. Southhampton, UK: Wessex Institute of Technology P, 2001.

Ross, Alex. "When Music Is Violence." *New Yorker*. 4 July 2016. Web. 5 July 2016. http://www.newyorker.com/magazine/2016/07/04/when-music-is-violence.

Royster, Jacqueline Jones. "When the First Voice You Hear Is Not Your Own." *College Composition and Communication* 47.1 (1996): 29–40.

S-Town. Host Brian Reed. Exec. Producers Brian Reed and Julie Snyder. *NPR*. 2017. Podcast.

Schafer, R. Murray. *Ear Cleaning: Notes for an Experimental Music Course*. Toronto: Clark and Cruickshank, 1967.

Schafer, R. Murray. *A Sound Education: 100 Exercises in Listening and Sound-Making*. Ontario: Arcana Editions, 1992.

Schafer, R. Murray. *The Soundscape: Our Sonic Environment and the Tuning of the World*. 1977. Rochester, VT: Destiny Books, 1994.

Schumacher, Angela. "Strong Brands = Smashable Brands." *Insight Creative*. 19 Mar. 2013. Web. 15 June 2015. http://insightcreative.com/blog/strong-brands-smash able-brands.html.

Selfe, Cynthia. "The Movement of Air, the Breath of Meaning: Aurality and Multimodal Composing." *College Composition and Communication* 60.4 (2009): 616–63.

Selfe, Cynthia, ed. *Multimodal Composition: Resources for Teachers*. Cresskill, NJ: Hampton P, 2007.

Selfe, Cynthia, Stephanie Owen Fletcher, and Susan Wright. "Words, Audio, and Video: Composing and the Processes of Production." *Multimodal Composition: Resources for Teachers*. Ed. Cynthia Selfe. Cresskill, NJ: Hampton P, 2007.

Selfe, Cynthia, and Gail Hawisher, eds. "Special Issue on the Influence of Gunther Kress' Work." *Computers and Composition* 22.1 (2005): 1–128.

Serial. Season 1. Host and Exec. Producer Sarah Koenig. *NPR*. 2014. Podcast.

Shadowlock. "iPod-iTunes Commercial: Dance." *YouTube*. 30 Nov. 2007. Web. 12 Oct. 2013. http://www.youtube.com/watch?v=64ue0LjcV-E.

Sheller, Mimi. "Automotive Emotions: Feeling the Car." *Theory, Culture, and Society* 21.4/5 (2004): 221–37.

Shepard, Mark. "Tactical Sound Garden." 2006. Web. 2 Apr. 2013. http://www.tacticalsoundgarden.net/.

Sheridan, David. "Fabricating Consent: Three-Dimensional Objects as Rhetorical Compositions." *Computers and Composition* 27.4 (2010): 249–65.

Shipka, Jody. "On Estate Sales, Archives, and the Matter of Making Things." *Provocations: Reconstructing the Archive*. Computers and Composition Digital Press (an imprint of Utah State UP). 2015.

Shipka, Jody. "Sound Engineering: Toward a Theory of Multimodal Soundness." *Computers and Composition* 23 (2006): 355–73.

Shipka, Jody. *Toward a Composition Made Whole*. Pittsburgh: U of Pittsburgh P, 2011.

Shivers-McNair, Ann. "What Can We Learn about Writing and Rhetoric from a Makerspace?" *Digital Rhetoric Collaborative*. 17 March 2016. Web. 1 Jan. 2017. http://www.digitalrhetoriccollaborative.org/2016/03/17/what-can-we-learn-about-writing-and-rhetoric-from-a-makerspace/.

Silva, Liana. "As Loud as I Want to Be: Gender, Loudness, and Respectability Politics." *Sounding Out: The Sound Studies Blog*. 9 Feb. 2015. Web. 10 Feb. 2015. https://soundstudiesblog.com/2015/02/09/as-loud-as-i-want-to-be-gender-loudness-and-respectability-politics/.

Silva, Liana. "Park Sounds: A Kansas City Soundwalk for Fall." *Sounding Out: The Sound Studies Blog*. 3 Dec. 2012. Web. 7 July 2016. https://soundstudiesblog.com/2012/12/03/park-sound-a-kansas-city-soundwalk-for-fall/.

Sirc, Geoffrey. *English Composition as a Happening*. Logan, UT: Utah State UP, 2002.

Siteur, Wouter. "Sonic Branding (3): Examples of Sonic Branding." *In Perfect Pitch* Blog. n.d. Web. 20 July 2016. https://www.inperfectpitch.com/sonic-branding/examples-of-sonic-branding/.

Smith, Bruce. *The Acoustic World of Early Modern England*. Chicago: U of Chicago P, 1999.

Snapes, Laura. "Glitter in the Dark." Pitchfork. n.d. Web. 15 Aug. 2016. http://pitchfork.com/features/cover-story/reader/bat-for-lashes/.

Souccar, Miriam Kreinin. "The Rise of the Outrageously Long Commute." *Atlantic*. 4 Oct. 2015. Web. 29 June 2016. http://www.theatlantic.com/business/archive/2015/10/extreme-commuting/408754/.

Sound Effects: An Interdisciplinary Journal of Sound and Sound Experience. Eds. Jacob Kreutzfeldt, Iben Have, Nina Gram et al. 2011. Web. 3 Nov. 2013. http://www.soundeffects.dk/.

Soundcities. Stanza. 2000. Web. 8 Aug. 2014. http://www.soundcities.com/.

Sounding Out: The Sound Studies Blog. Eds. Jennifer Stoever, Liana Silva, and Aaron Trammell. 2009. http://soundstudiesblog.com/.

Stedman, Kyle, and Courtney Danforth, eds. *Soundwriting Pedagogies: Strategies, Lessons, Practices*. 2017. Web.

Sterne, Jonathan. *The Audible Past: Cultural Origins of Sound Reproduction*. Durham: Duke UP, 2003.

Sterne, Jonathan, ed. "Sonic Imaginations." *The Sound Studies Reader*. New York: Routledge, 2012: 1–17.

Sterne, Jonathan. "Sounds like the Mall of America: Programmed Music and the Architectonics of Commercial Space." *Ethnomusicology* 41.1 (1997): 22–50.

Sterne, Jonathan, and Mitchell Akiyama. "The Recording That Never Wanted to Be Heard and Other Stories of Sonification." *The Oxford Handbook of Sound Studies*. Eds. Trevor Pinch and Karin Bijsterveld. Oxford: Oxford UP, 2013: 544–60.

Stocker, Michael. *Hear Where We Are: Sound, Ecology, and Sense of Place*. New York: Springer, 2013.

Stockfelt, Ola. "Cars, Buildings, Soundscapes." *Soundscapes: Essays on Vroom and Moo*. Ed. H. Jarviluoma. Tampere, Finland: Tampere UP, 1994.

Stoever, Jennifer Lynn. *The Sonic Color Line: Race and the Cultural Politics of Listening*. New York: New York UP, 2016.

Stoever, Jennifer Lynn. "Toward a Civically Engaged Sound Studies, or Resounding Binghamton." *Sounding Out: The Sound Studies Blog*. 18 Aug. 2014. Web. 5 Aug. 2016. https://soundstudiesblog.com/2014/08/18/toward-a-civically-engaged-sound-stud ies-or-resounding-binghamton/.

Stone, Jonathan. "Listening to the Sonic Archive: Rhetoric, Representation, and Race in the Lomax Prison Recordings." *Enculturation: A Journal of Rhetoric, Writing, and Culture* 19 (2015): n. pag. Web. 12 Nov 2016.

Stratton, Ollie. "Techniques for Literate Listening." *English Journal* 37.10 (1948): 542–44.

Sullivan, John Jeremiah. "The Ballad of Geeshie and Elvie." *New York Times*. 13 Apr. 2014. Web. 7 July 2016. http://www.nytimes.com/interactive/2014/04/13/maga zine/blues.html.

Sun Eidsheim, Nina. *Sensing Sound: Singing and Listening as Vibrational Practice*. Durham: Duke UP, 2015.

Swanson, David. Personal Interview. 9 Feb. 2012.

Symanczyk, Anna. "The Sound of Stuff—Archetypical Sound in Product Sound Design." *Journal of Sonic Studies* 10 (2015): n. pag. Web. 7 Dec. 2016.

Syverson, Margaret. *The Wealth of Reality: An Ecology of Composition*. Carbondale: Southern Illinois UP, 1999.

Szendy, Peter. *Listen: A History of Our Ears*. New York: Fordham UP, 2008.

Taimi, Michael. "BMW Luxury Car Commerical 2D." *YouTube*. 23 Sept. 2011. Web. 13 Nov. 2013. https://www.youtube.com/watch?v=t7d528bYisg.

Tallman, Marion L. "Teaching Discriminating Radio Listening." *English Journal* 37.8 (1948): 408–12.

Thomas, Douglas, and John Seely Brown. *A New Culture of Learning: Cultivating the Imagination for a World of Constant Change*. CreateSpace, 2011.

Thompson, Emily. *The Soundscape of Modernity: Architectural Acoustics and the Culture of Listening in America, 1900–1933*. Cambridge, MA: MIT P, 2002.

"Todd Selby x Christine Sun Kim." *Nowness*. Nov. 2011. Web. 7 Oct. 2013. https:// www.nowness.com/story/todd-selby-x-christine-sun-kim.

Toker, Franklin. *Pittsburgh: An Urban Portrait*. Pittsburgh: U of Pittsburgh P, 1986.

Toop, David. *Sinister Resonance: The Mediumship of the Listener*. New York: Continuum, 2011.

Touch the Sound: A Sound Journey with Evelyn Glennie. Dir. Thomas Riedelsheimer. Docudrama, 2005. DVD.

Trower, Shelley. *Senses of Vibration: A History of the Pleasure and Pain of Sound.* New York: Bloomsbury Academic, 2012.

Truax, Barry. *Acoustic Communication.* New York: Ablex, 1984.

Truax, Barry, ed. *Handbook for Acoustic Ecology.* Vancouver: A.R.C., 1978.

Urry, John. "Inhabiting the Car." *Sociological Review* 54.1 (2006): 17–31.

VanHemert, Kyle. "GE's New Emphasis on Appliances: Sound Design." *Fast Company Design.* 6 Dec. 2012. Web. 26 Nov. 2013. https://www.fastcodesign.com/1671333/ges-new-emphasis-in-appliances-sound-design.

VanKooten, Crystal. "Singer, Writer: A Choric Exploration of Sound and Writing." *Kairos: A Journal of Rhetoric, Technology, and Pedagogy* 21.1 (2016): n. pag. Web. 8 Aug. 2017.

"Visitor's Guide." University of Maryland-Baltimore County Official Website. n.d. Web. 11 July 2016. http://about.umbc.edu/visitors-guide/.

Vitanza, Victor. "From Heuristics to Aleatory Procedures; Or Toward Writing the Accident." *Inventing a Discipline.* Ed. Maureen Daly Goggin. Urbana, IL: NCTE, 2000: 185–206.

Vitanza, Victor. *Negation, Subjectivity, and the History of Rhetoric.* Albany: State U of New York P, 1997.

Vitanza, Victor. "Three Countertheses: Or, A Critical In(ter)vention into Composition Theories and Pedagogies." *Contending with Words.* Eds. Patricia Harkin and John Schlib. New York: MLA, 1991: 139–72.

Voegelin, Salomé. *Listening to Noise and Silence: Towards a Philosophy of Sound Art.* New York: Bloomsbury Academic, 2010.

Voegelin, Salomé. *Sonic Possible Worlds: Hearing the Continuum of Sound.* New York: Bloomsbury Academic, 2014.

Vogt, Nancy. "Audio: Fact Sheet." *Pew Research Center.* Pew Research Center. 29 Apr. 2015. Web. 29 June 2016. http://www.journalism.org/2015/04/29/audio-fact-sheet-2015/.

Wargo, Jon M. and Cassie J. Brownell. "#hearmyhome." 2016. Web. 18 Aug. 2017. http://hearmyhome.matrix.msu.edu/.

Weheliye, Alexander G. *Phonographies: Grooves in Sonic Afro-Modernity.* Durham: Duke UP, 2005.

Westerkamp, Hildegard. "Soundwalking as Ecological Practice." Proceedings of the International Conference on Acoustic Ecology. Hirosaki University, Japan. 2–4 Nov. 2006. Web. 10 July 2015. http://www.sfu.ca/~westerka/writings%20page/articles%20pages/soundasecology2.htm.

Whiplash. Dir. Damien Chazelle. Perf. Miles Teller, J.K. Simmons, Melissa Benoist. Blumhouse Productions, 2014. Film.

Wible, Scott. "Design Thinking in the Writing Course: Transforming Knowledge through Mobile Research Practices." Thomas R. Watson Conference. University of Louisville. Louisville, KY. 21 Oct. 2016. Keynote address.

Wise, Pascal. "What Will Our Cities Sound Like in the Future." *Guardian*. 13 Mar. 2014. Web. 4 Apr. 2014. https://www.theguardian.com/cities/2014/mar/13/sounds-city-technology-urban-centres-peaceful.

"World Soundscape Project." n.d. Web. 7 July 2010. https://www.sfu.ca/~truax/wsp.html.

Worsham, Lynn. "The Question Concerning Invention: Hermeneutics and the Genesis of Writing." *PRE/TEXT* 8 (1987): 197–244.

WTF with Marc Maron. Episode 613. "President Barack Obama." Host Marc Maron. Exec. Producer Brendan McDonald. 22 June 2015. Podcast.

Wysocki, Anne, ed. *Writing New Media: Theory and Applications for Expanding the Teaching of Composition*. Logan: Utah State UP, 2004.

Ximm, Aaron. "Tips for Recording in the Field." *Quiet American*. n.d. Web. 7 June 2015. http://www.quietamerican.org/links_diy-rec_tips.html.

Yancey, Kathleen Blake and Matthew Davis. "Notes toward the Role of Materiality in Composing, Reviewing, and Assessing Multimodal Texts." *Computers and Composition* 31 (2014): 13–28.

Yergeau, Melanie. "Shiny Rhetorics." 21st Century Englishes Graduate Student Conference. Bowling Green State University. Bowling Green, OH. 4 Oct. 2014. Keynote address.

Yergeau, Melanie et al. "Multimodality in Motion: Disability and Kairotic Spaces." *Kairos: A Journal of Rhetoric, Technology, and Pedagogy* 18.1 (2013): n. pag. Web. 14 March 2015.

Zdenek, Sean. *Reading Sounds: Closed-Captioning Media and Popular Culture*. Chicago: U of Chicago P, 2015.

Zwhalen, Christie. "Listening to and through 'Need': Sound Studies and Civic Engagement." *Sounding Out: The Sound Studies Blog*. 6 Apr. 2015. Web. 18 Aug. 2016. https://soundstudiesblog.com/tag/christie-zwahlen/.

INDEX

Abel, Jessica, 150

Abumrad, Jad, 150

accessibility, 35–36, 55–56, 61–62, 77–78, 96–97, 147–48, 158–59nn5–6, 163n25

acoustemology, 157n5

acoustical technologies, 81–82, 161–62nn10–13

acoustic design: of consumer products, 106–7, 121–22; and experimentation, 75–76; and holistic sonic experiences, 48–49, 76–78; as practice, 72–73, 161n7; purpose and meaning in, 78–79; and spatial environment, 73–75, 161n9. *See also* automotive acoustic engineering

acoustic ecology, 70, 160n3

affordances, as term, 155n2

agency, studies on, 18–20

agility, listening, 145–47

Ahern, Kati Fargo, 42, 88

Alexander, Jonathan, 42, 156n5

Arola, Kristin, 8, 109

Arola, Kristin L., 9

artist statement: assignment guidelines for, 53–54, 92–93; as compositional practice, 55, 94–95

attention: directed by sound, 19; and hierarchy of senses, 56–57; in sonic environments, 81–82; and ubiquitous listening, 157n4

audiences, embodied, 43–45, 147–48, 152–53

audio essays, 41, 159n8

automotive acoustic engineering: diminishing sensory experiences, 115–17, 164–65nn6–7; and holistic sonic experiences, 113–15, 164n5; manipulation of sound, 111–12, 118–21, 165n8, 165n10; and sonic branding, 112–13; and soundscapes, 110–11, 165n10. *See also* acoustic design; Sonic Objects

Ball, Cheryl E., 9, 109

Barnett, Scot, 20, 109

bass culture, 120

Beckerman, Joel, 112–13

Bergson, Henri, 37

Bialostosky, Don, 40

Bickford, Tyler, 163n24

Bijsterveld, Karin, 107, 112, 113–14, 115, 116, 118, 164n3, 164n6

Bingham, David, 122

Blair, Carole, 21

Blake, Art, 58

Blesser, Barry, 101, 114

body/embodiment: bodily learning, 36–40; embodied audiences, 43–45, 147–48, 152–53; embodied ear concept, 64; feeling sound, 30–31, 32–33, 79, 119–20, 160n13; in feminist rhetorical scholarship, 16–17; and mind-body complex, 47–48, 148; seeing sound, 31, 33–34; and sound absorption, 162n15; and soundwalking, 95–96; and unique interactions with sound, 31–32, 35–36, 158–59nn5–6. *See also* My Listening Body

Boffone, Trevor, 158n4

Bosch dishwashers, 140–41

Bowen, Tracey, 9

Bowman, John, 69

Boyle, Casey, 20, 55, 109

Britton, Terry A., 140

Brooks, Christopher, 77

Brown, John Seely, 147

Bull, Michael, 110, 119, 165n8

Burt, Henry, 141

Cardinale, Cara Lynne, 158n4

career options, 149–51

Carney, Shawn, 113

cars. *See* automotive acoustic engineering

car seat (student project), 137–38

Cathedral of Learning, 68–69, 161n11

churches, sound in, 78–79

Cintron, Ralph, 120

Cleophas, Eefje, 107, 115, 164n3

commercial spaces, sound in, 84, 162–63n18

communication, 156–57n2

community projects, sound-based, 152–53, 167n6

Composing (Media) = Composing (Embodiment) (Arola and Wysocki), 8

composition studies. *See* rhetoric and composition studies

Comstock, Michelle, 42

consumer products, 106–7, 121–22, 140–42, 163–64nn1–2. *See also* automotive acoustic engineering

Corbin, Alain, 157n5

Coudriet, Greg, 73, 74, 75, 82–83

Cowan, James, 75

Cox, Trevor, 46–47, 161n9

Daughtry, J. Martin, 17, 18–19, 31, 32

Davidson, Cathy, 37

Davis, Diane, 19

deafness, and sound studies, 31–32, 158n4

defamiliarization, 40

design. *See* acoustic design

Dewey, John, 40, 146

Dickinson, Greg, 21

digital audio technologies: availability/presence

of, 148–49; impact on sound and listening, 3–5; MP3 players/iPods, 86–87, 118–19, 163n21, 163nn23–24. *See also* automotive acoustic engineering

digital production, of scholarship, 22–25, 157n6

digital sound maps, 93. *See also* Mapping Sound

digital spaces: aesthetics of, 74; vs nondigital, 23–24, 72; as soundscapes, 22, 45–46

Dobrin, Sidney, 71

drivers, as acoustic engineers, 118–21, 165n8, 165n10

Dunn, Patricia, 9, 159–60n11

Dyson, Frances, 18

ear-ing, 6, 155n4

ecology: acoustic, 70, 160n3; of composition, 71–72, 95; of sound, 73–75; of soundscapes, 22, 70–72

Eisenberg, Andrew J., 157n5

electric cars, 116–17

Ellsworth, Elizabeth, 146

embodied audiences, 43–45, 147–48, 152–53

embodied ear concept, 64

embodiment. *See* body/embodiment

Enculturation (journal), 22

Enoch, Jessica, 21

Farman, Jason, 24

Feld, Steven, 157n5

feminist rhetoric scholarship, 16–17, 157n3

Fleckenstein, Kristie, 9

Fleischer, Stephanie Owen, 41

Fleming, David, 21

Ford, 112–13

frequencies, sonic, 30–31, 39–40, 120, 158n2, 159n7

Friedner, Michele, 31–32

Frith, Jordan, 21, 88

Fuchs, Helmut, 73

Gauntlett, David, 148

gender, 16–17, 58, 64, 152

General Electric (GE), 121–22

Gibson, James, 155n2

Glenn, Cheryl, 16

Glennie, Evelyn: on deafness, 158n1; as example of multimodal listening, 29–30, 32, 58, 63; on multimodal listening, 32–34; on sonic excess, 37–40, 159n7

Goodman, Steve, 17, 18, 31, 158n2, 162n16

Gordon, Kara, 116

Gries, Laurie, 19–20, 109, 161n6

Haas, Christina, 9, 108

Hagood, Mack, 86, 162n14

Halbritter, Bump, 41

Hawhee, Debra, 47–48

Hawisher, Gail, 8–9

Helmreich, Stefan, 31–32

Henriques, Julian, 10, 17

Hesse, Doug, 109

Hocks, Mary, 42

Howes, David, 164n2

ice cream trucks, 141–42

inclusivity, 35–36, 55–56, 61–62, 77–78, 96–97, 147–48, 158–59nn5–6, 163n25

iPods/MP3 players, 86–87, 118–19, 163n21, 163nn23–24

Jones, Douglas, 78–79

Kähler, Magnus, 141
Kairos, Computers and Composition Online (journal), 22
Kassabian, Anahid, 157n4
Kerschbaum, Stephanie, 44, 63
Kirschenbaum, Matthew, 7
Krebs, Stefan, 133
Kress, Gunther, 8, 156n7

LaBelle, Brandon, 111, 120, 164n5
Lalwani, Mona, 166n4
language, for describing sound, 133–35
LaSalle, Diana, 140
Leverenz, Carrie, 109
listening: agility in, 145–47; rhetorical, 152; selective, 4; studies on, 15–18, 25–26, 157n4; ubiquitous, 157n4. *See also* multimodal listening
lobbies, sound in, 82–83
Lunsford, Andrea, 157n3
Lutkewitte, Claire, 9

Maly, Tim, 116
Mapping Sound (assignment): assignment guidelines, 91–93; challenges, 95–97; design and purpose, 93–95; evaluation, 102–3; resources, 103–4; student work examples, 97–102
Marback, Richard, 109
Marco Polo (student project), 59–62
materiality: impact on sound, 114–15; manipulated in cars, 118–21; of rhetoric and composition, 108–10; of sound,

30–32; of soundscapes, 71, 162n15; and sound studies, 18–19. *See also* Sonic Objects
McCarthy, John, 35, 44
meaning-making, 8–9, 18, 41–42, 50
memory, bodily, 36–37
metacognitive writing, 55
Mills, Mara, 158n4
mind-body complex, 47–48, 148
Mountford, Roxanne, 21
"The Movement of Air, the Breath of Meaning: Aurality and Multimodal Composing" (Selfe), 41–42, 57
MP3 players/iPods, 86–87, 118–19, 163n21, 163nn23–24
Multimodal Composition: A Critical Sourcebook (Lutkewitte), 9
Multimodal Composition: Resources for Teachers (Selfe), 9
multimodality: and digital vs nondigital spaces, 23–24, 72; scholarship on, 8–9, 156nn5–7; as term, 6–8
multimodal listening: connection to multimodal production, 17–18; defined, 3, 6; Glennie on, 32–34; value of, 35
multimodal listening pedagogy: acoustic design practices applied to, 73–80; automotive acoustic engineering practices applied to, 111–18; and career options, 149–51, 166n2; cultivating awareness, 151–53; cultivating listening agility, 145–47; cultivating production of multimodal work, 147–49; current practices in, 41–42; emphasizing felt experience, 17, 20; foundational practices of, 144; scholarship on, 25–26; and situation-specific practices, 35–36,

158–59nn5–6; and unlearning listening habits, 36–40; value of, 43–49. *See also* Mapping Sound; My Listening Body; Sonic Objects

Multimodal Literacies and Emerging Genres (Bowen and Whithaus), 9

multimodal soundness, 129–30

Murray, Joddy, 156n7

music halls, sound in, 83

Muzak, 84, 162nn16–17

My Listening Body (assignment): assignment guidelines, 51–54; challenges, 56–59; design and purpose, 54–56; evaluation, 65–66; resources, 67; student work examples, 59–65

Neely, Daniel, 141

Netinga, Myron, 46–47

New London Group, 8–9, 109

Norman, Don, 117

notebook (student project), 135–36

Objective Evaluation of Interior Car Sound (OBELICS), 114–15

Oliveros, Pauline, 25–26

Ott, Brian, 21

Ouzounian, Gascia, 93

Palmeri, Jason, 144, 156n5

pedagogy. *See* multimodal listening pedagogy

podcasts, 41, 149–50, 159n8, 165–66nn1–3

Porcello, Thomas, 134

Price, Margaret, 159n6

Prins, Kristin, 109

Pullin, Graham, 48

Purdy, James, 109

quietness/loudness, 58, 116, 161–62n12

race, 16–17, 64, 120, 121, 152

Ratcliffe, Krista, 16, 152

reverberation: adjustment of, 69, 75, 77, 78, 81, 161n11; as term, 11

Reynolds, Nedra, 21

rhetorical listening, 152

rhetorical ontology, 109

rhetoric and composition studies: on agency, 18–20; digital scholarship in, 22–23; as discipline, 156–57n2; and ecology, 71; growing connection with sound studies, 27, 157n7; on listening, 16–17; on materiality and design, 108–9; sound pedagogy in, 25; on space, 21

Rhodes, Jacqueline, 156n5

rhythm (student project), 62–64

Rickert, Thomas, 6, 19, 20, 72, 80, 109, 160n12

Riedelsheimer, Thomas, 32

Rivers, Nathaniel, 95

Rosenblatt, Adam, 157n3

Rosenhouse, G., 73

Royster, Jacqueline Jones, 16

Salter, Linda-Ruth, 101, 114

Schafer, R. Murray, 21, 25, 70–71, 95, 160n2

Schulze, Gerhard, 107

Schumacher, Angela, 140

selective listening, 4

Selfe, Cynthia, 8–9, 41–42, 57

semiotics, 8–9, 18, 41–42

Sheller, Mimi, 163–64n1

Shepard, Mark, 88, 89

Sheppard, Jennifer, 9, 109

Sheridan, David, 109

Shipka, Jody, 42, 72, 108–9, 129–30, 131, 156n5

Shivers-McNair, Anne, 109

Shkolovsky, Viktor, 40

Silva, Liana, 58

Sirc, Geoffrey, 72

Snapple cap, 140

Sommers, Nancy, 109

sonic branding, 112–13

sonic design. *See* acoustic design; automotive acoustic engineering

sonic environment, as term, 71. *See also* soundscapes

"Sonic Imaginations" (Sterne), 57

Sonic Objects (assignment): assignment guidelines, 124–26, 127–29, 132; commentary, 126–27, 129–31, 133–35; evaluation, 138–40; resources, 140–42; student work examples, 135–38

sonic objects, defined, 123

sonic rhetorics, 82–85, 113, 127

sonification, 158n3

sound: affective potential of, 43–45, 46–47, 76–77; agency of, 19; in churches, 78–79; in commercial spaces, 84, 162–63n18; describing, 133–35; detached from space, 81; diminishing of, 115–17, 164–65nn6–7; ecology of, 73–75; experimentation with, 75–76; impacted by materiality, 114–15; in lobbies, 82–83; manipulated in cars, 111–12, 118–21, 165n8, 165n10; meaning in, 78–79; as mode of disengagement, 3–4; in music halls, 83; and sonic branding, 112–13; and sonic excess, 37–40, 159n7; and sonic holistic experiences, 48–49, 76–78,

113–15, 164n5; tactile experiences of, 30–31, 32–33, 79, 119–20, 160n13; visual experiences of, 31, 33–34

sound apps, 2, 155n3

sound clouds, 77

sounding, as term, 10

Sounding Out forum, 58

soundscapes: of cars, 110–11, 165n10; digital spaces as, 22, 45–46; materiality of, 71; and personal devices, 86–88, 163n19, 163n21, 163nn23–24; social, 88–90, 163n25; sonic rhetorics of, 82–86; studies on, 70–71, 160n2; as term, 21, 70, 157n5. *See also* Mapping Sound

sound studies: on agency, 18–19; and deafness, 31–32, 158n4; digital scholarship in, 23, 157n6; as discipline, 14–15, 27, 156n1; growing connection with rhetoric and composition studies, 27, 157n7; on listening, 15–16, 17; and multisensoriality of experience, 24–25; pedagogy in, 25–26; on space, 21

soundwalking, 95–96

space/spatiality: sound detached from, 81; studies on, 21–22, 157n5. *See also* acoustic design; digital spaces; soundscapes

spatial rhetorics, 21–22

Sterne, Jonathan, 14, 27, 57, 84, 157n5, 158n4, 162–63n18

Stocker, Michael, 87

Stockfelt, Ola, 106

Stoever, Jennifer, 17, 64, 152

storytelling, 150–51, 166–67nn4–5

SunChips bag, 141

Sun Eidsheim, Nina, 17

Sun Kim, Christine, 31